IMAGES
of America

MARIN HEADLANDS

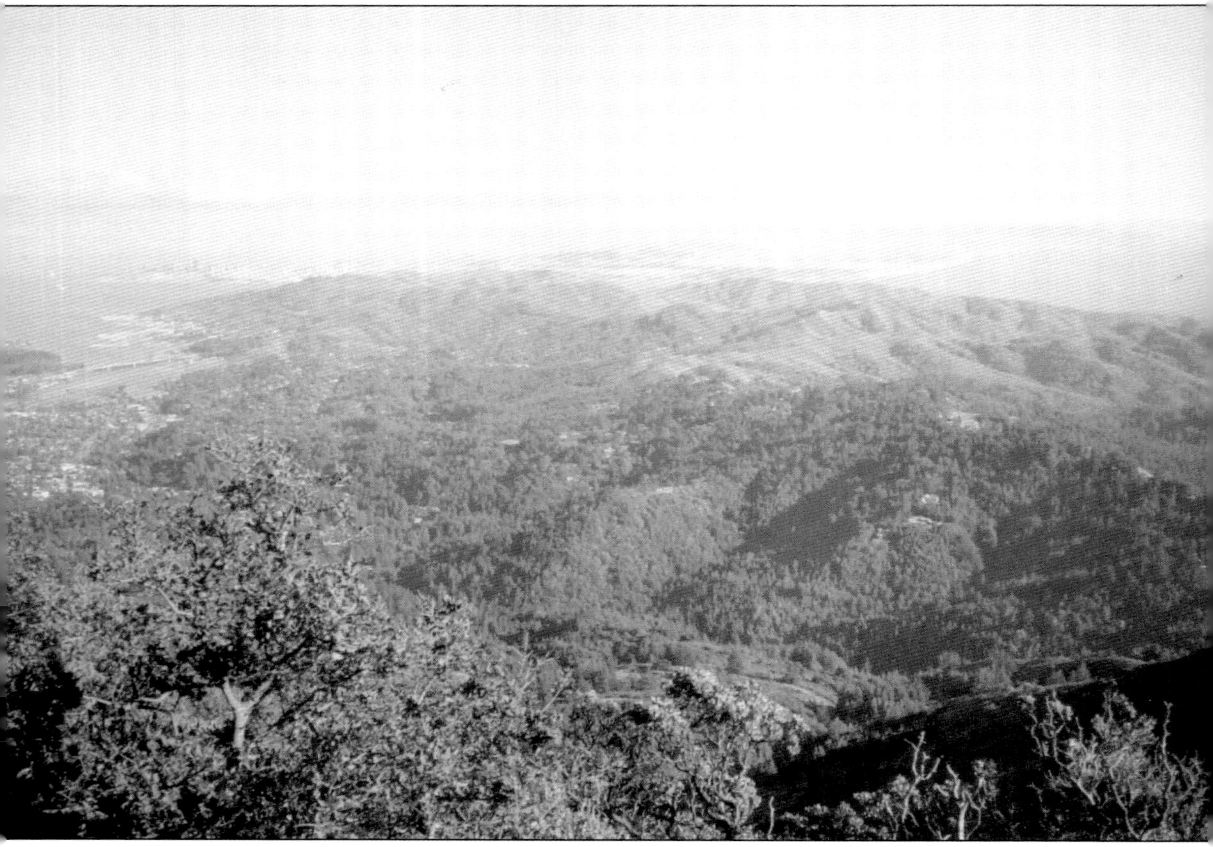

This view of the Headlands from the east peak of 2,571-foot-high Mount Tamalpais shows descending ridges going in different directions. The break-off where the Pacific Ocean enters through the Golden Gate to San Francisco Bay is at upper left. (Photograph by Dorothy Gibson.)

ON THE COVER: The north side of the picturesque Tennessee Valley Beach is pictured here with its dramatic arching rock sentinel. There is a World War II–era gun emplacement atop this rock, which is composed mostly of chert and is estimated to be 90 million years old. The hole in the center may possibly have been caused by softer material or "pillows" being washed out over the eons from tidal action. (Photograph by Dorothy Gibson.)

IMAGES
of America

MARIN HEADLANDS

Dorothy E. Gibson

ARCADIA
PUBLISHING

ISBN 978-0-7385-7024-2

Published by Arcadia Publishing
Charleston, South Carolina

Printed in the United States of America

Library of Congress Control Number: 2009922894

For all general information contact Arcadia Publishing at:
Telephone 843-853-2070
Fax 843-853-0044
E-mail sales@arcadiapublishing.com
For customer service and orders:
Toll-Free 1-888-313-2665

Visit us on the Internet at www.arcadiapublishing.com

Dedicated to all those who simultaneously love, enjoy, and care for Mount Tamalpais

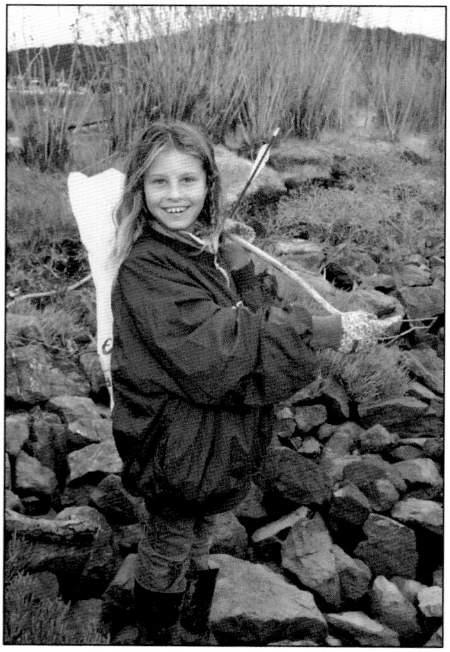

A young volunteer is pictured helping out with coastal cleanup in Marin County. (Courtesy San Francisco Bay Model Visitor Center, San Francisco District, U.S. Army Corps of Engineers.)

Contents

ACKNOWLEDGMENTS

It has been an intense, exciting, and gratifying time preparing *Marin Headlands*. Many people from multiple sources of information have been involved, joining in the search for representative photographs of the area and offering their knowledge.

First it was Carol Hayes, curator of the Sausalito Historical Society Archives, who joined in the search and then offered her husband, Allan, for technical work. It has been a compatible team. Other docents joined in: Pres. Larry Clinton, Vicki Nichols, Jeanne Fidler, and Doris Berdahl.

The rangers at Golden Gate National Recreation Area (GGNRA) Headlands contributed: Will Elder, Ph.D., and Roxanne Farwell on geology and Solange Russek and Sarah Koene on Point Bonita. Amanda Williford, reference archivist at the Presidio in San Francisco's GGNRA Archive, introduced me to a wealth of army life. Chris Gallagher, manager of the San Francisco Bay Model at the U.S. Army Corps of Engineers in Sausalito, offered historical material and Earth Day photography. Ranger Elizabeth Evans took me on a walk around a water-filled San Francisco Bay Model. A visit to Point Reyes National Seashore's Kule Loklo was helpful.

Mary Mergand, director of the library archives at North Baker Research Library in San Francisco, found a photograph of Stephen Richardson (author of *The Days of the Dons*), Capt. William Richardson's son. At San Rafael's Marin History Museum, Holly Gallagher found photographs of Marin City. Marin City Library offered information. Carol Uhrmacher, digital archivist in San Rafael's Civic Center Library History Room, found a colorful account of life. The Marin County Assessor's Office located dairy properties in Tennessee Valley, and David Grossman and Barbara Ford, docents at Mill Valley Library's History Room, had dramatic newspaper accounts.

Sausalito City departments were consistently helpful: director Mary Richardson and her library staff and Jeremy Grave's staff at Community Development. San Francisco's Maritime Museum and Library was a colorful place and the library staff generous in helping. Dave Hull is the principal librarian, and Ted Miles is reference librarian. The Marin Museum of the American Indian offered a display of Native American work and suggestions.

Individuals who gave information and photographs included John Martini, historian and photographer; Thomas S. Tyree, Jewelers; Gene Poole; Ed Ashoff; Konrad Knudsen; Ted Wurn; Roland Beisenstein; Linda Pfeiffer; and Louis Wilkinson. It was Linda Bonnett who guided me when searching for a publisher of a map linking Sausalito trails with the Marin Headlands and Arcadia editor John Poultney who picked up on it!

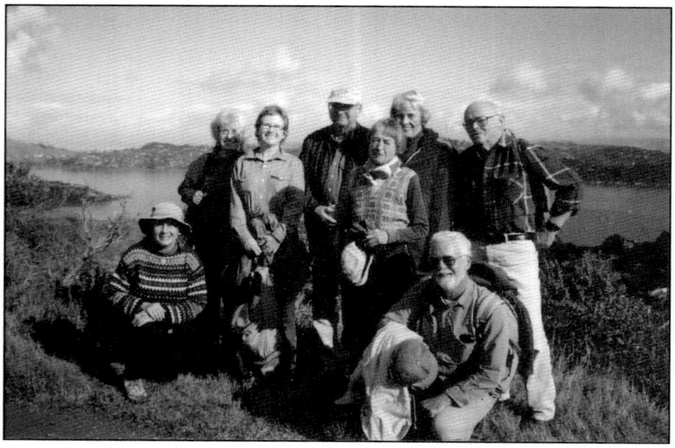

Dorothy Gibson leads a historic walk around Sausalito. The photograph shows a group at Cavallo Point. Dorothy is in the center with Lou Wilkinson to her left. Others and the photographer are unidentified. (Photograph by Dorothy Gibson.)

INTRODUCTION

The history of the headlands is the history of the Earth during the Jurassic period of the Mesozoic era, some 200 million years ago, when the one continent in one ocean broke up to form the continents. The history of the Earth can be read in the cliffs at the Golden Gate and the Pacific Ocean. It can be read in the sands that one feels in the palm of the hand, the bits of shells, and the color of pebbles. It can be read in the variety of the native and exotic plant life—the Spanish ice plant and the English ivy—and in the animal life—what was once here and what no longer roams the headlands. It can be read in the objects, the names, and the places where people came and went, and in the Native Americans' tightly woven baskets, so delicately painted. It can be read in the Spanish names like Cavallo (*caballo*) and Rodeo, and in the names of the settlers and their descendants: English names like Baker and Harrison, Scottish names like Wallace, Portuguese names like Silva, French names like Truette, and Italian, German, and Chinese names as well.

The Golden Gate Bridge is a dramatic reminder of the history of transportation—the little sailboats and huge vessels that go under it and the automobiles that go over it.

The water is different now, not clear as it was—the air also. Most of the stars cannot be seen at night now, and there are "Spare the Air" days. Plastic debris is on the beaches and in the water, animals wash ashore, and some fish are rare or extinct. The weather changes, and there is worry over water shortages, global warming, and technology. Where will it lead next, and what will the layer of our lives look like on those cliffs and in the sand?

About the Author

Since childhood on a farm in central Ohio, Dorothy Gibson has been fascinated by the vicissitudes of nature, including human nature. As a clinical social worker and resident of California and Sausalito after World War II, she has been involved in environmental and social issues. She has served on numerous committees and commissions as well as making professional studies of homelessness, housing, waterfront use, and transportation (water, roads, and paths).

She was a founding member of Mount Tamalpais State Park's Interpretive Association, and as a six-year member of the board of the Sausalito Historical Society, she took many oral histories.

An avid world traveler (she goes it alone), she has visited more than 50 countries on four continents, camping in more than 80 national parks.

Since the publication of her *Sausalito Paths and Walkways* in 2001, she has led historic walks annually.

One

Geology

The headlands draw people in, creating amateur geologists. From the top of Mount Tamalpais, they stare down southward, wondering why the descending ridges go every which way. At the base of Baker's Beach, looking north across the Golden Gate, that final drop-off is parallel to the top of the mountain flowing from east to west—like twins, Mount Tamalpais and the headlands.

Its history goes back to the Jurassic period of the Mesozoic era. Then, 200 million years ago, there was one continent, Pangaea, in one ocean, which began to break up into North and South America, Europe and Asia, Africa and Australia. Rocks from this period extend from the headland area (latitude 37° 49′ N, longitude 122° 29″ W) northward to Oregon and from the Pacific Ocean to Sacramento Valley and the foothills of the Sierra. They include sandstone, shale, chert, basalt, dark igneous rock, granite, and serpentine. This was complicated 16 to 33 million years ago when volcanic activity in the higher ranges of North America created the Sierra. Then, 21 million years ago on the coastal side, largely due to fault activity of the Pacific plate as it moved northwest, grinding against the continental plate (called the San Andreas Fault Line), the Coastal Ranges were created as the Earth's crust was shifted, broken, slipped, moved, and thrust upwards.

Other activities along the coast included volcanoes, geysers, fumaroles, and hot springs originating below the Earth's crust. Volcanic activity continued through the ice ages. It was during the Pleistocene epoch, 1.8 million years ago, that glaciers buried the northern half of North America at least four times. While most of the lower ranges were not covered, they were affected by the melts, the flow of water, and the changing climate—valleys filled with floods and debris and sea levels rose and fell and carried back and forth sediments and rubble.

The California River, which deeply eroded the valley, reached the Pacific shoreline at the edge of the continental shelf, about 15 to 20 miles west of the present coast, around 8,700 years ago. There is a large semicircular bar 5 to 6 miles off the Golden Gate, barely 35 feet below the water's surface. At midpoint of the Golden Gate, there is a chasm 630 feet deep. Very recent findings of geologists have lead to the conclusion that the Headlands Block has rotated 130 degrees since 95 million years ago.

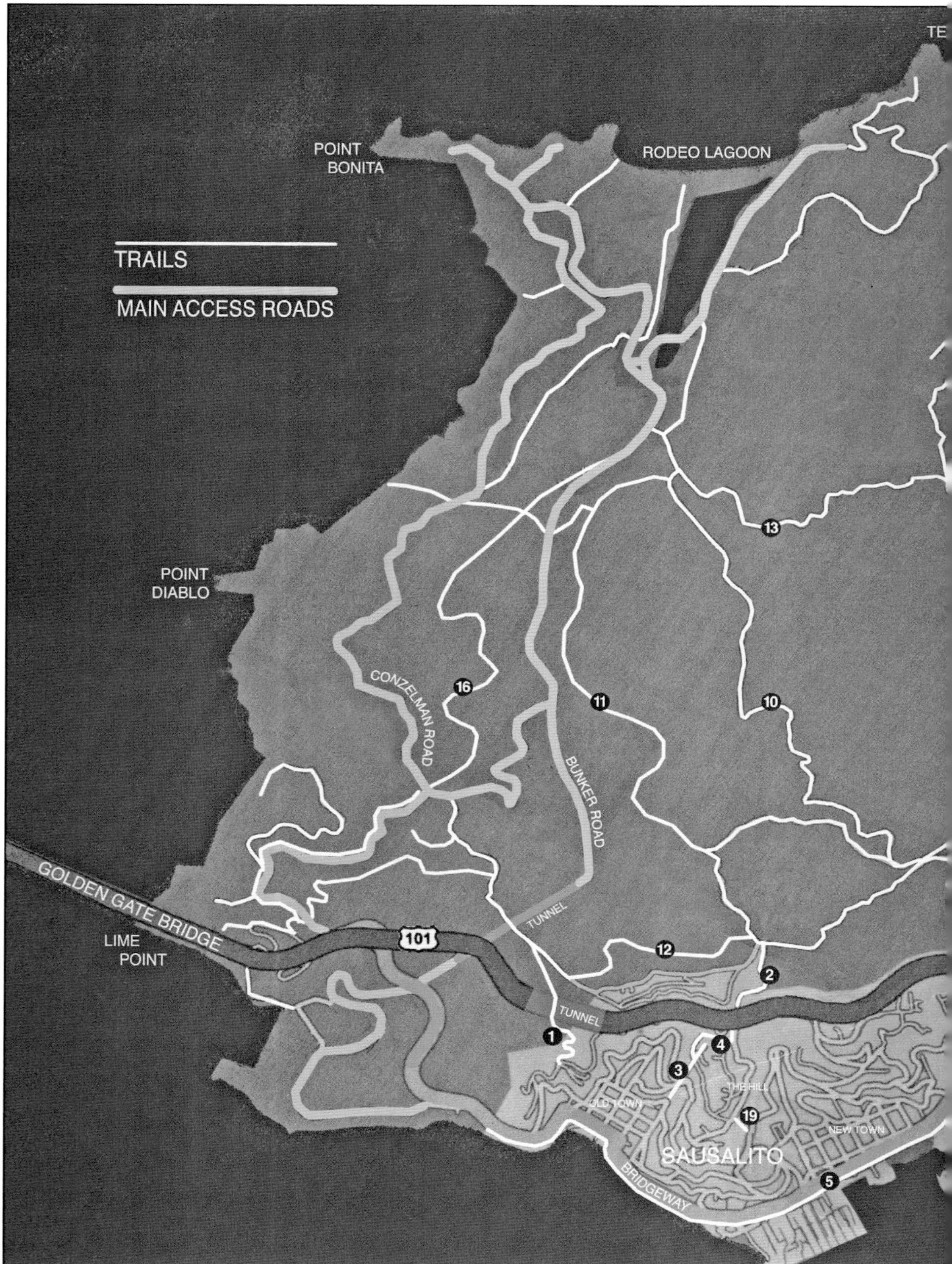
TE
POINT BONITA
RODEO LAGOON
TRAILS
MAIN ACCESS ROADS
POINT DIABLO
CONZELMAN ROAD
BUNKER ROAD
GOLDEN GATE BRIDGE
LIME POINT
101
TUNNEL
TUNNEL
OLD TOWN
THE HILL
NEW TOWN
SAUSALITO
BRIDGEWAY
1
2
3
4
5
10
11
12
13
16
19

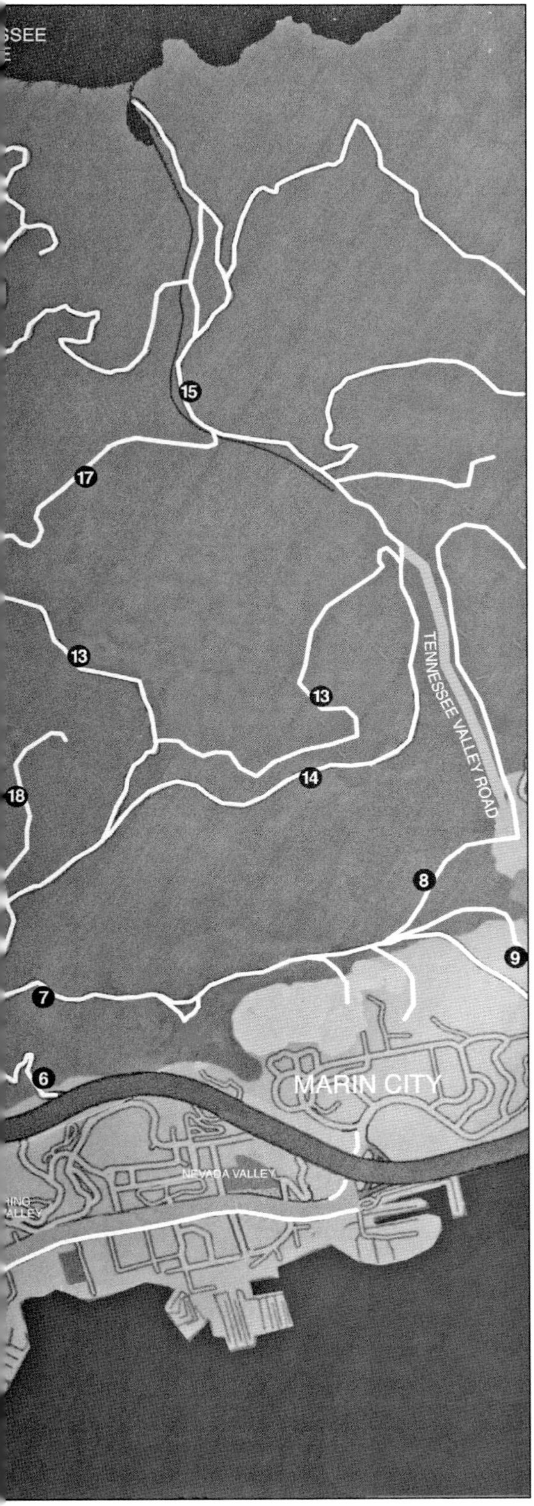

The headlands trails are as follows: 1. Old Fire Road; 2. Morning Sun Trail; 3. Cable Railway; 4. Prospect Steps; 5. Bridgeway; 6. Rodeo Avenue; 7. Alta Avenue; 8. To Fernwood Cemetery; 9. To Marin City; 10. Bobcat Trail; 11. Rodeo Valley Trail; 12. Student Conservation Trail; 13. Marincello/Miwok Trail; 14. Oakwood; 15. Tennessee Valley Road; 16. Coastal Trail; and 17. Old Springs Trail. (Courtesy Sausalito Historical Society, GGNRA, and the Sausalito Department of Public Works.)

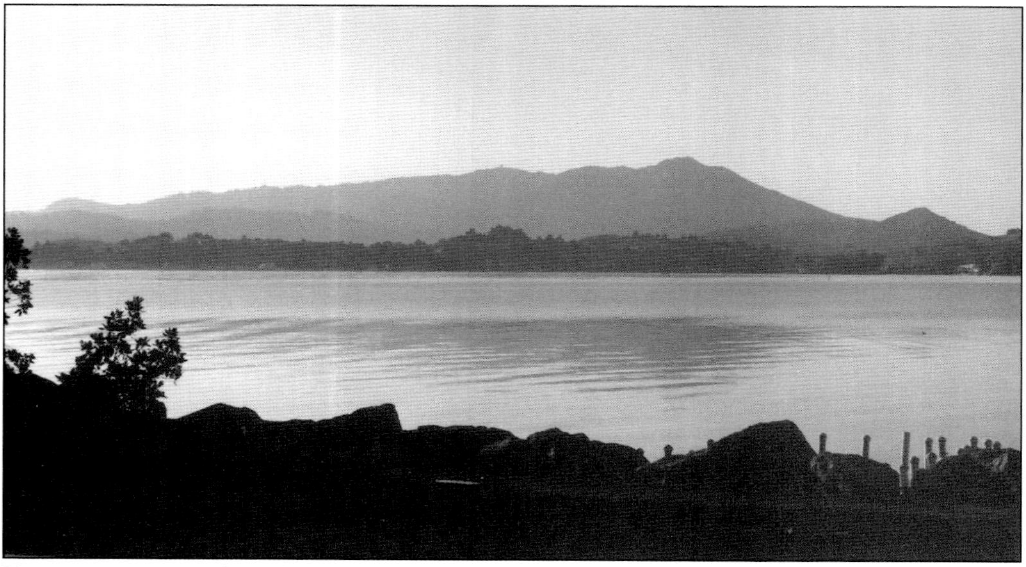

Here is Mount Tamalpais from Tiburon, looking to the west. The mountain's name is believed to come from the Miwok Indian words *Tamal*, meaning "bay," and *Pais*, meaning "country." There is a legend (which was written down and performed at the Cushing Mountain Theater after 1913) that relates the tale of a god in the heavens who falls in love with a Native American princess. He changes himself into an eagle, swoops down, and tries to carry her up to the heavens. Not calculating the height of the mountain with the weight, he cannot continue. She is left lying on the mountain—the "Sleeping Lady" with her head, her bosom, her stomach, thighs, and legs toward the ocean—hence the reference to the mountain as the Sleeping Lady ever since. (Photograph by Dorothy Gibson.)

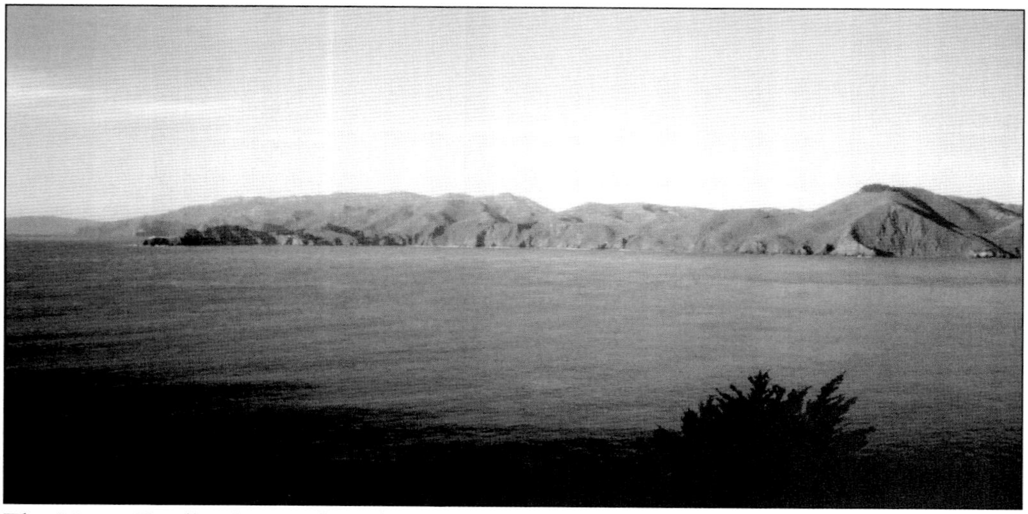

The Marin Headlands, seen here from Land's End in San Francisco across the Golden Gate, looms before Mount Tamalpais in the background. Note the similar shape of the mountain and the headlands. The following pages illustrate the specific characteristics of the cliffs, the soil, and the sand—the geology of the headlands. The commentary is with the guidance of the Golden Gate National Park's Geology Educational Department at Fort Cronkite. (Photograph by Dorothy Gibson.)

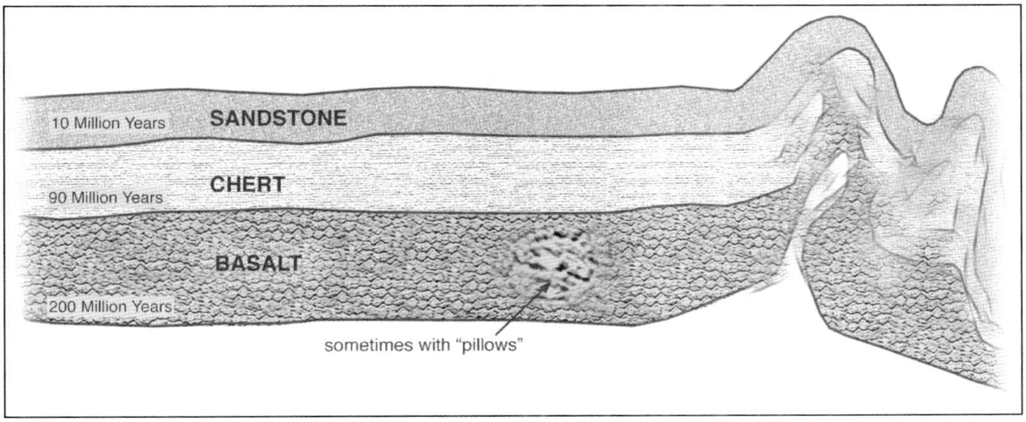

This geological drawing of the Earth's strata at the Marin Headlands shows basalt, a hard, dense volcanic rock, and chert, a sedimentary rock common on California and Oregon coasts. Color variations resistant to erosion stand out in relief on weathered surfaces, containing microscopic ocean sediments and organisms. Also present is sandstone, variously colored sedimentary rock composed of sand-like quartz grains cemented by lime, silica, and other matter. (Courtesy GGNRA Education and Interpretation.)

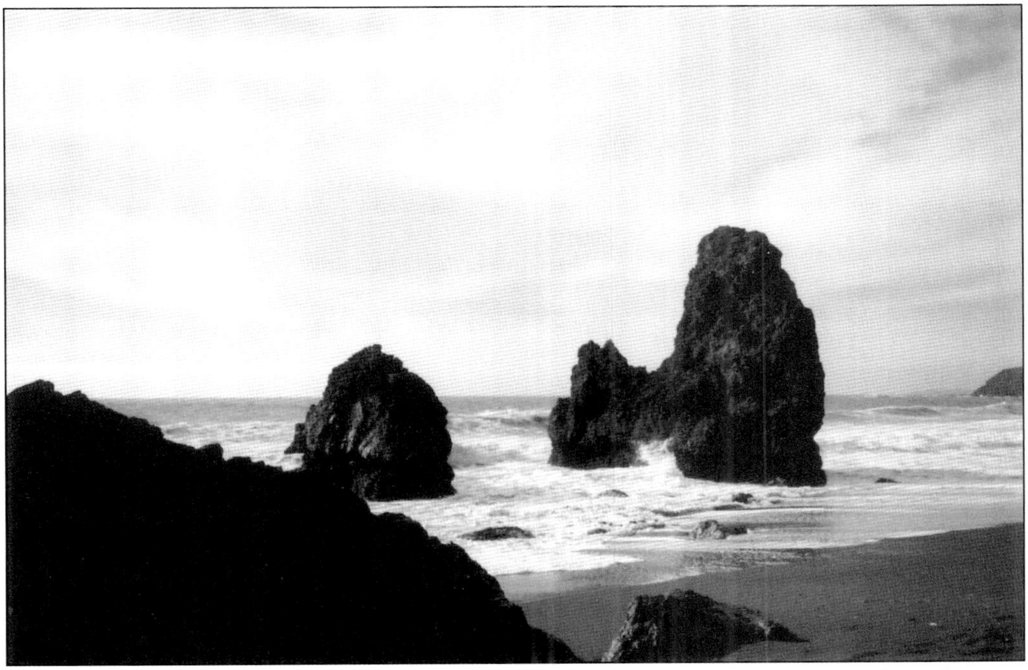

Pictured is basalt from Tennessee Valley Beach's south area. The rock comes from Pacific underwater volcanoes. (Photograph by Dorothy Gibson.)

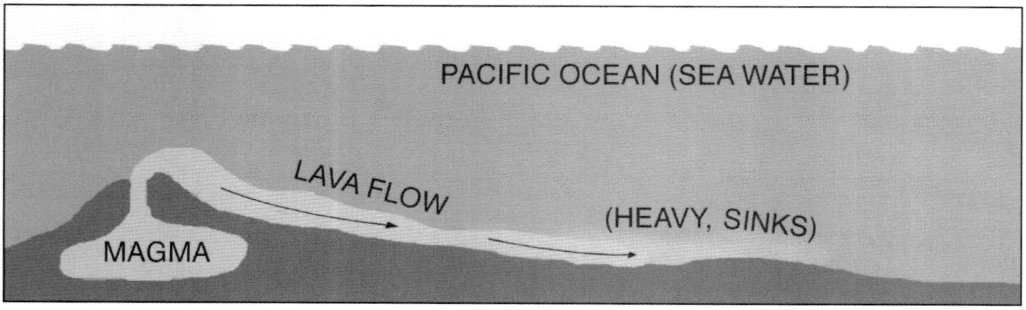

This diagram shows how ancient underwater lava flows formed distinctive outcropping formations in the area of Tennessee Valley Beach. (Courtesy GGNRA Education and Interpretation.)

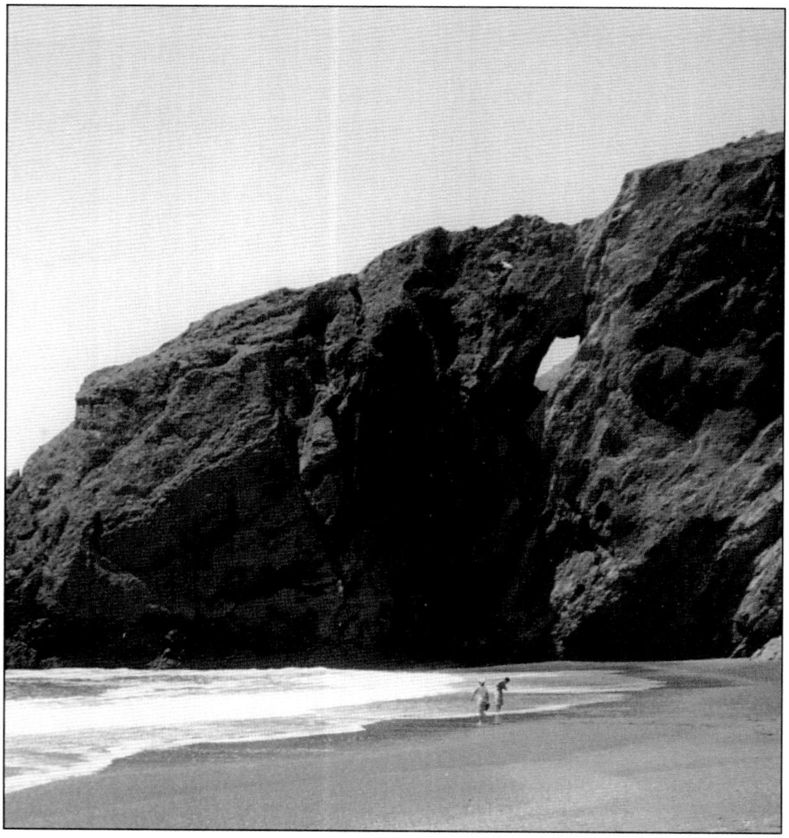

This image captures Tennessee Valley Beach's north end at low tide. The rock is mostly chert, estimated to be 90 million years old. The cause behind the hole in the center is open to speculation; possibly softer material or "pillows" may have been washed out over the eons from tidal action. (Photograph by Dorothy Gibson.)

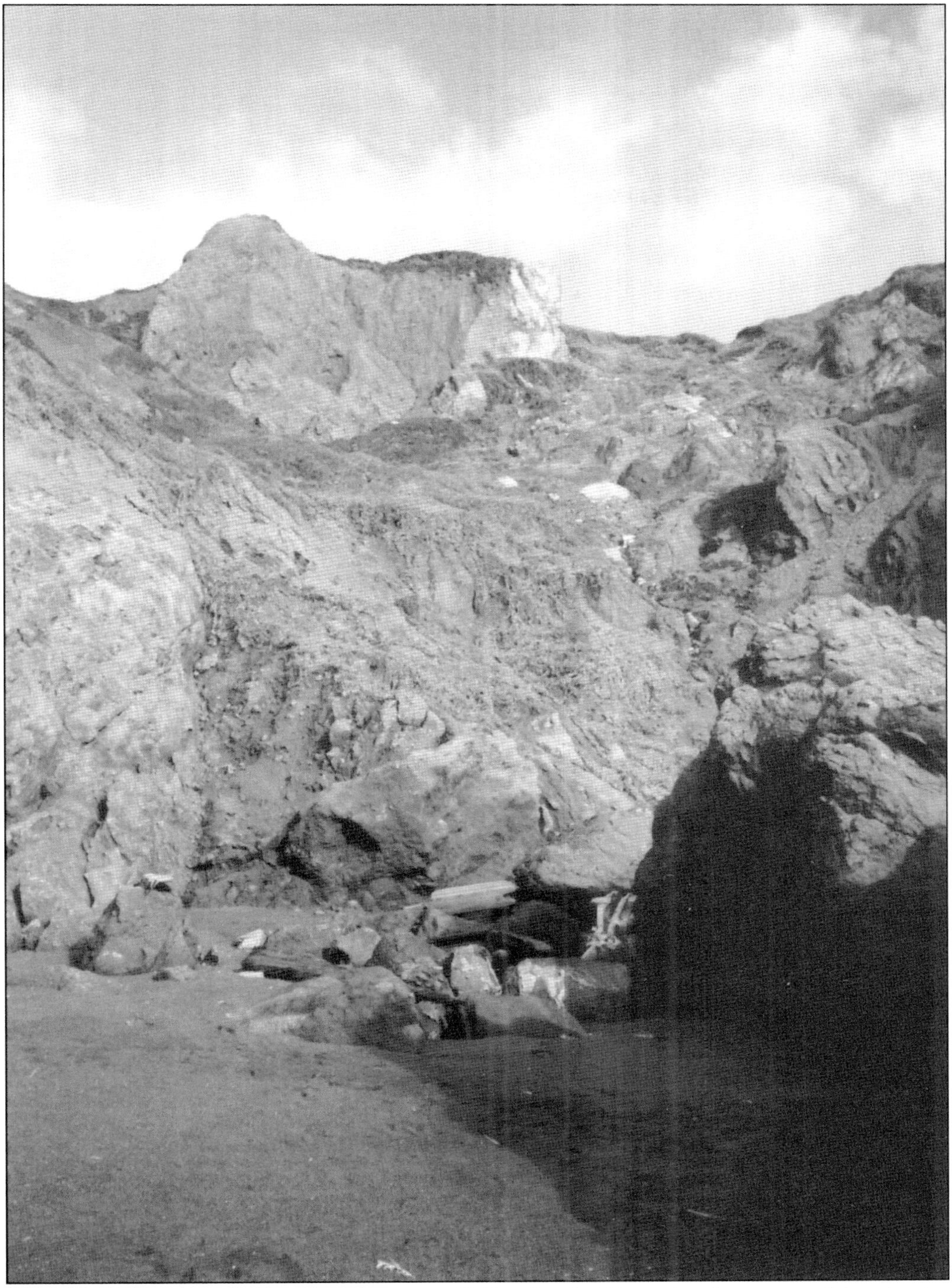

This is a cliff at the south end of Tennessee Valley Beach. The colors here are mild and quite varied, as is the soil's texture. It looks like the chief ingredients are "pillow" basalt and maybe green chert. (Photograph by Dorothy Gibson.)

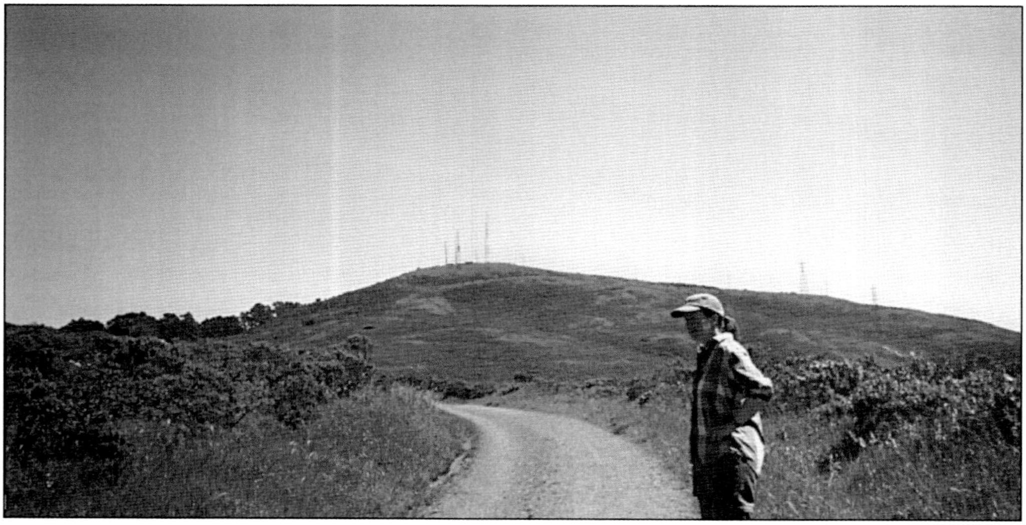

Here is Alta Avenue, also known as Alta Road, looking north, with an unidentified walker. The roadbed, like many in the headlands, is probably chert with a periodically scraped gravel surface. (Photograph by Dorothy Gibson.)

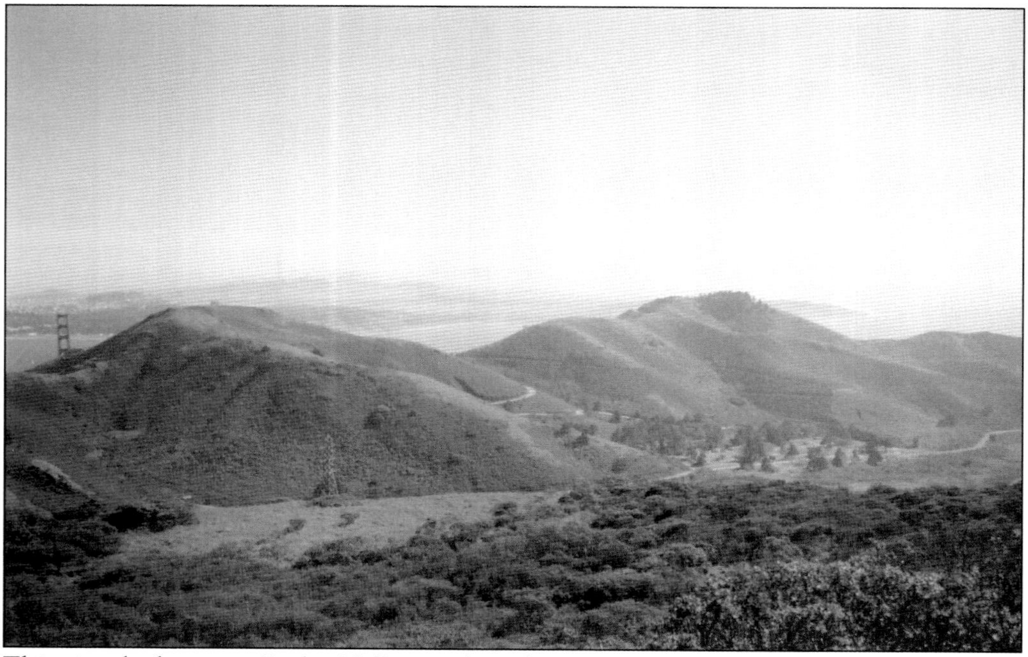

This view looks across Rodeo Valley south and across to the Golden Gate from the federal aviation tower. The one-lane tunnel through the mountain, constructed by the U.S. Army Corps of Engineers from West Fort Baker/Fort Barry to East Fort Baker, was cut through serpentine, a shiny greenish-brownish mineral/rock. (Photograph by Dorothy Gibson.)

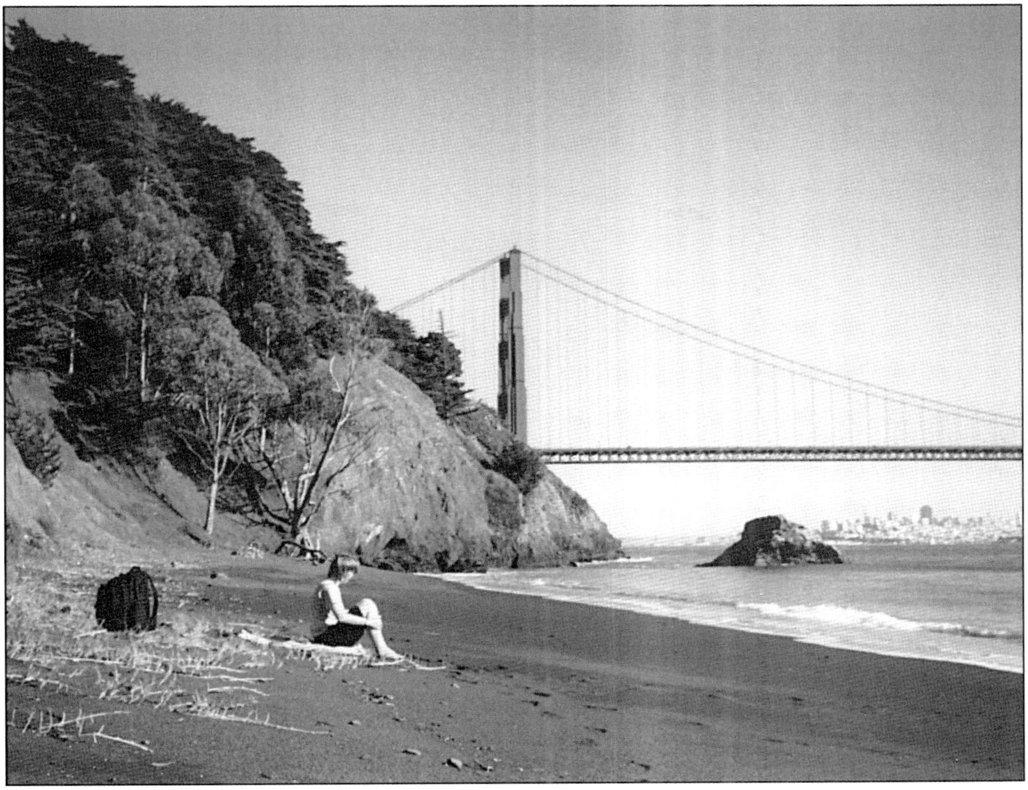

Kirby Cove Beach, also known as Gravelly Beach, has colorful sand with a mix of chert, basalt, and other sands. San Francisco is seen in the distance, and Battery Spencer is to the left above. (Photograph by Dorothy Gibson.)

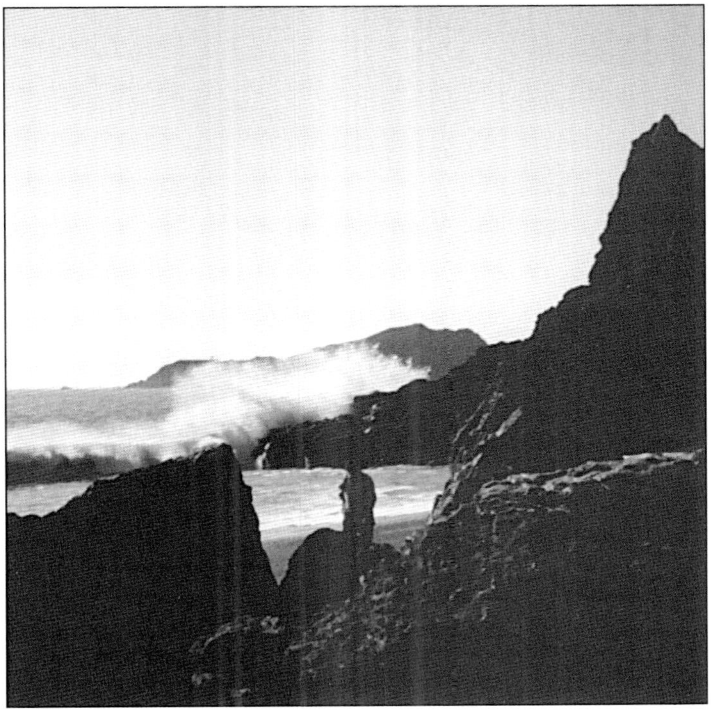

Black Sand Beach at the east end of Bonita Cove has a rock formation with a pillow basalt "spine." It is reached by a steep staircase off Conzelman Road. Farther on is Naked Beach. (Photograph by Dorothy Gibson.)

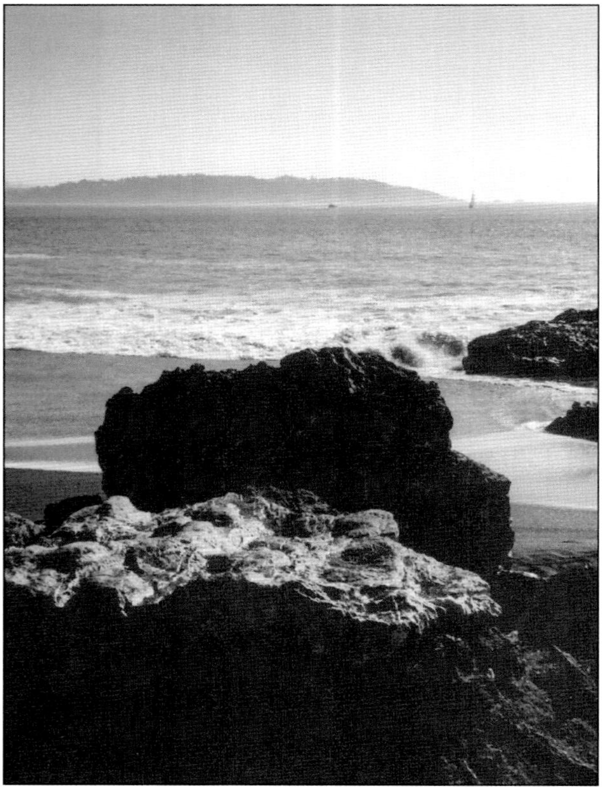

Black Sand Beach is directly across the Golden Gate opposite San Francisco's Land's End. The white rock overlay in the foreground is thought to be Franciscan limestone. (Photograph by Dorothy Gibson.)

There is much evidence of cliff erosion on South Rodeo Beach, where the rocks show layers of green chert (indicating reduced iron) and red chert with pillow lavas above. This beach is reached by a trail and steep staircase adjacent to a parking area to the north of Conzelman Road near the trail to Point Bonita Lighthouse or from Rodeo Beach proper at low tides. (Photograph by Dorothy Gibson.)

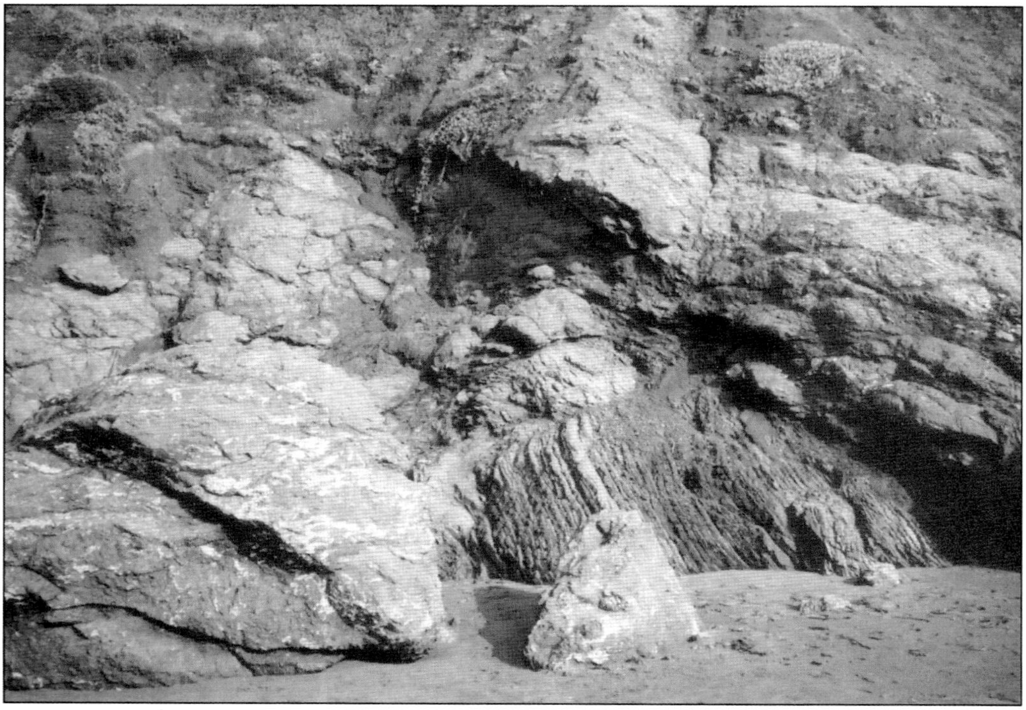

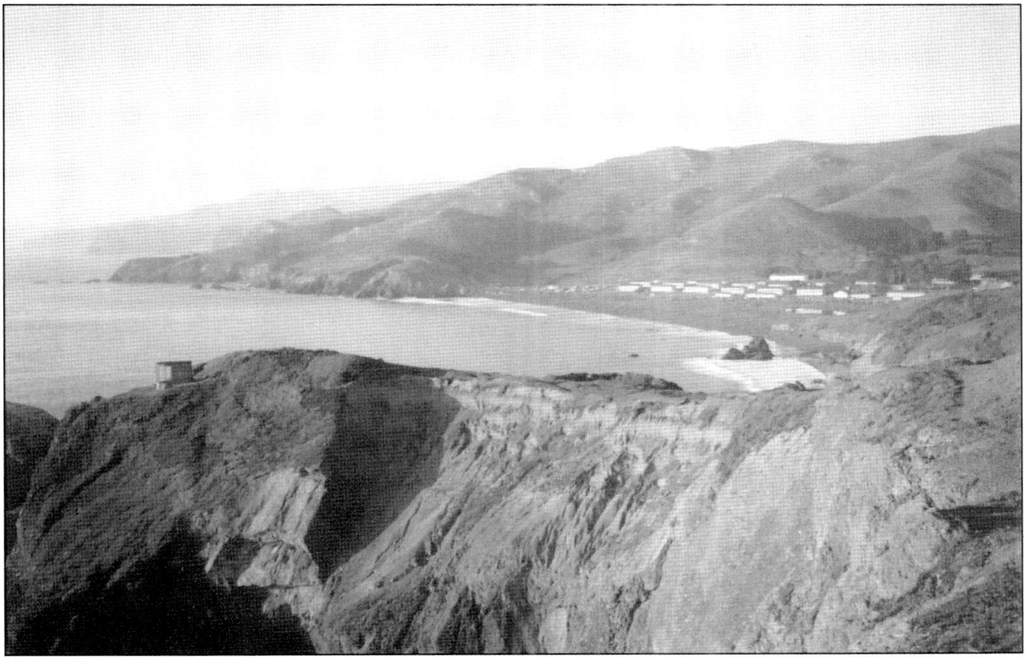

Bird Rock is also called Elephant Rock for its shape as seen from below. Birds frequent here. It is between South Rodeo Beach and Point Bonita. The formation is a pillow basalt marine terrace. (Photograph by Dorothy Gibson.)

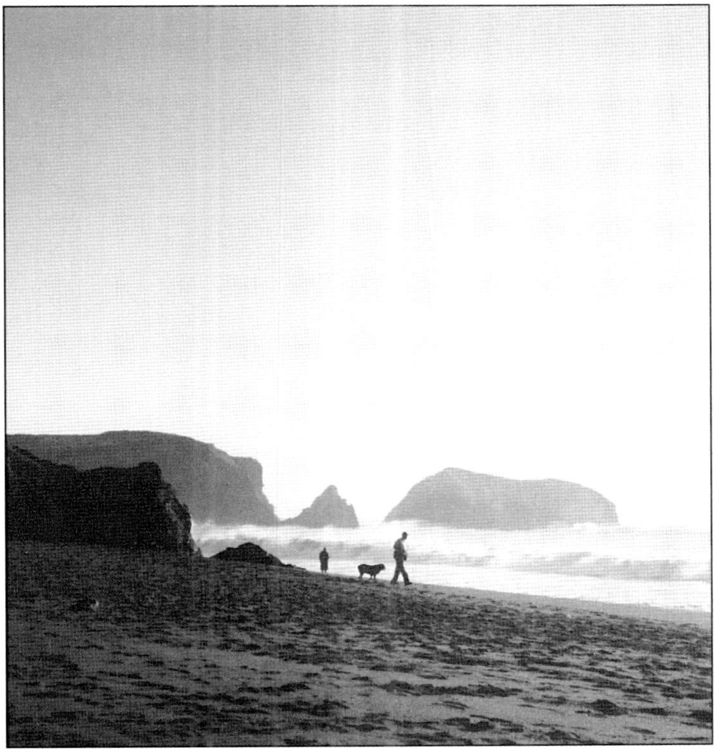

Pictured here is Elephant (Bird) Rock on Rodeo Beach at Fort Cronkite with high surf. The main ingredient is pillow basalt, a hard, dense, dark volcanic rock. (Photograph by Dorothy Gibson.)

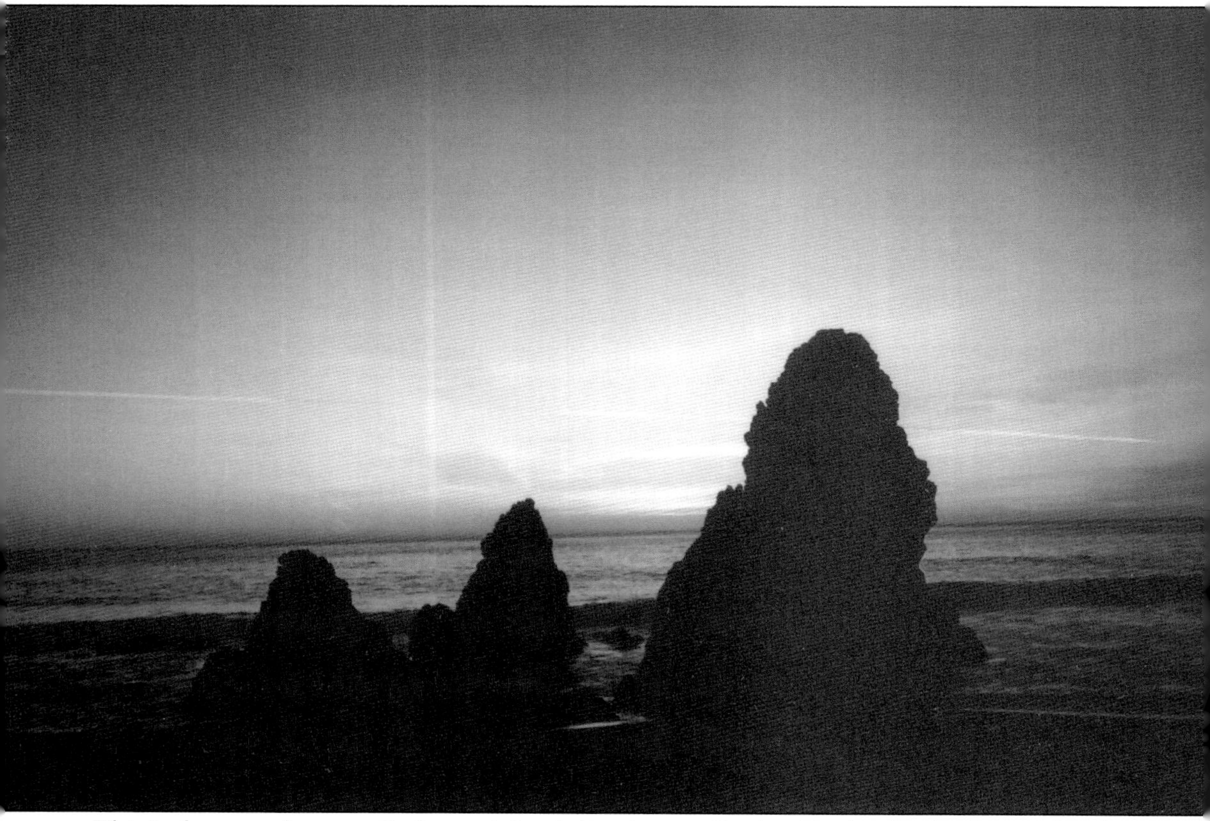

This is the scene between Rodeo and South Beaches via Bunker Road or Rodeo Lagoon Trail. The geological material is mostly pillow basalt and diabase. (Photograph by Dorothy Gibson.)

Two

Flora and Fauna

Botanists have determined that the rise of the ocean and its entrance into California's great valley had little influence on the plant life, which had been established previously. The rocks, the soil, the marshlands, the streams, the precipitation, the fog, and the mild but varying climate—all of these factors set the stage for the variety of native vegetation found in the headlands. Here, also, are now found additional species introduced by the early settlers both intentionally and accidentally. Since the Spanish, botanists have visited the area from time to time. One, Alice Eastwood of the California Academy of Science, began focusing on Marin County in 1842. In January 1855, Dr. Gilbert Kellogg described *Antirrhinum vexilla*—calyculatum, a lavender flower that grows in gravelly or rocky serpentine soil on sunny slopes in Sausalito and Mount Tamalpais. Over 100 other flowers may be found, such as California wild rose, ice plant, sticky monkey flower, California blackberry, Douglas iris, wild onion, miner's lettuce, wild strawberry, fennel, and purple and silver bush lupine.

Many animal species are here as well; the sea lion barks on the south side announce the entrance into San Francisco Bay, and harbor seals bask in the sun on flat rocks just to the north under the protection of Point Bonita. Both flop around in a seemingly boisterous way. In Sausalito and neighboring Strawberry Point, these and other sea life have been displaced and precariously overfished. Whaler's Cove in Sausalito, also known as Hurricane Gulch and Old Town, got its name from the butchering of whales for their blubber and hide. There salmon, sturgeon, steelhead, rockfish, herring, and crab are still taken from the shore and from small boats in Richardson Bay's Sausalito and Fort Baker area. Mussels still cling to rocks at the ocean-side beaches, as do barnacles around pilings. Grizzly bears were hunted to extinction. Black bears and elk have disappeared. Black-tailed deer are still here and have adapted, eating grass in the open, daring to descend into Sausalito and still swimming back and forth to Angel Island. Coyotes, raccoons, skunks, mice, rats, fox, opossum, rabbits, squirrels, bobcats, and an occasional mountain lion are also here. Currently, the Audubon Society reports 310 native bird species. The California Valley quail (*Callipepla californica*) was designated the state bird by the legislature in 1931. Ladybugs, spiders, flies, mosquitoes, butterflies—monarch and little blue, though endangered—are still here.

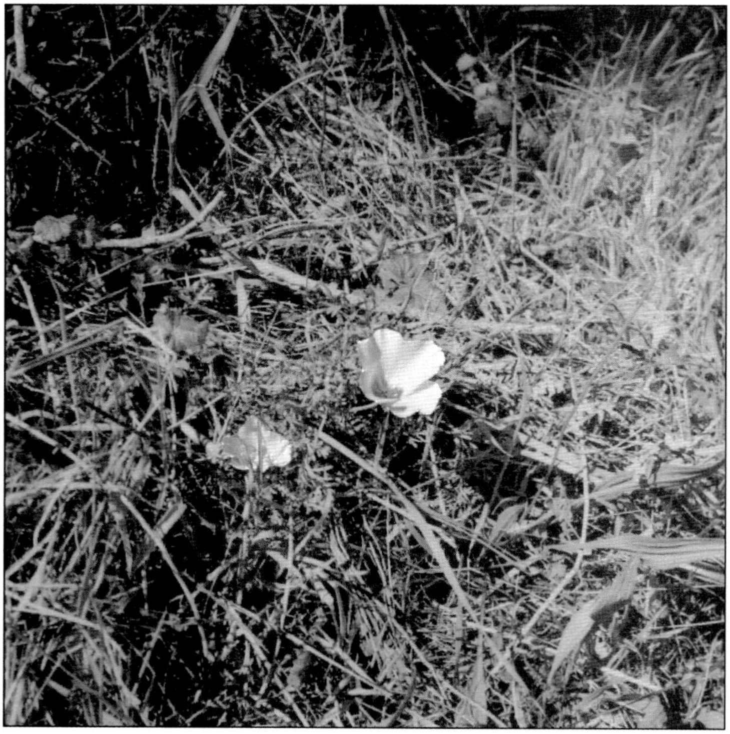

This California poppy is on the upper hillside of the Alexander area in Fort Baker near the tunnel to West Fort Baker and Fort Barry. The California poppy became California's state flower in 1903 when the legislature officially adopted it. Golden poppies (*Eschscholzia californica*), according to the *California Almanac and State Fact Book*, are "found throughout the state on any day throughout the year . . . bright with the gleam of our gold mines, warm with the radiance of our sunshine, typify the ideal of California." (Photograph by Dorothy Gibson.)

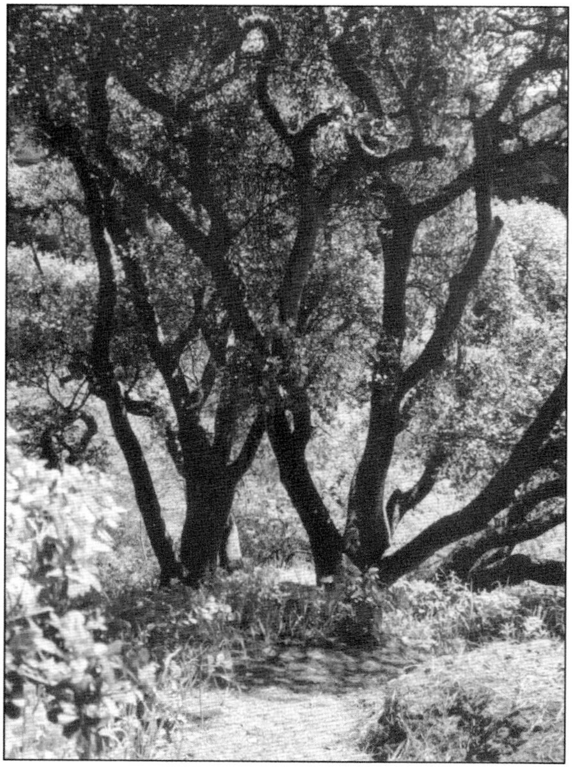

Here is a live oak, typical of many down the creek bed from Alta Road to Tennessee Valley Road (Oakwood Valley). The Miwok Indians depended upon the acorns as a basic food supply. They would be leached to take away the wild bitterness and pounded into flour for bread and cakes. The limbs always form a graceful pattern from the base. (Photograph by Dorothy Gibson.)

Purple thistles adorn Tennessee Valley in the autumn. This view is on the road/walkway down to the lagoon and the beach. Hikers are advised to appreciate the beauty of this plant but not to touch, for obvious reasons. (Photograph by Dorothy Gibson.)

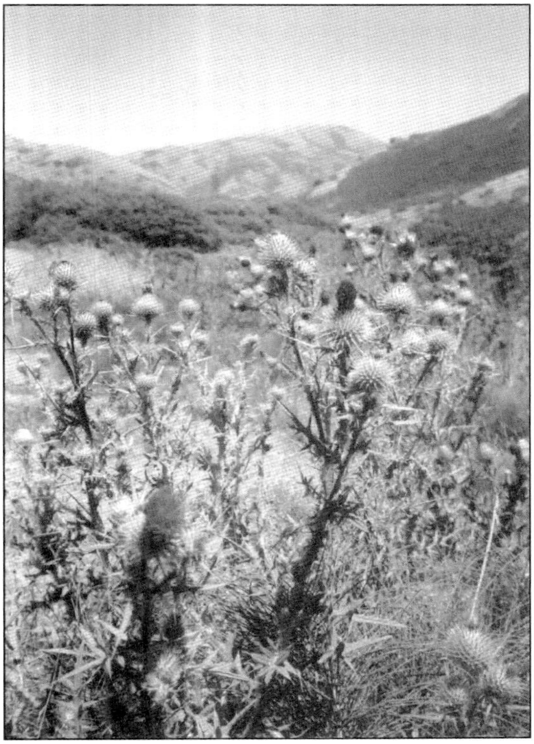

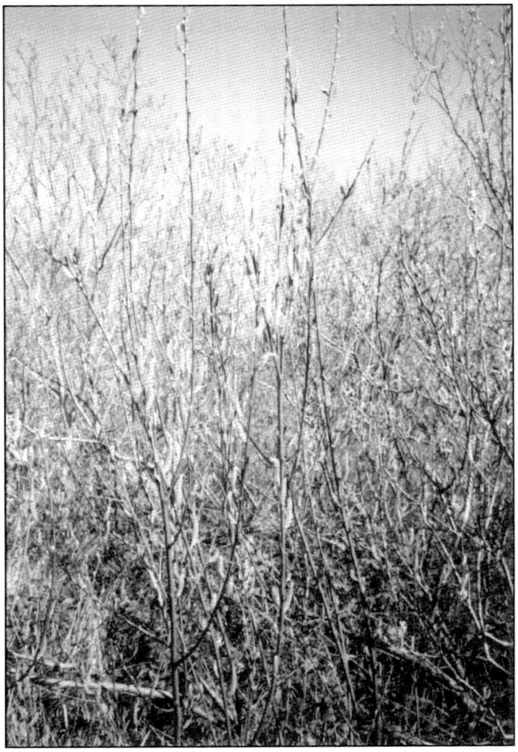

This image depicts pussy willows but not the weeping willow variety (which come from Italy; these are native). Sausalito was named with the Spanish word for "little place of willows." No doubt they were in abundance in the valley in Whaler's Cove (Old Town), where the two streams came down to form one to go to the San Francisco Bay. There are some still in Nevada Valley in Sausalito, such as at Bridgeway and Nevada Streets. (Photograph by Dorothy Gibson.)

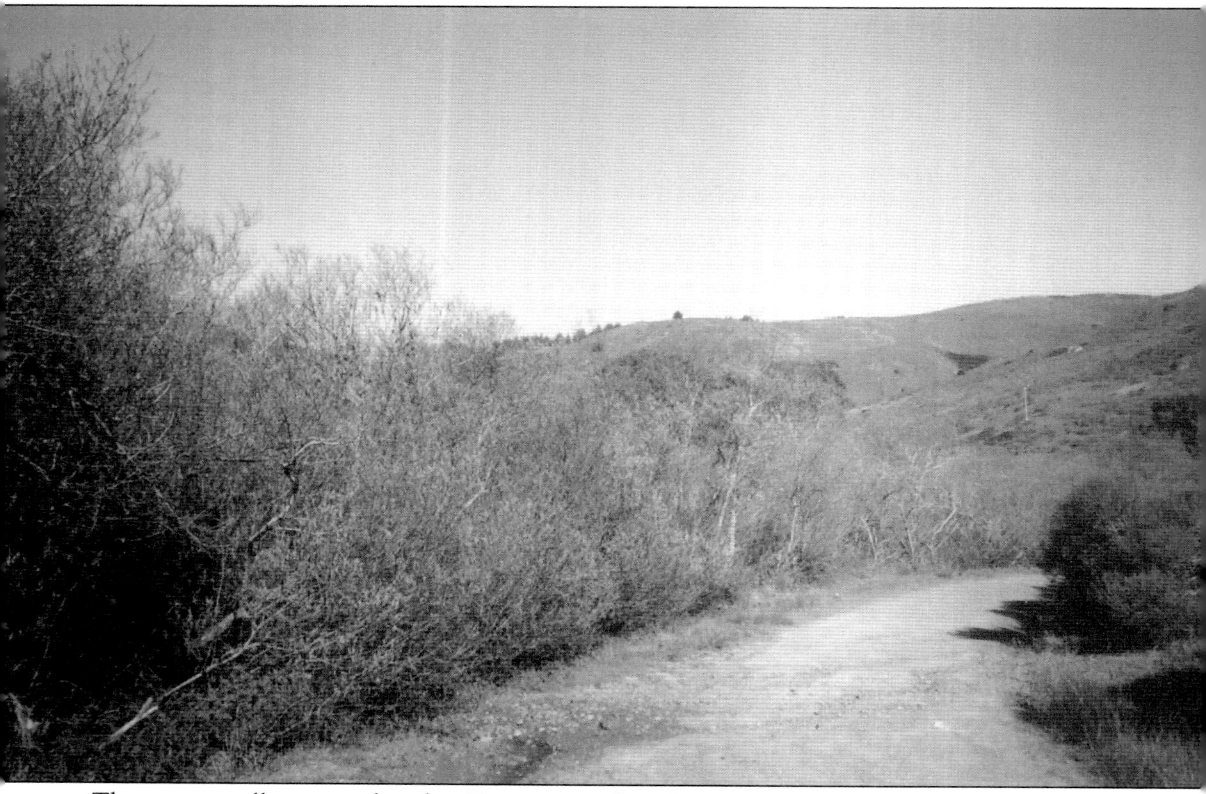

These pussy willows were found in Tennessee Valley along the little creek beside the road going up the hill on the way to the lagoon and beach. (Photograph by Dorothy Gibson.)

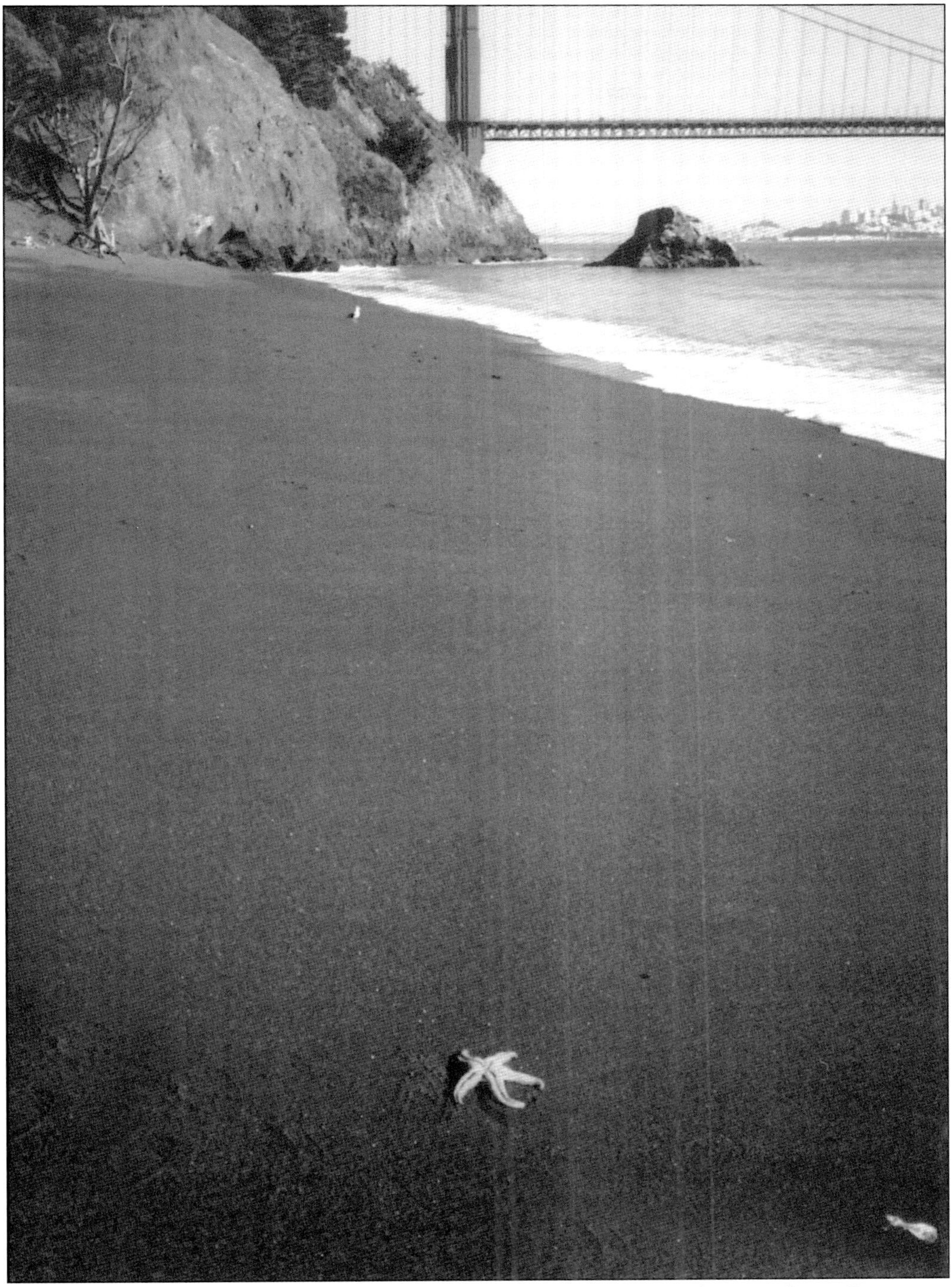

Starfish appear at low tide on Kirby Cove, also known as Gravelly Beach, west of Lime Point near the Golden Gate's north tower. (Photograph by Dorothy Gibson.)

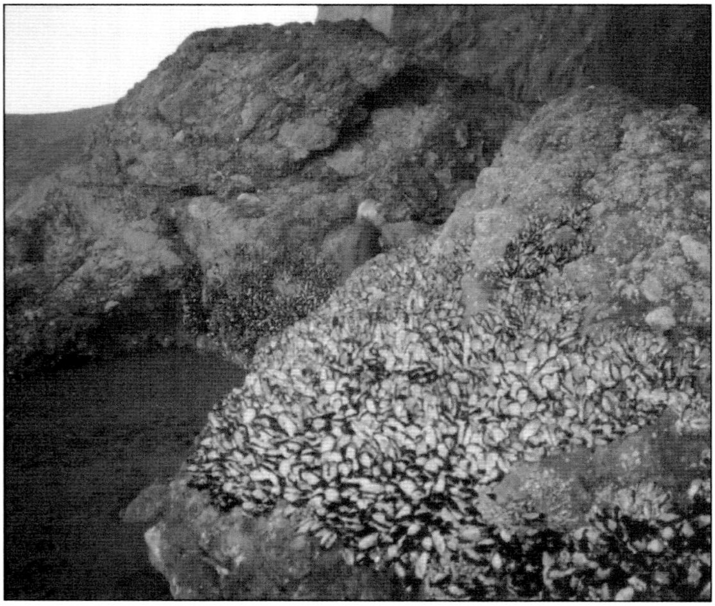

The rock at Rodeo Beach, also known as Fort Cronkite, is mostly "blobby"—that is, hard-to-erode bulbous basalt with mussels attached. (Photograph by Dorothy Gibson.)

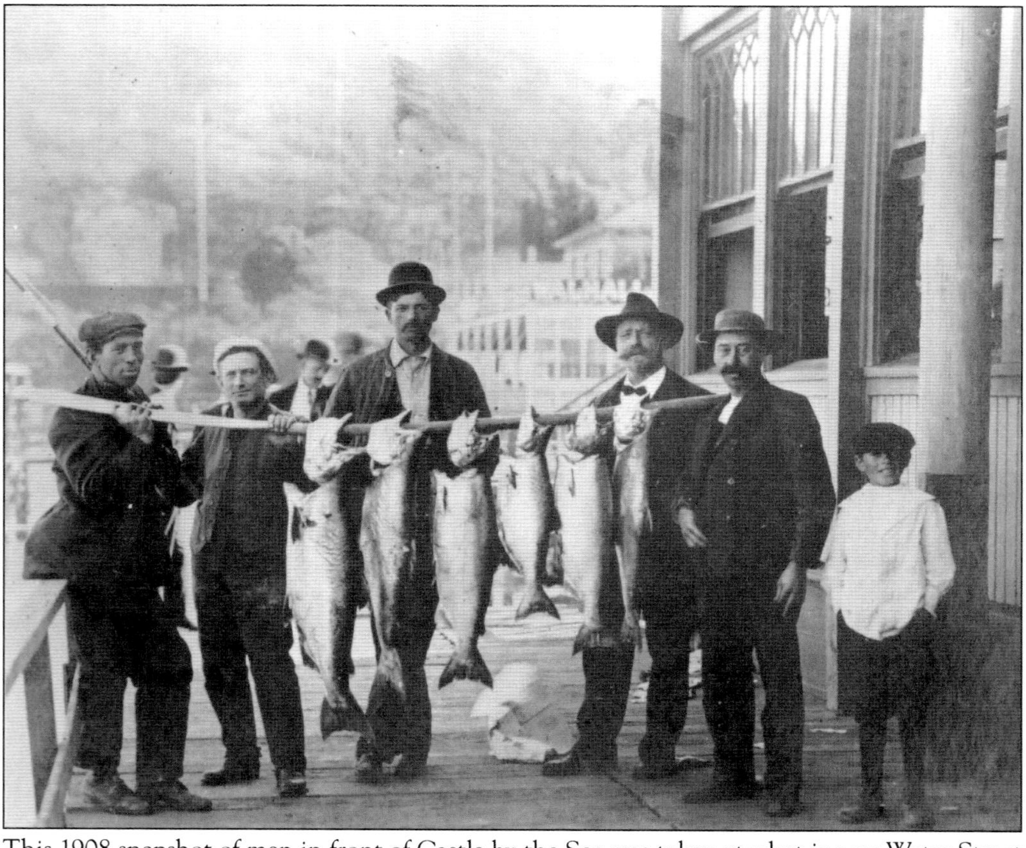

This 1908 snapshot of men in front of Castle by the Sea was taken at what is now Water Street in Old Town Sausalito, or Whaler's Cove. (Courtesy Sausalito Historical Society, 84-116.)

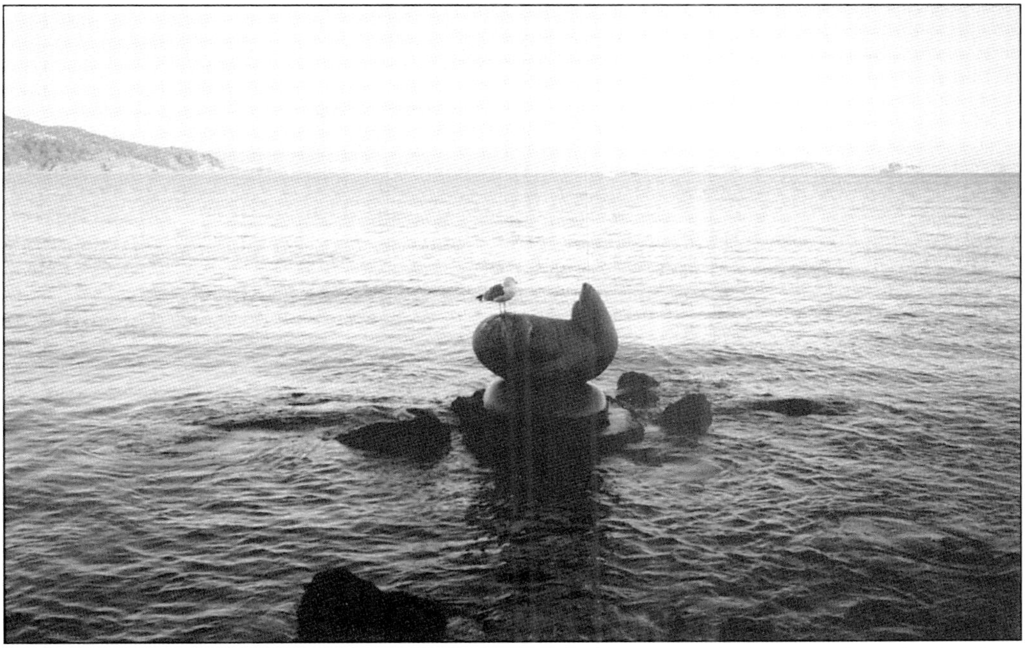

This western seagull is perched on top of Sausalito's sculpture on Bridgeway, along Richardson Bay from Old Town to Sausalito Point (Princess Street downtown). The bronze plaque reads, "Sausalito Sea Lion Sculpture, Al E. Sybrian, Sculptor, Bronze casting 1996, Foundry 3, San Francisco, Sponsored by the Sausalito Foundation." (Photograph by Dorothy Gibson.)

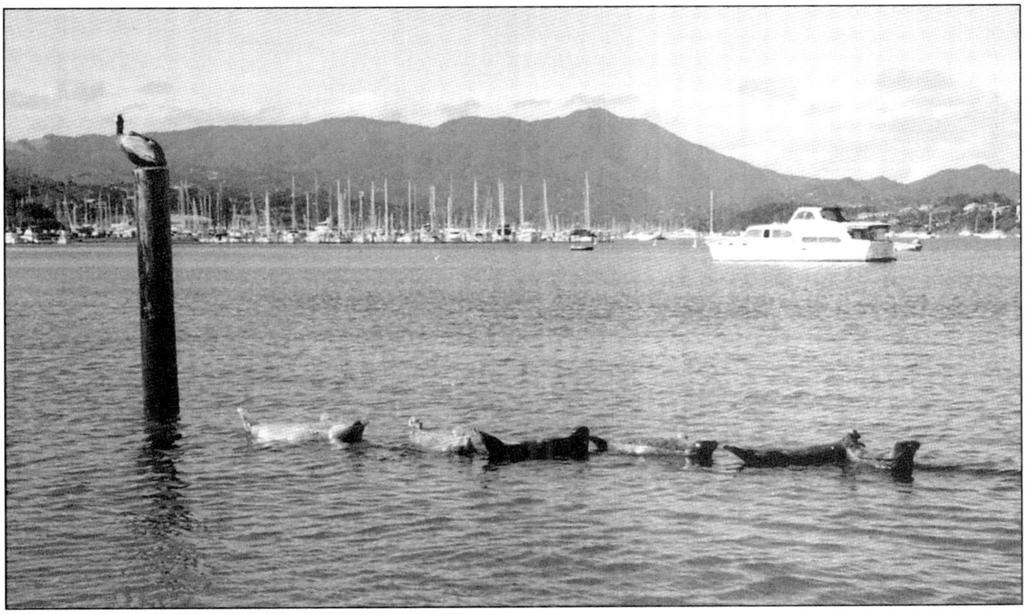

A brown-billed pelican rests on a piling while harbor seals lounge on an old plank underneath at Pelican Harbor in Sausalito. Mount Tamalpais is pictured in the background. The area is noted for eelgrass, a necessary diet for aquatic life. Many locals hope this will become a sanctuary area. (Photograph by Dorothy Gibson.)

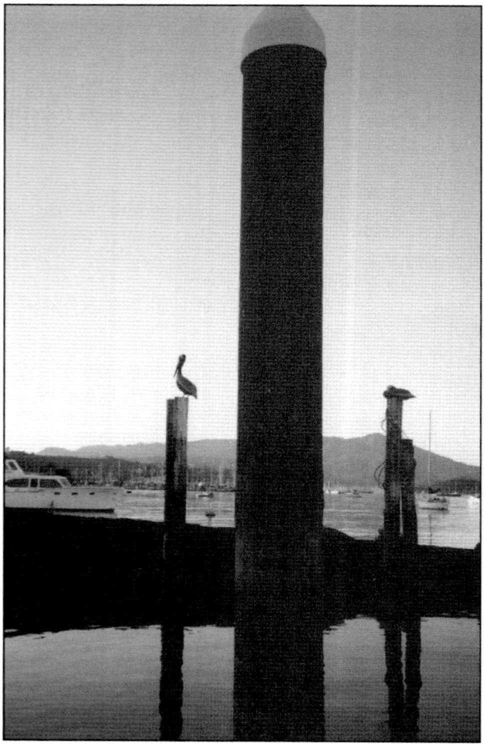

Here are some common visitors (and residents) of the headlands—a pelican with a California gull. (Photograph by Dorothy Gibson.)

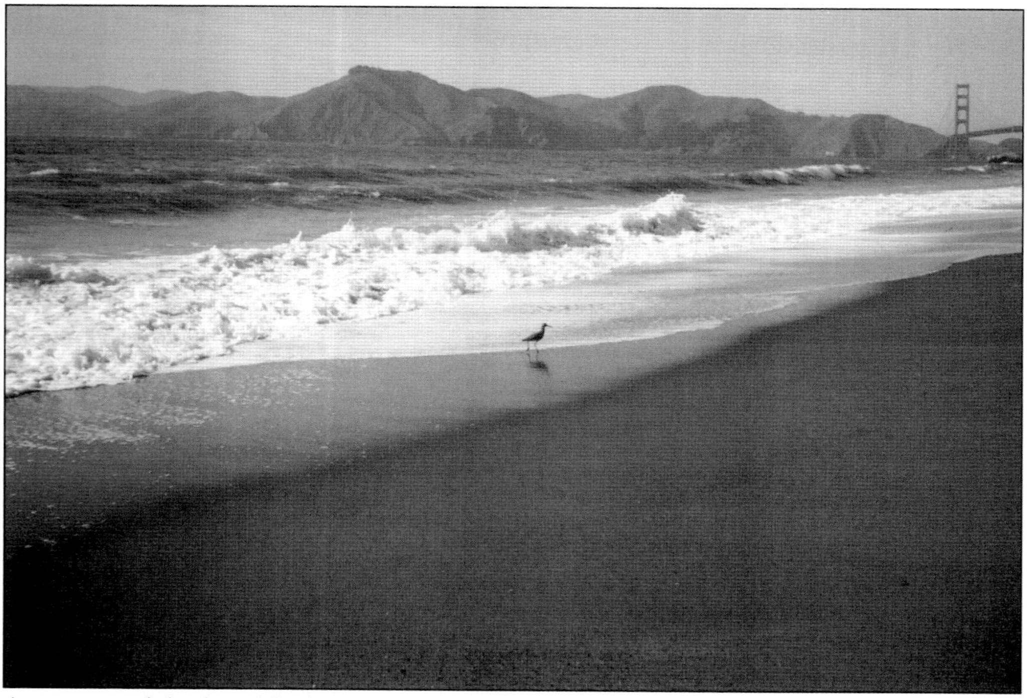

As waves wash back and forth at Baker Beach in San Francisco, a sandpiper catches comestibles across from the headlands. (Photograph by Dorothy Gibson.)

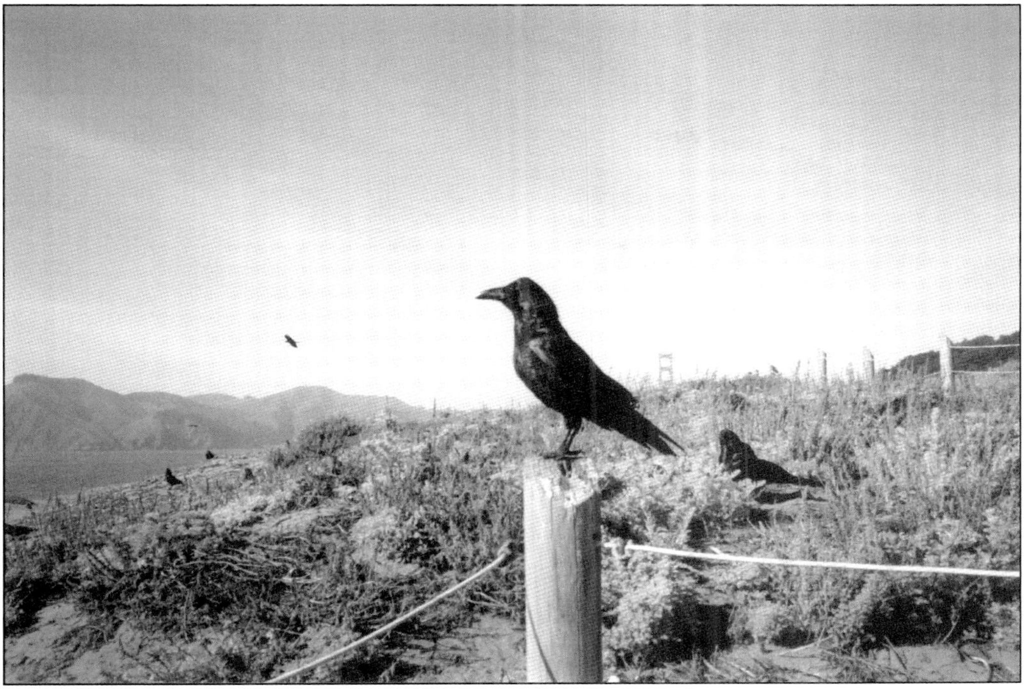
Here a black crow sits on a beach post, one of a larger flock moving in for a feast very likely left by picnickers at Baker Beach. (Photograph by Dorothy Gibson.)

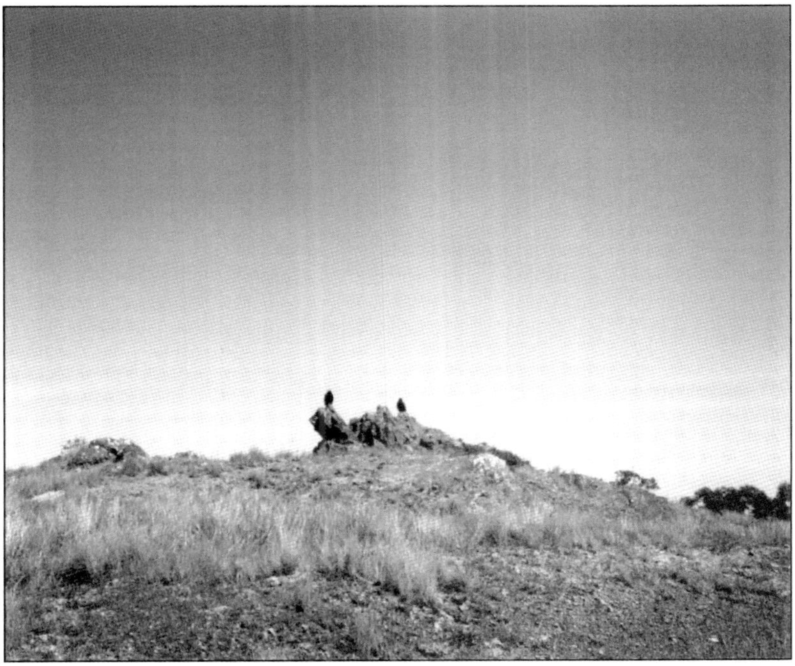
Turkey vultures roost along the Student Conservation Trail on Wolfback Ridge above Rodeo Valley to the east. (Photograph by Dorothy Gibson.)

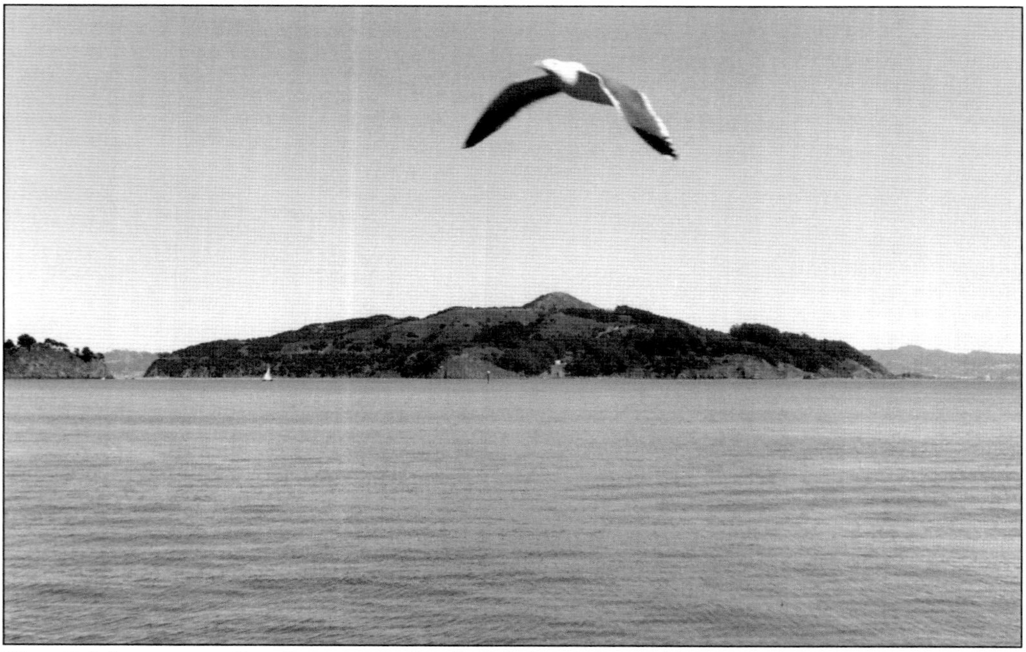

This California seagull is floating on the draft behind the Golden Gate Ferry to San Francisco. Angel Island is seen in the background. (Photograph by Dorothy Gibson.)

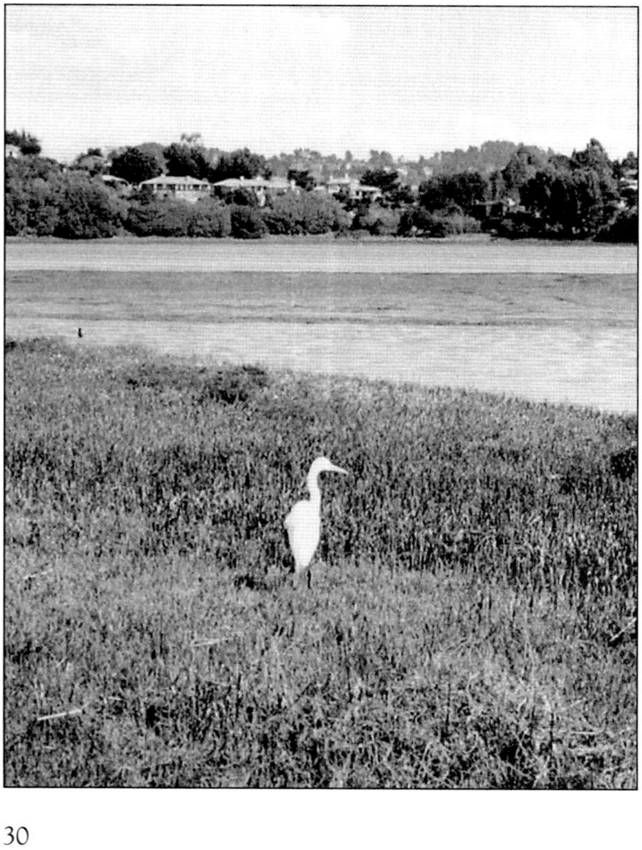

A familiar sight around the headlands are great egrets, such as this one in a marsh in upper Richardson Bay opposite Strawberry Point. (Photograph by Dorothy Gibson.)

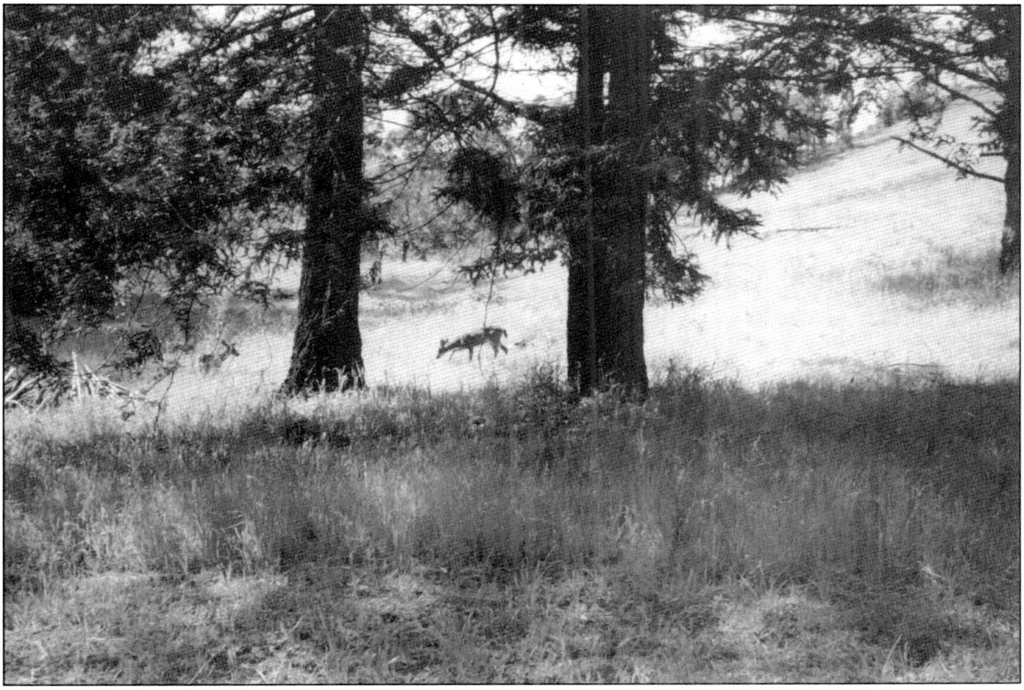

Female deer congregate on the grassy slope at East Fort Baker. These animals have been seen going down through the trees and swimming all the way across Richardson Bay to Angel Island. (Photograph by Dorothy Gibson.)

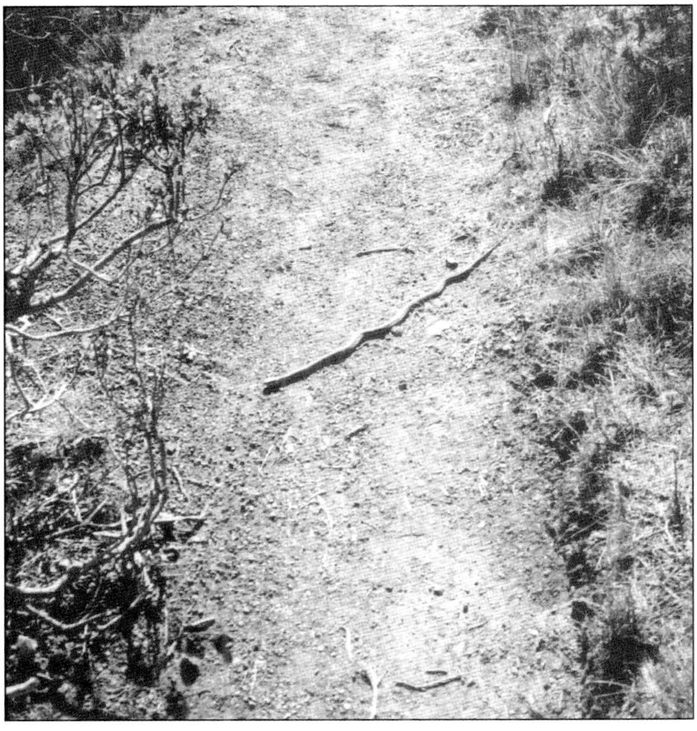

A western aquatic garter snake crosses the narrow path above Bonita Cove. Note its characteristic bright yellow and black stripes. (Photograph by Dorothy Gibson.)

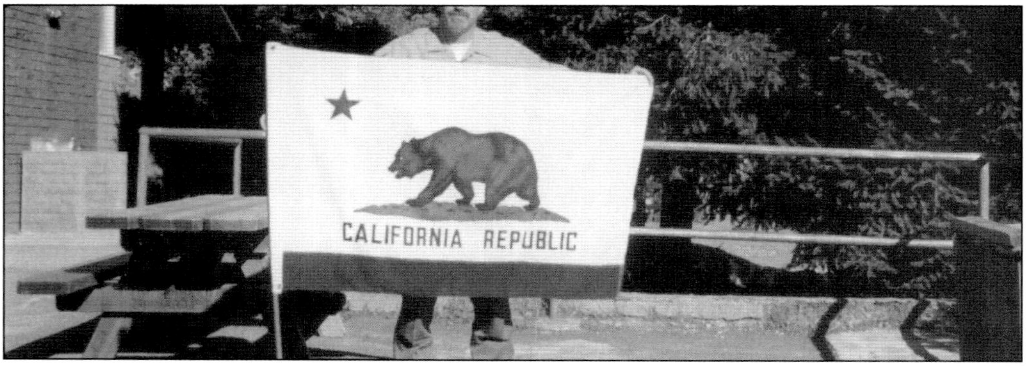

From Mount Tamalpais's East Peak Visitor Center area, an unidentified hiker poses with a newly purchased California flag. The California grizzly bear was made an official symbol by the California State Legislature in 1911 after the Bear Flag Revolt of 1846. Black bears are no longer known to be in Marin County, but several years ago, one young male did appear on Eldridge Grade. The rangers carefully and firmly escorted him back north. (Photograph by Dorothy Gibson.)

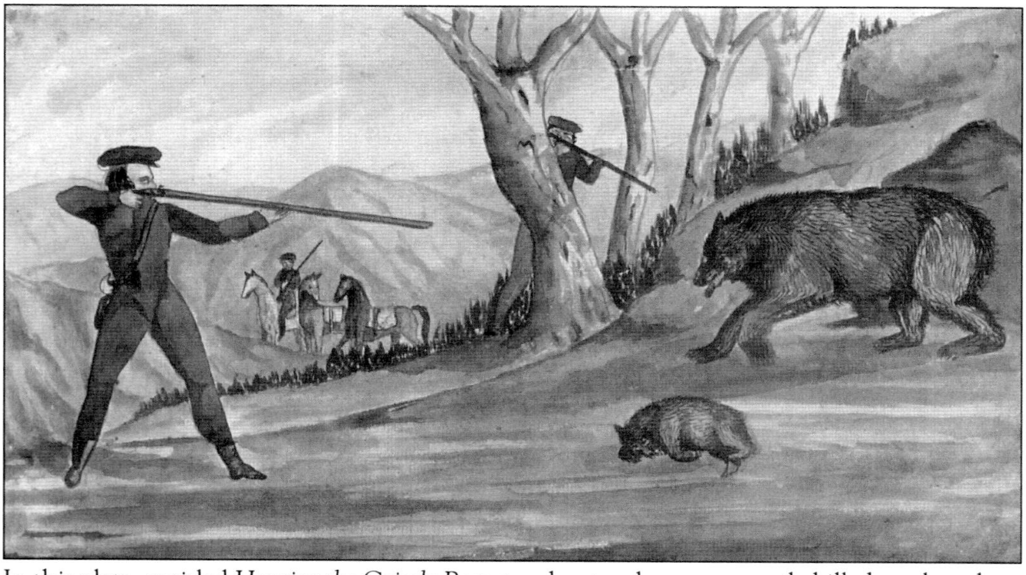

In this plate, entitled *Hunting the Grizzly Bear*, two hunters have apparently killed a cub and are now both aiming at the mother bear, as a third hunter sits astride his horse in the distance and holds the horses of the two men who have dismounted. Noted watercolorist William H. Meyers, who created this plate, indulged in this most dangerous and exciting of field sports with his friends while in California. His journal refers repeatedly to bear hunting while his vessel *Cyane* was anchored off Sausalito in 1842 and 1843. Book Club of California reproduced this plate in 1955. (Courtesy Roland C. Beisenstein collection, Mill Valley.)

Three

THE FIRST PEOPLE OF MARIN

The Native Americans lived in protected shoreline areas near fresh water. Archeological sites have been found in the southern Marin County area, including Mill Valley, Silva Island (the oldest is 5,000 years), Sausalito, Belvedere, and Tiburon. The Native Americans here and in the headlands were a branch of the Miwoks called the Huiman tribe (pronounced Wee-men). Chief Marin, a leader of the Huiman, was considered colorful, defiant, brave, and clever by Mariano Vallejo, the former Mexican commandant general who, in 1850, proposed his name for that of the county to the north of the San Francisco Presidio and the Golden Gate. Early explorers and sailors found the Native Americans friendly, gentle, and even childlike as they exchanged objects. Later, with the establishment of the Spanish-Mexican presidio and mission system, they were further enticed by the baptismal ceremony and then coerced into the formal everyday agrarian life of providing for the lands, buildings, horses, and cattle of the system. For women, there were the traditional homemaking roles. For men with special skills, there were some ventures with the military on sea and land expeditions. Those who rebelled and resisted were punished. Those who escaped were captured.

In 1821, Mexico succeeded in its rebellion against Spain, and the new government took over. In the 1830s, the Mexican government began dismantling and secularizing the mission system and promising the Miwok their private lands. It never came to pass. American settlers moved in, seizing horses meant for the mission militia and forming a group that arrested and jailed Gen. Mariano Vallejo, commandant of Northern California, as they carried a flag with the California bear painted on it. This was followed by a routing of the California militia at Olompali and by Gen. John C. Fremont's storming the Mission San Rafael Arcangel, where historic documents were destroyed. Commodore J. D. Sloat of the U.S. Navy arrived from Mexico and ordered the American flag flown over Monterey, the capital. Mexican rule came to a close in January 1847. In 1850, California was accepted as a state. In 1920, the United States purchased 15.45 acres at Graton in Sonoma County for the landless Native Americans. Years went by. In 1993, the Native American descendants rallied around an exhibit at a small museum in Bolinas and through their congressional representatives petitioned for federal recognition granting them full constitutional rights. Pres. Bill Clinton signed the legislation in 2000. They are now known as the Federated Indians of Graton Rancheria.

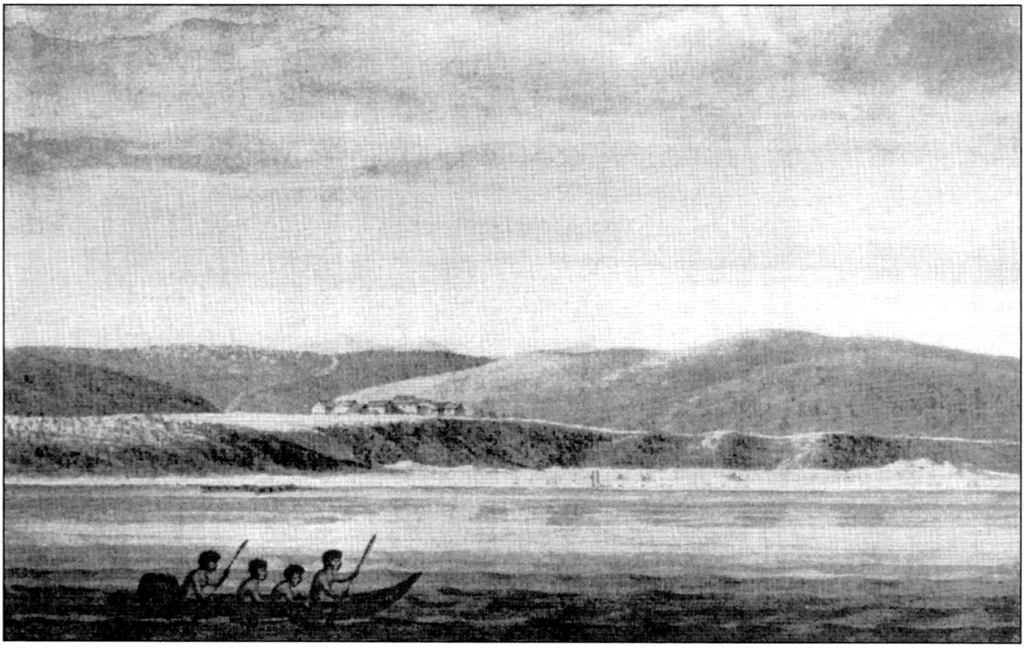

In this illustration by Dr. Georg Heinrich Langsdorff from John Haskla Kimble's *San Francisco Bay, A Pictorial Maritime History*, a Native American boat made of tule is propelled by double-bladed paddles along the bay shore. The presidio is in the background. (Courtesy San Francisco Maritime Museum.)

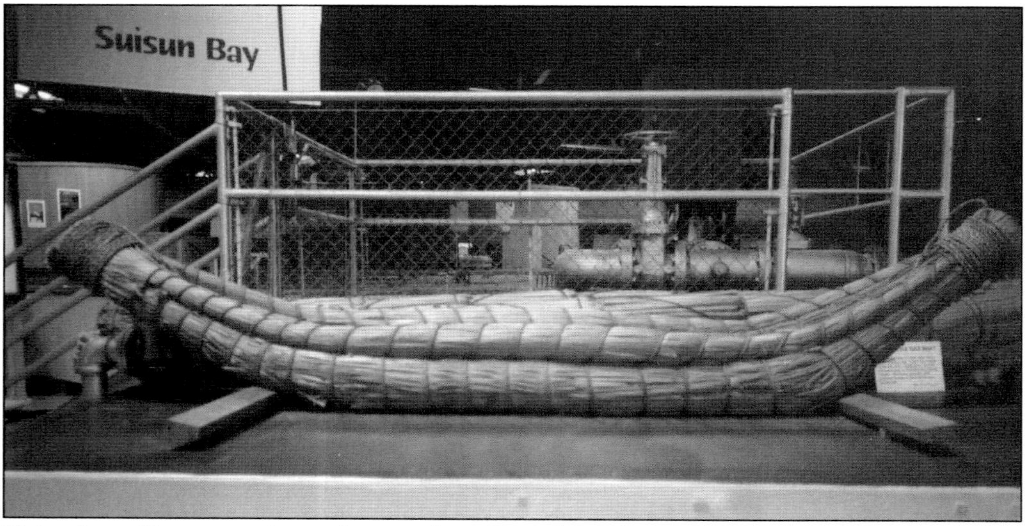

This tule reed boat is similar in shape to those formerly used on San Francisco Bay but has features more typical of Bolivian reed boats, such as an even number of bundles and a spiral binding. The end bindings are of cattail and the spiral bindings of commercial rope. This boat is on exhibit at the San Francisco Bay Model Visitor Center, San Francisco District, U.S. Army Corps of Engineers, in Sausalito. (Photograph by Dorothy Gibson.)

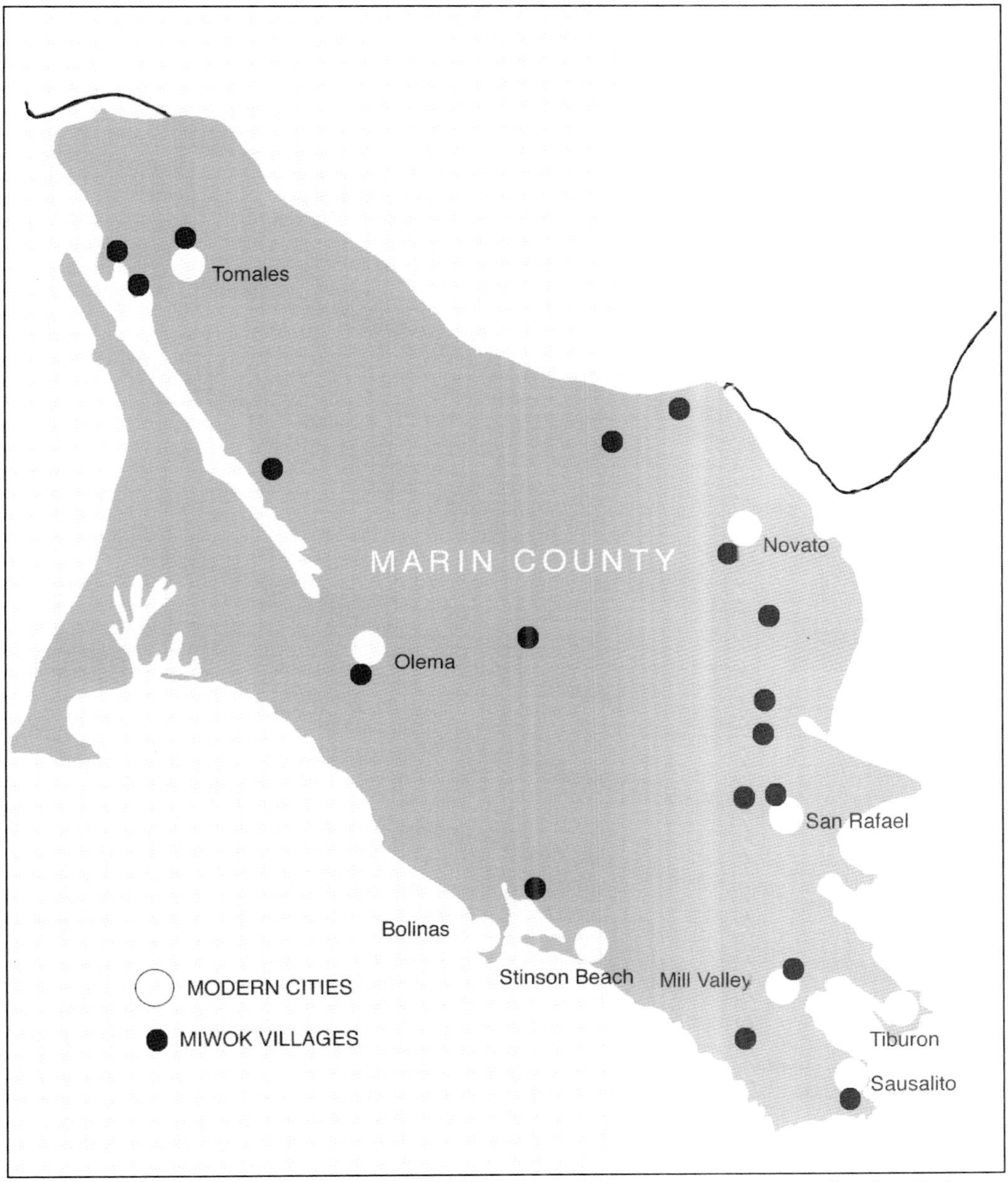

The known Miwok village sites in Marin County, California, are shown on this detailed map adapted from *Coast Miwok of Marin* by Iva Pace. (Courtesy Mill Valley History Room, Mill Valley Public Library.)

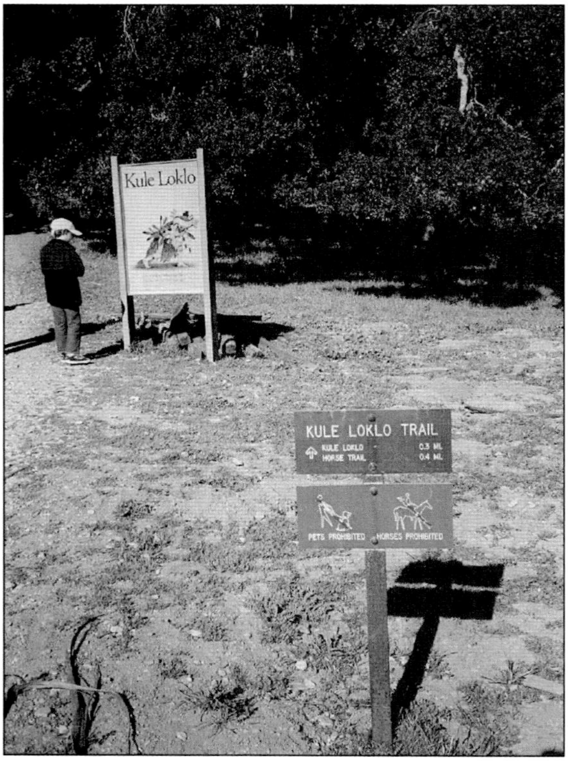

This walkway—Kule Loklo (Bear Valley)—at Point Reyes National Seashore, close to the visitor center, allows visitors to see what the headlands area was like 200 years ago. The trail leads past a group of trees on the right to an area where educational posters are placed. (Photograph by Dorothy Gibson.)

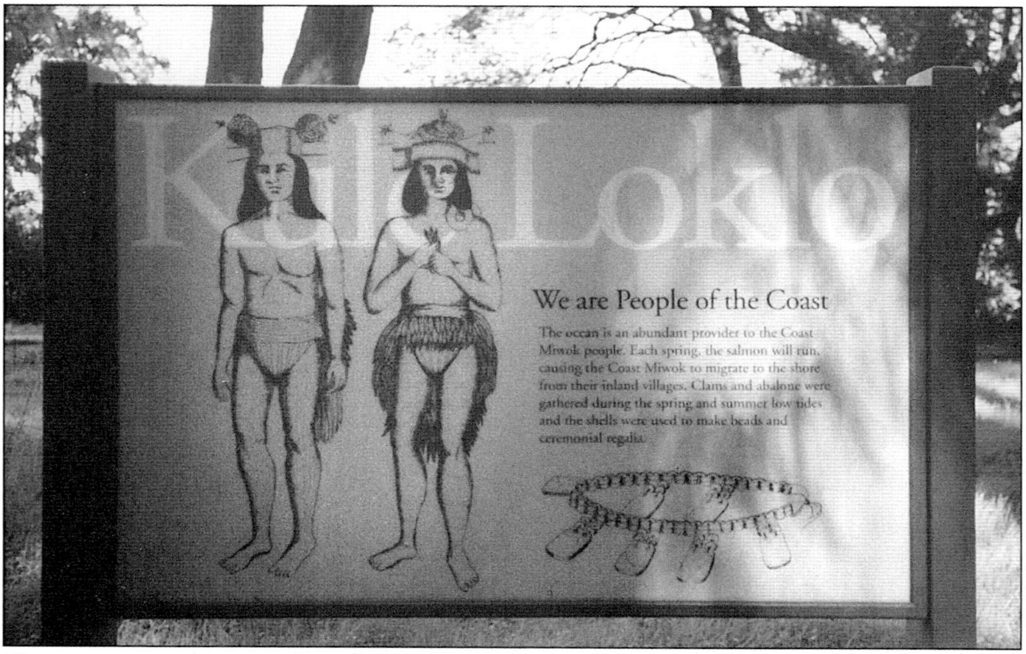

This opening in the trees along the trail holds a clearing, a small meadow, a community of tule *kotca* (houses), a large rack for drying things (like skins), and elevated planks for worktables. (Photograph by Dorothy Gibson.)

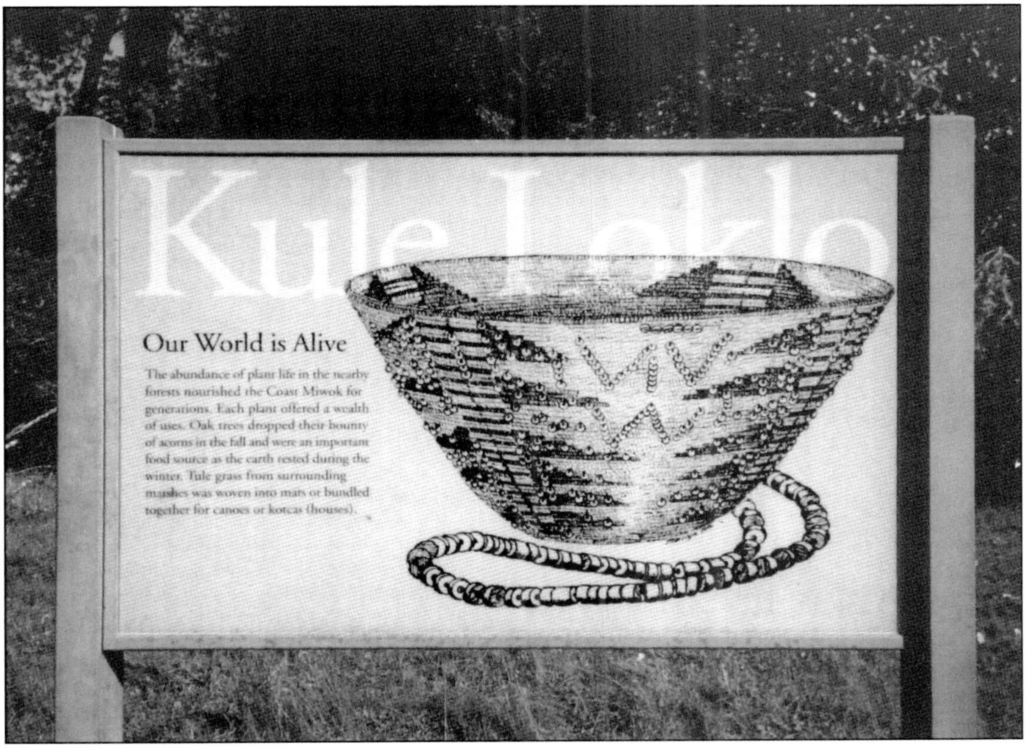

This sign discusses the living world of the Point Reyes National Seashore, in particular the varied plant life used by the coastal Miwoks. (Photograph by Dorothy Gibson.)

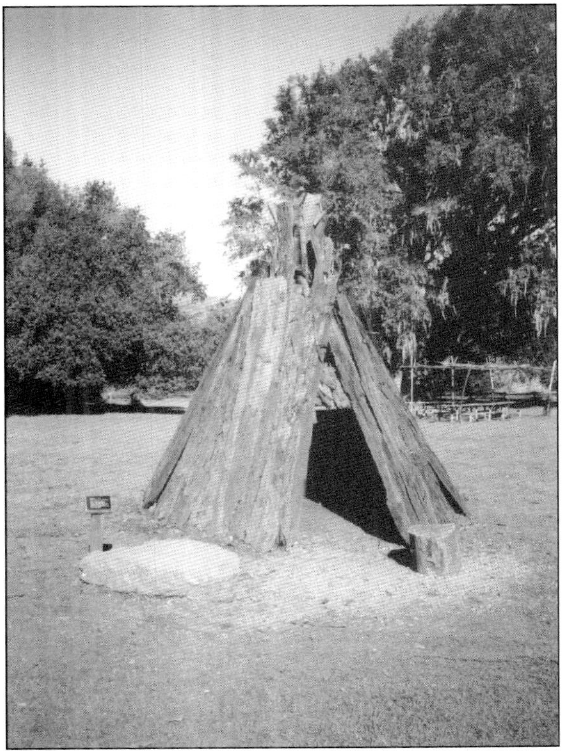

With their open entrances, these tule kotca invite visitors to come in and "play house," so to speak. Despite their primitive appearance, they actually make for a very congenial environment. (Photograph by Dorothy Gibson.)

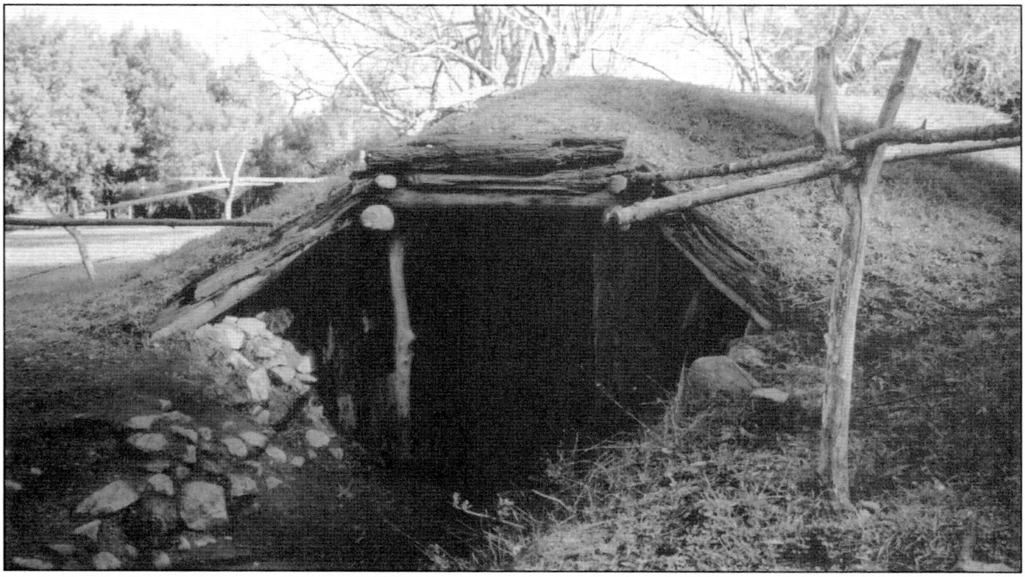

This is a sweat house (sometimes called a sweat lodge), designed for ceremonial rituals of Native American men. A fire is built inside, and water is poured on to hot stones to create steam. Some gatherings involve complete silence and meditation, while others include talking, chanting, or drumming. Women are not allowed to enter except on special occasions. (Photograph by Dorothy Gibson.)

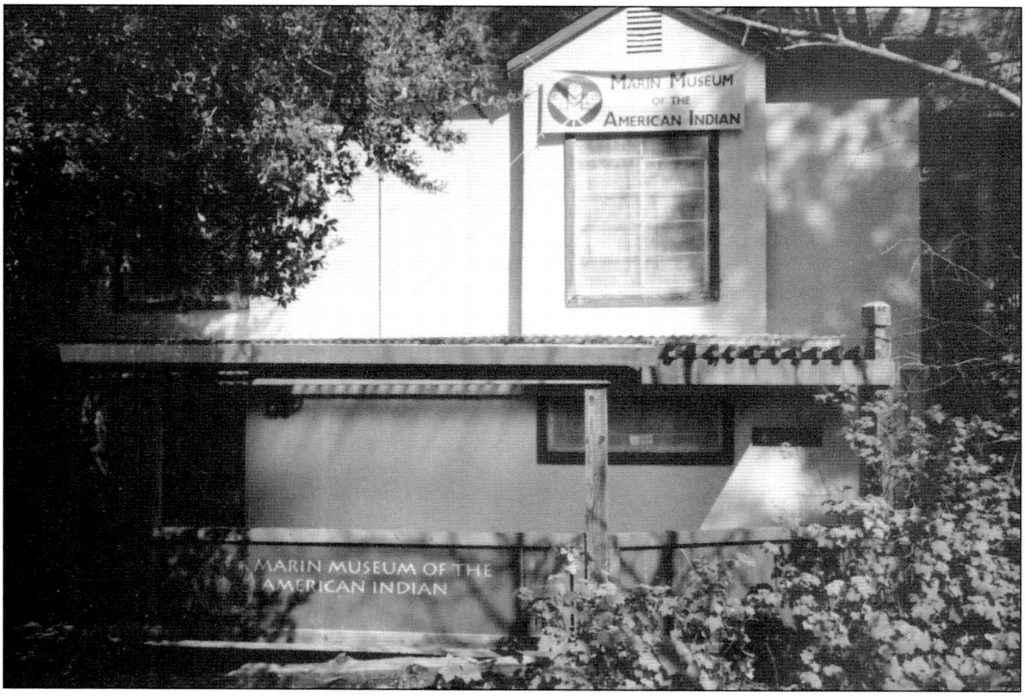

This small two-story house, shaded by trees, is on the grounds of Miwok Park in Novato. There are picnic tables and a path nearby, as well as a creek lined with trees. Inside the museum are permanent and temporary exhibits dedicated to the local Native Americans. (Photograph by Dorothy Gibson.)

Four

Those Enduring Explorers and Settlers

In 1542, Juan Rodriguez Cabrillo, by order of the viceroy of New Spain, led an expedition up towards Northern California and got as far as Mendocino. He was looking for a northwest passage from the Atlantic to the Pacific. He did not find it. In 1564, Miguel Lopez de Legazpi led an expedition securing a foothold in the Philippines—a stopover from Spain to Acapulco, Mexico, via Manila. In 1578, Sir Francis Drake proceeded to navigate the world for Queen Elizabeth I. After some troubles at the strait, he proceeded north, captured several Spanish ships, searched for the Northwest Passage, did not find it, repaired his ship after taking possession for the queen, and returned to England via the Moluccas, around the Cape of Good Hope, and up the African coast. Queen Elizabeth knighted him.

Two hundred years later, Spanish settlers, soldiers, and missionaries moved up the coast at the direction of the viceroy, Marquis de Monte Claro, who thought it the best way of not calling attention to competitors. Spain had charted San Diego, Monterey, and Punta de los Reyes (Drake's Bay). Discovering no direct Asia–to–North America connection, others explored the far north for Russia, which was laying claim to North America. They persevered, eventually finding what was to be called the Bering Sea as well as Native Americans on the coastline of North America. Spain resumed its naval exploration with success when Lt. Juan Manuel de Ayala, captain of the *San Carlos*, entered San Francisco Bay, anchored in a cove (Angel Island), and stayed from August 13 to September 7, 1775. The first survey was made of San Francisco Bay. In his diary, Ayala spoke favorably of the climate and of the people encountered as always friendly. On March 27, 1776, Spanish captain Juan Bautiste de Anza with Fr. Pedro Font and an advance party of soldiers ended a difficult nine-month trek from Mexico to San Francisco Bay, camping for two days at Mountain Lake. Three months later, 103 settlers arrived and staked out the ground for the presidio. Father Font wrote in his diary expressing pleasure for the area. Nearby there would be the mission called Dolores.

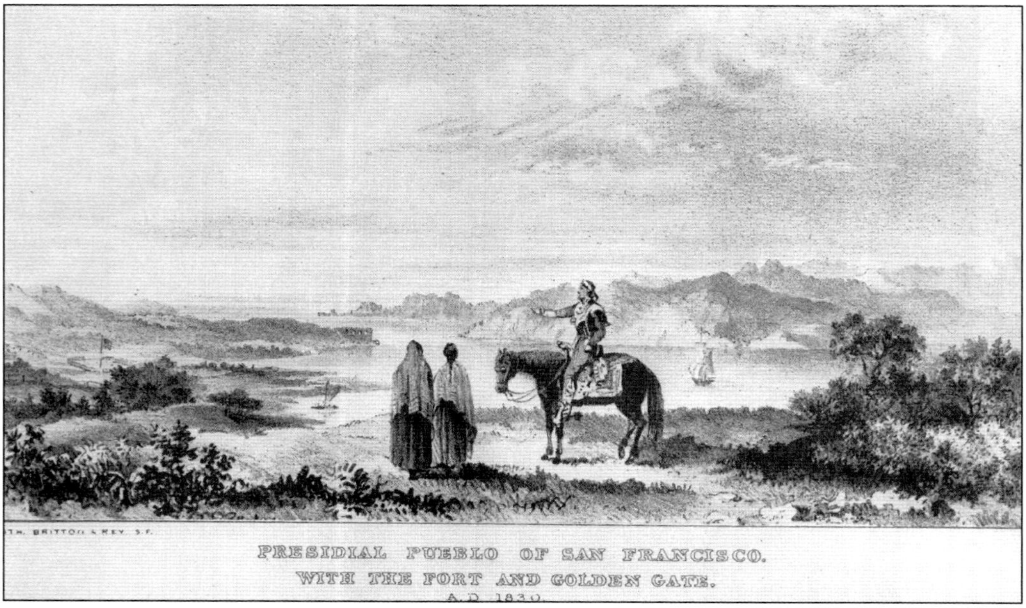

The detail of this painting, *Presidial Pueblo of San Francisco with the Fort and Golden Gate A.D. 1830*, shows Point Bonita on the far opposite shore and closer to what would be called the Marin Headlands today. Fort Point is on the opposite side of the Golden Gate. On the rise is a Spanish caballero on horseback gesturing with two women, probably Native Americans. (Courtesy GGNRA Archives, manuscript 324562a.)

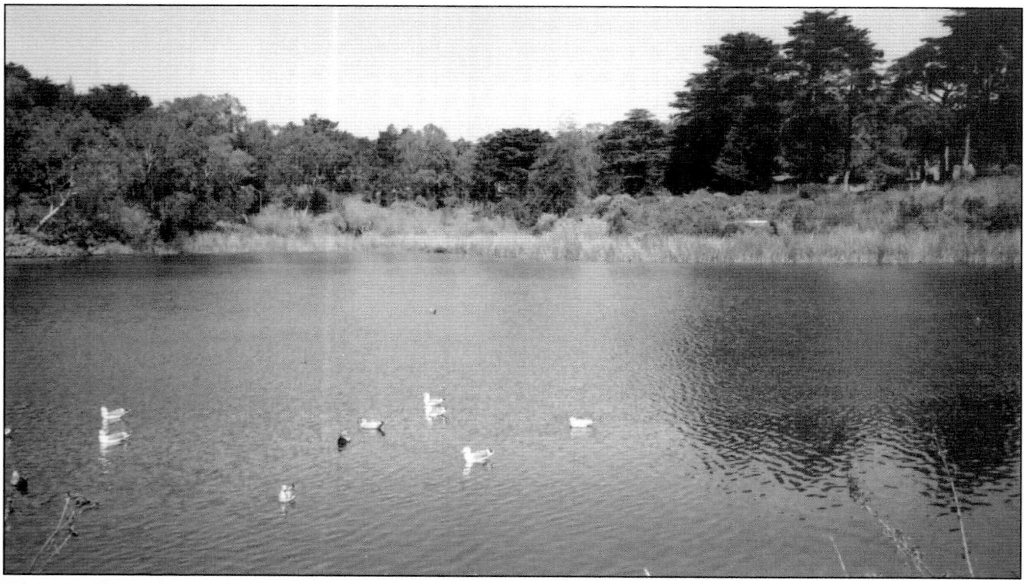

The modern-day Lake Park at Funston and Lake Streets in San Francisco is the spot where Spanish captain Juan Bautista de Anza, with Fr. Pedro Font and an advance party of soldiers, ended a nine-month trek from Mexico. They camped here for two days. Father Font, writing of the area, praised it as perfect for a presidio and mission. The presidio was built a little farther north on a rise overlooking the bay. Mission Dolores was established nearby on March 27, 1775. (Photograph by Dorothy Gibson.)

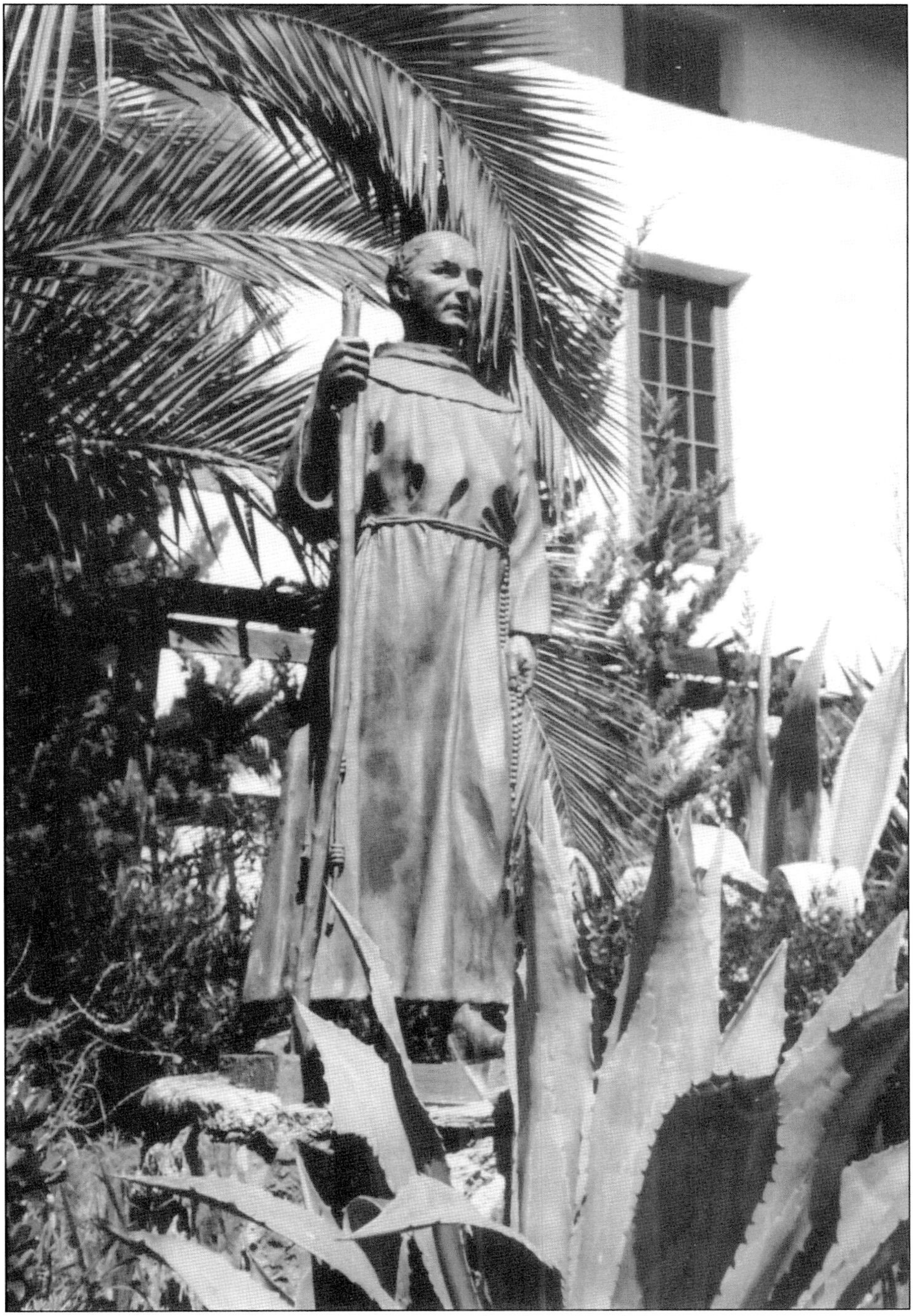

Here is a memorial statue of Fr. Junipero Serra, the founder of the Franciscan mission chain, who accompanied Don Gaspar de Portola in securing California for Spain through the mission system. The soldiers would establish a military post—a presidio—and the mission close by. Native Americans were persuaded into baptism and became workers on the mission grounds, gardening, cooking, and the like. (Photograph by Dorothy Gibson.)

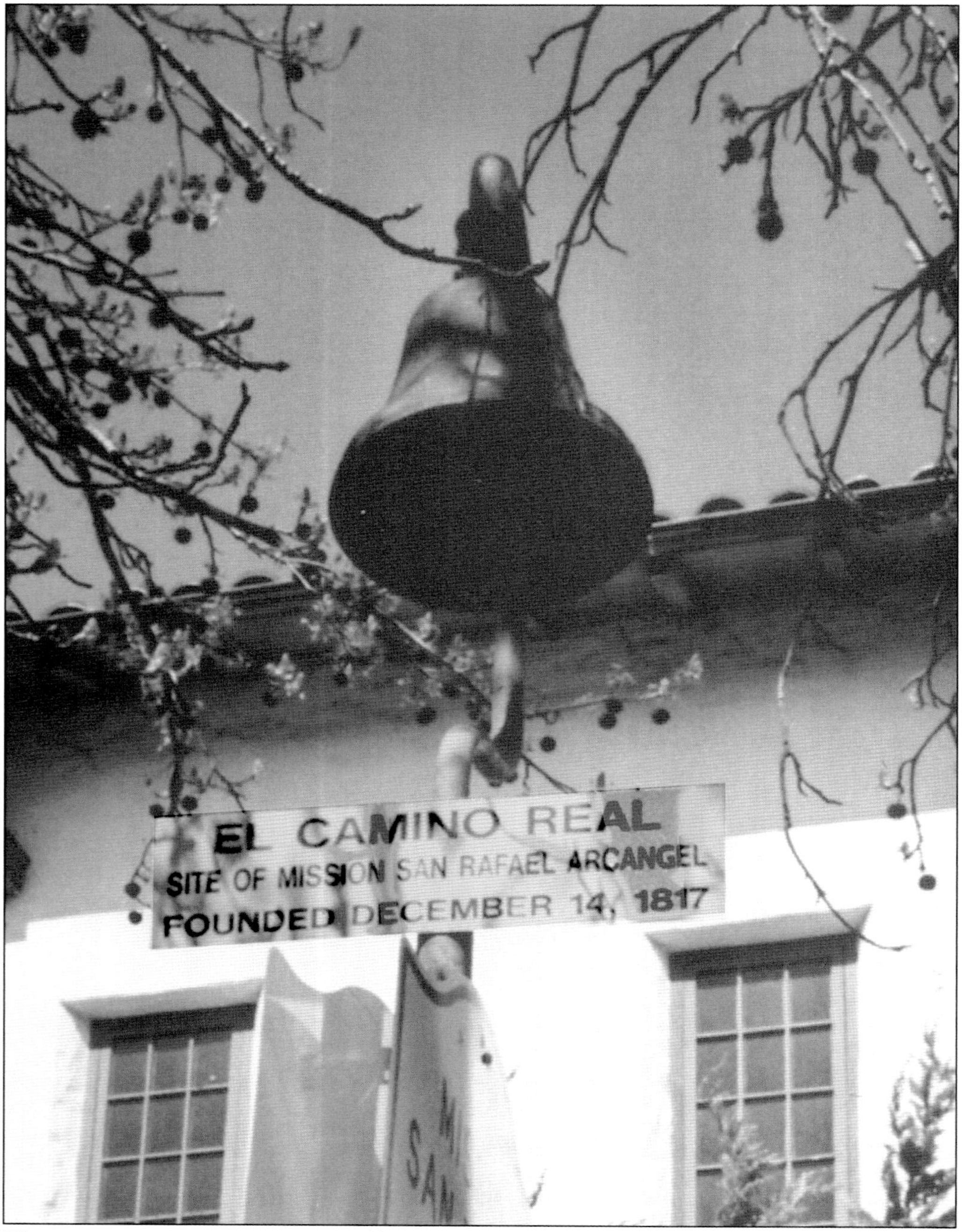

There were two more missions established by the Fathers after Dolores—San Miguel in San Rafael and San Francisco de Solano. El Camino Real (the Royal Way) ran the entire length of the missions from San Diego, and bells were posted at each mission—20 in all. This bell and sign mark the location of Mission San Rafael Arcangel. Founded December 14, 1817, it was the first to be secularized under the Mexicans. (Photograph by Dorothy Gibson.)

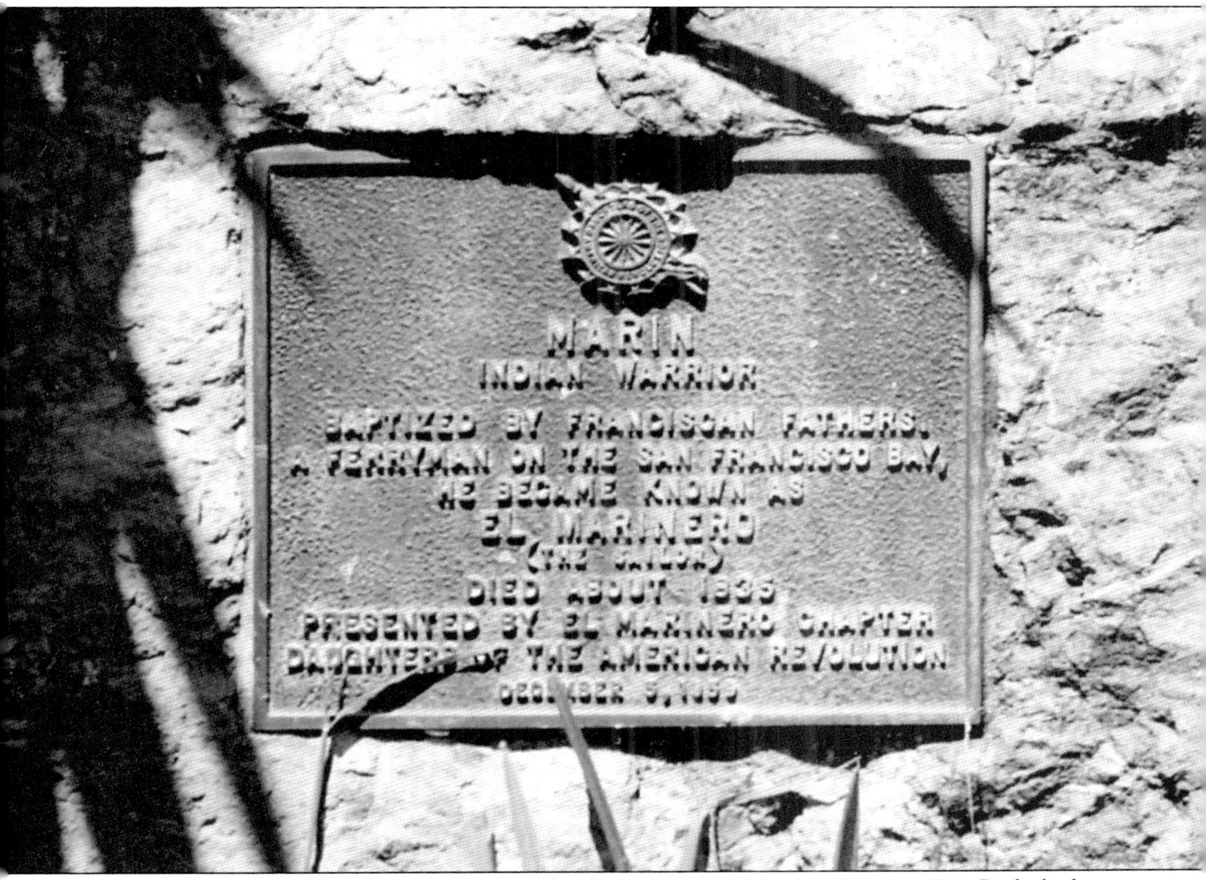

This is a bronze memorial plaque on the side of a building on Mission Street in San Rafael where the original San Rafael Arcangel stood. (Photograph by Dorothy Gibson.)

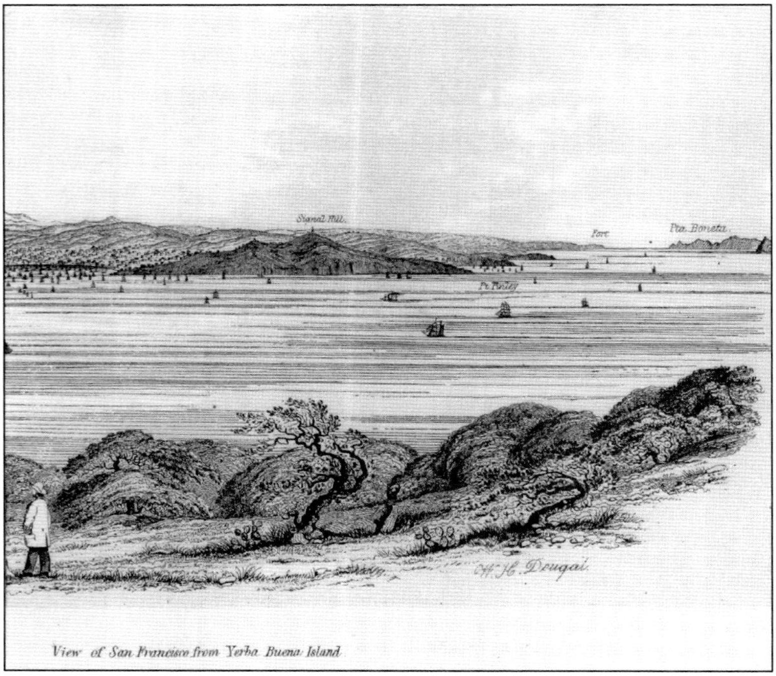

In this undated view of San Francisco from Yerba Buena Island, drawn by W. H. Dougal, Signal Hill (Telegraph Hill), Fort Point, and Point Bonita are visible on the north side. (Courtesy GGNRA Archives, 32456b.)

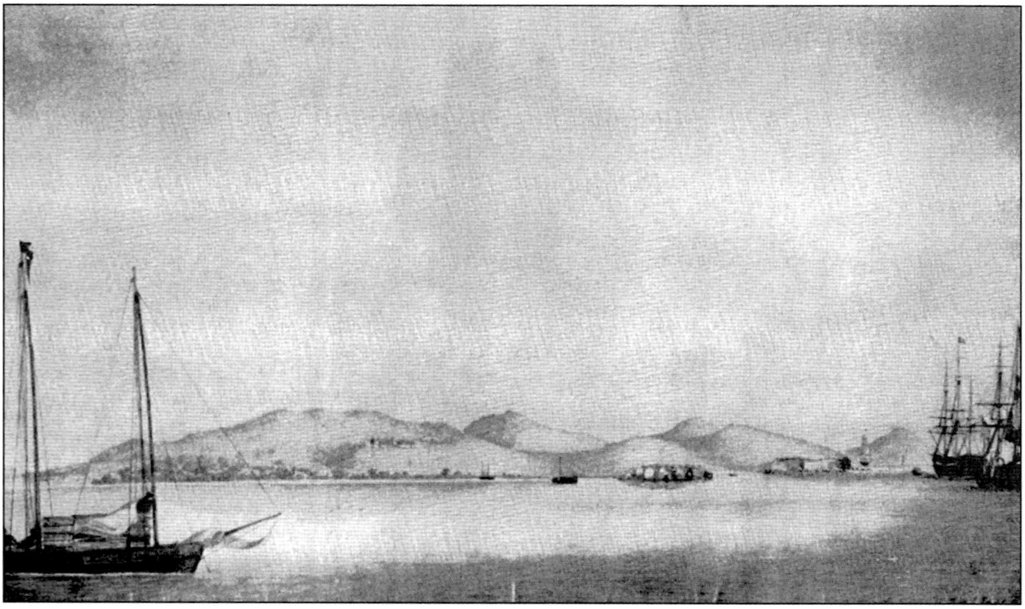

This watercolor by Jean Jacques Vioget, master of the Ecuadorian brig *Delmina*, shows the village of Yerba Buena with two houses. This would be after 1835, when William Richardson petitioned for a house lot there. The schooner at left has a deck load of hides. (Courtesy San Francisco Maritime Museum, Harry C. Peterson Collection.)

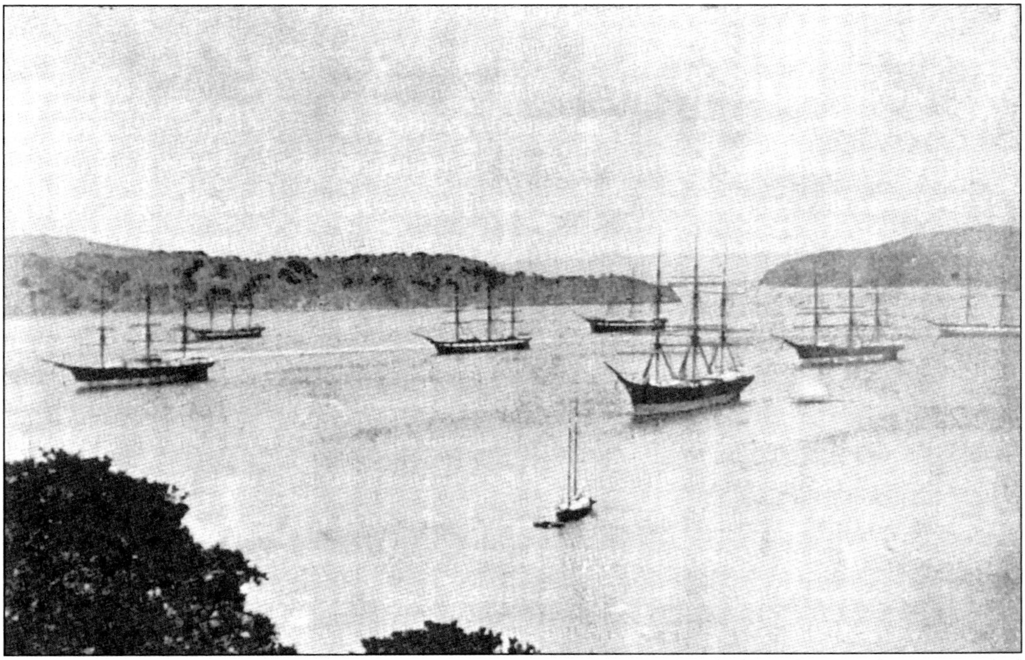

The vessels in this undocumented, undated painting are probably whaling ships or ships intended to carry hides. (Courtesy San Francisco Maritime Museum.)

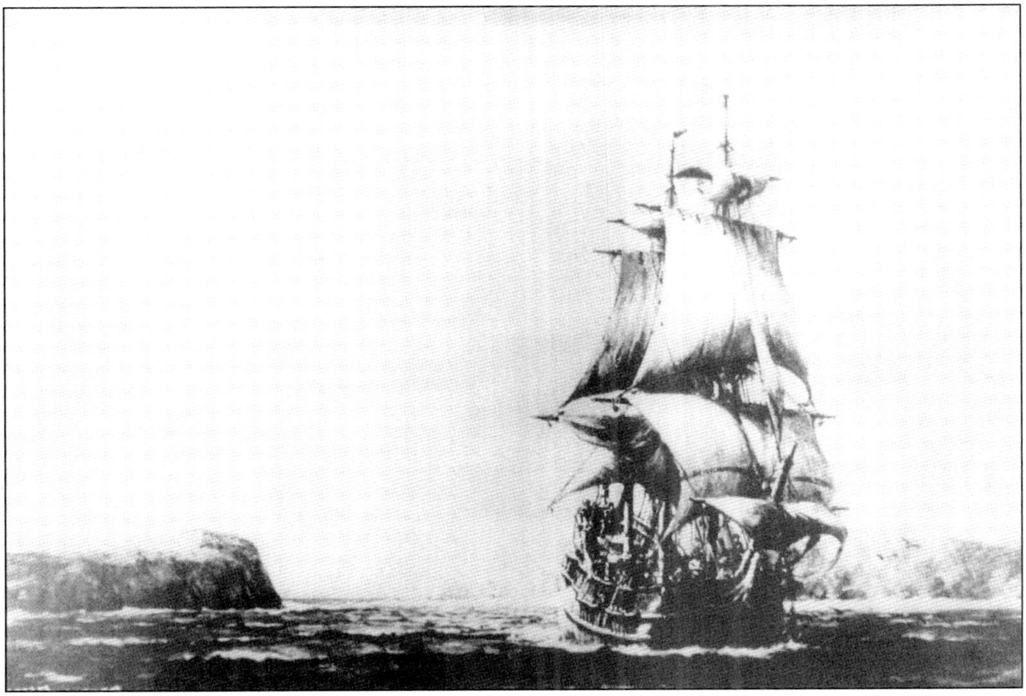

A square rigger enters San Francisco through the Golden Gate in this mid-1800s painting by W. Francis. The ship is accompanied, as would be the case today, by gulls. (Courtesy Sausalito Historical Society, 95.135.)

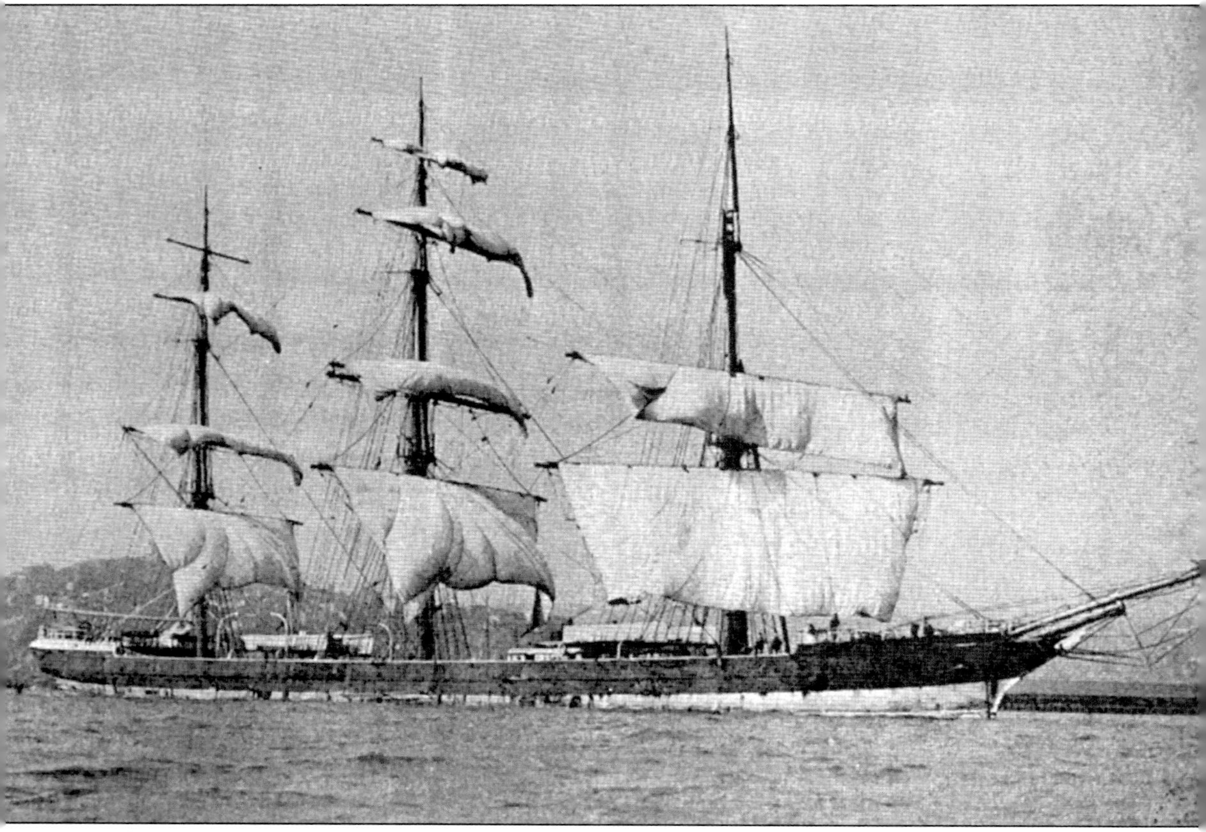

Lady Isabella, a British grain ship built in Scotland in 1882, heads into San Francisco. (Courtesy Morton Waters Company and San Francisco Maritime Museum, from *Francisco Bay* by John Haskell Kemble.)

Five

Coastal Defense

Within 71 years, the possession of California went from Spain to Mexico to the United States. Mexico, after winning independence from Spain in 1821, took over the presidios and began secularizing the missions. Then, within 26 years, newly arrived and impatient Americans combined with the U.S. Navy's Pacific Squadron, the U.S. Army officer John C. Fremont, and Thomas O. Larkin, the U.S. consul for California, determined to create bedlam to claim the territory for California and the United States: the Bear Flag Revolt. Commodore J. D. Sloat ordered the raising of the American flag over San Francisco's port on July 9, 1846. Rebuilding the presidio was the first order: a third system fort with thick walls and a hundred cannons in tiers of casements with a barbette tier on top. After the Civil War (1865) came a new fort system: guns and powder magazines behind earthworks reinforced with brick and granite.

After 10 years of negotiations, the Lime Point Tract (north side of the Golden Gate) was purchased for $200,000 on July 21, 1866. It contained 1,700 acres. The new Fort Baker was built with new batteries: Cavallo, Ridge, Cliff, and Gravelly Beach. After 1866, to keep up with technology, 35 gun batteries, electric searchlights, and telephones were added. In the headlands the batteries included Duncan, Yates, Wagner, Spencer, Kirby, McIndoe, Mine Casement, Alexander, Mendell, Searchlight, Smith Guthrie, and O'Rorke on Bird Island.

After World Wars I and II, advances in battleship guns and aircraft brought antiaircraft technology: thick concrete shields, observation aircraft, additional searchlights, antiaircraft guns, underwater mines, and antisubmarine nets. The cold war brought aerial bombers with nuclear weapons. Antiaircraft missiles were guided by radar, and 12 sites were installed around the Bay Area. In the 1970s, intercontinental ballistic missiles replaced bombers. Four installations were in the headlands: SF-88 radar and launcher and SF-87 radar and launcher. The last Nike missile sites were taken out in 1974 (Fort Point, Point Reyes, Point Bonita, Point Montaro, and Point Año Nuevo). The initial construction, periodic updating of the defense installations, and the building of Forts Baker, Barry, and Cronkite with their associated services (residences, chapels, hospitals, and service centers) were the responsibility of the U.S. Army Corps of Engineers. In addition, the corps built the roads, the tunnel from Baker to Barry, and the lighthouse stations. The U.S. Coast Guard arrived in the San Francisco Bay in 1854, erecting Alcatraz, the first of 16 lights on the coast. Those on the headlands are Lime Point, Point Diablo, and Point Bonito.

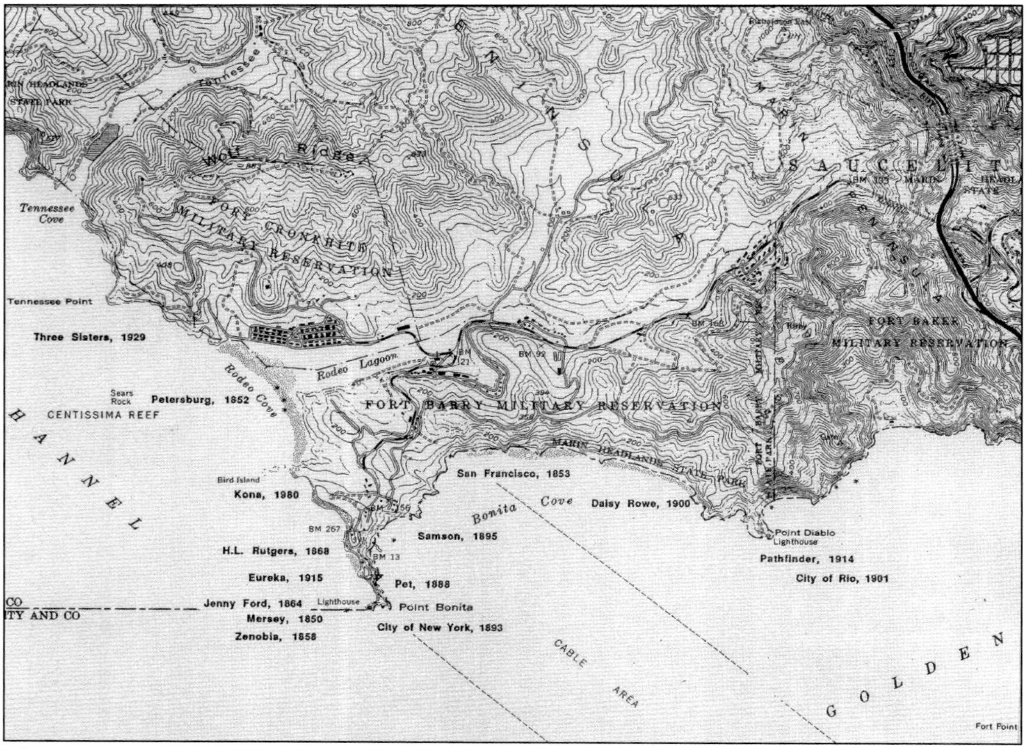

There are many shipwrecks along the Golden Gate, which is known to navigators as a treacherous place. The channel is narrow, the surrounding cliffs harsh, and the area to the north (the famous "potato patch," named for vegetables on ships being thrown about) is shallow. And there is the fog—always coming, always going. This map pinpoints the known wrecks; there is no doubt that there have been more. (Courtesy San Francisco Maritime Museum, from *Shipwrecks at the Golden Gate*.)

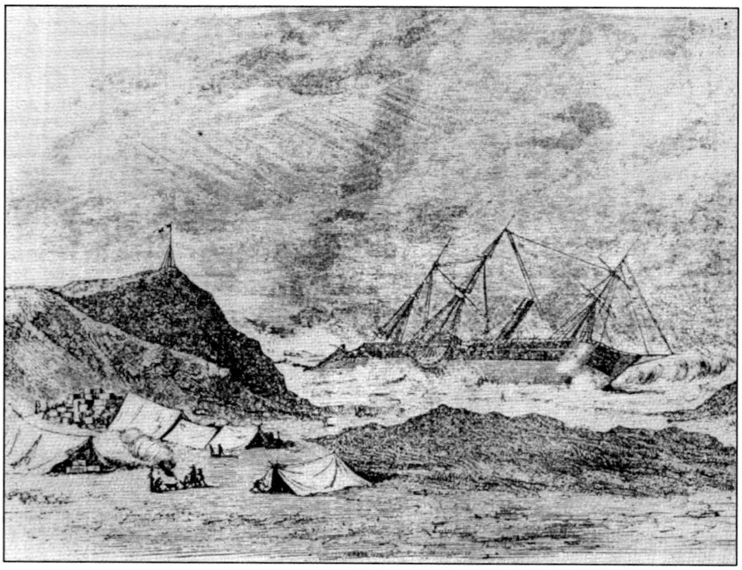

The March 1853 wreck of the Pacific Mail steamer *Tennessee* in the second cove north of the Golden Gate prompted rescuers to rename the cove, the lagoon, and the road leading to it "Tennessee." The ship's run was from Panama to San Francisco. At low tide, a rusting piece is still visible. (Courtesy San Francisco Maritime Museum, from *Shipwrecks at the Golden Gate*.)

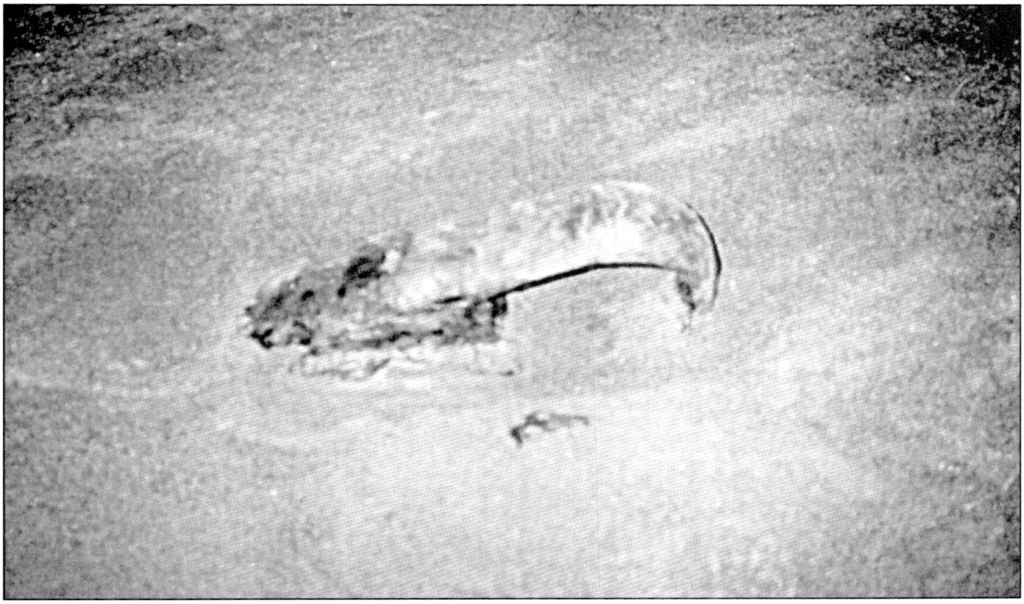

Here is a rusted piece of the Pacific Mail Steamship Company's ill-fated *Tennessee* at Tennessee Valley Beach during low tide. (Photograph by Dorothy Gibson.)

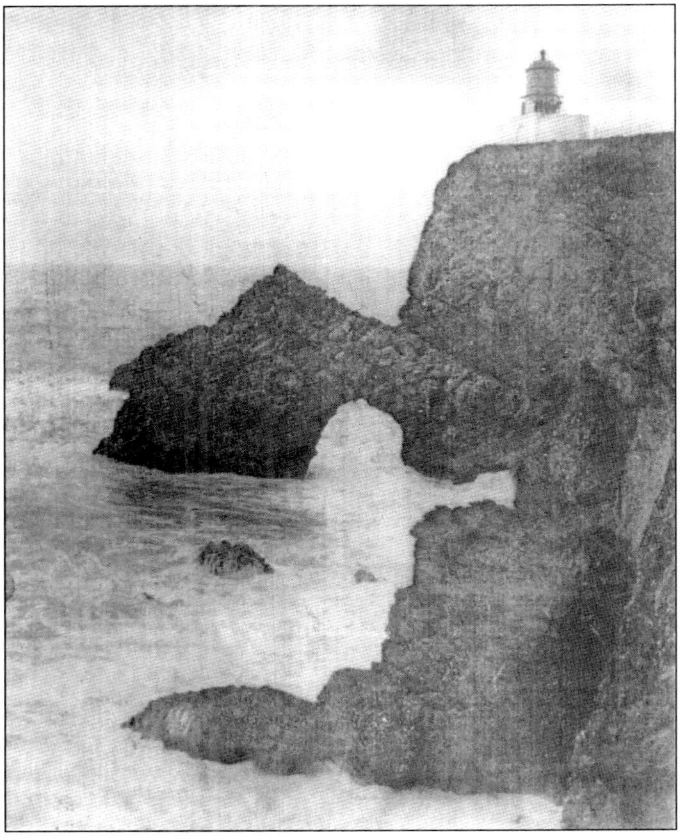

Within two years after the *Tennessee* wrecked, the first Point Bonita Lighthouse was lit on May 21, 1855. It had a French Fresnel lens and could be seen 18 miles away. It proved to have been placed too high, though, and the heavy fog blocked it. It was rebuilt lower down on the southern tip of the point. (Courtesy GGNRA Archives, PMH3db.)

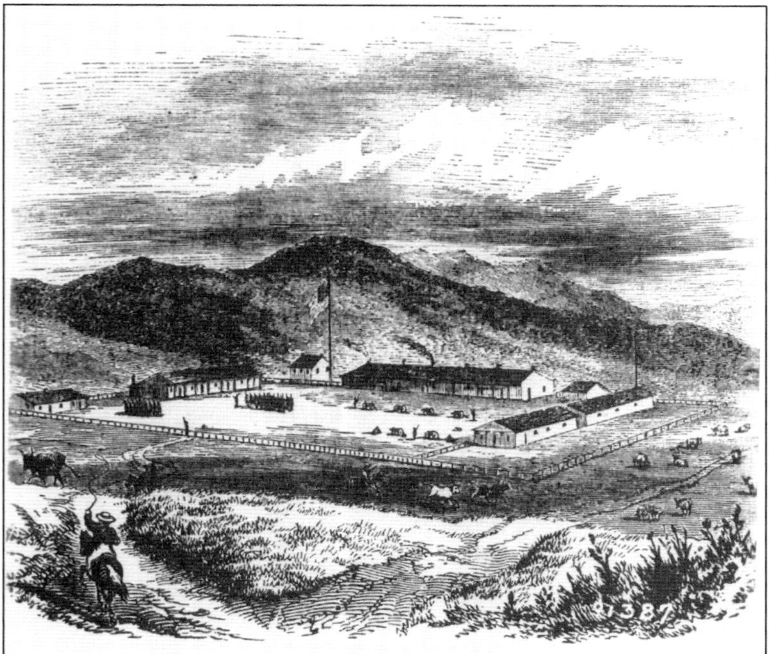

The Presidio of San Francisco.

This copy of a painting entitled *Presidio of San Francisco* shows a vaquero (cowboy) on horseback roping a cow in the foreground. This depicts life around 1820 and suggests what was to follow at Point Cavallo and the Fort Baker region. (Courtesy GGNRA Archives, 32456c.)

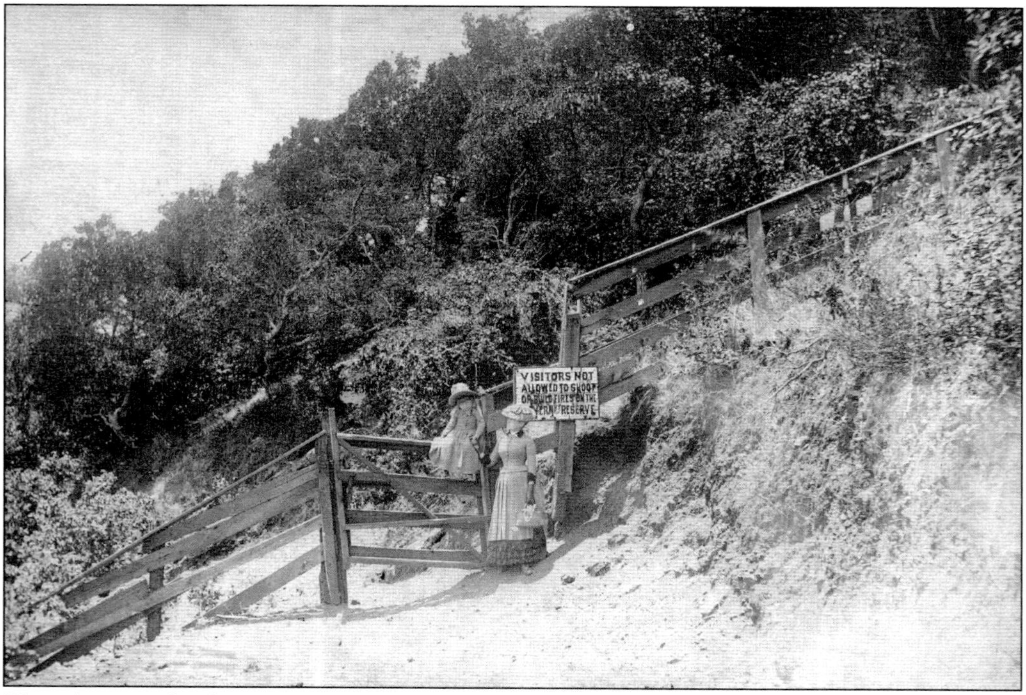

This photograph of a woman holding a picnic basket and two children was taken between the Edwards-Harrison Tract and Fort Baker, according to an inscription on the back. There is no date, but it can be deduced that it is post-1866, when the U.S. government purchased the land. (Courtesy Sausalito Historical Society, 81.131.)

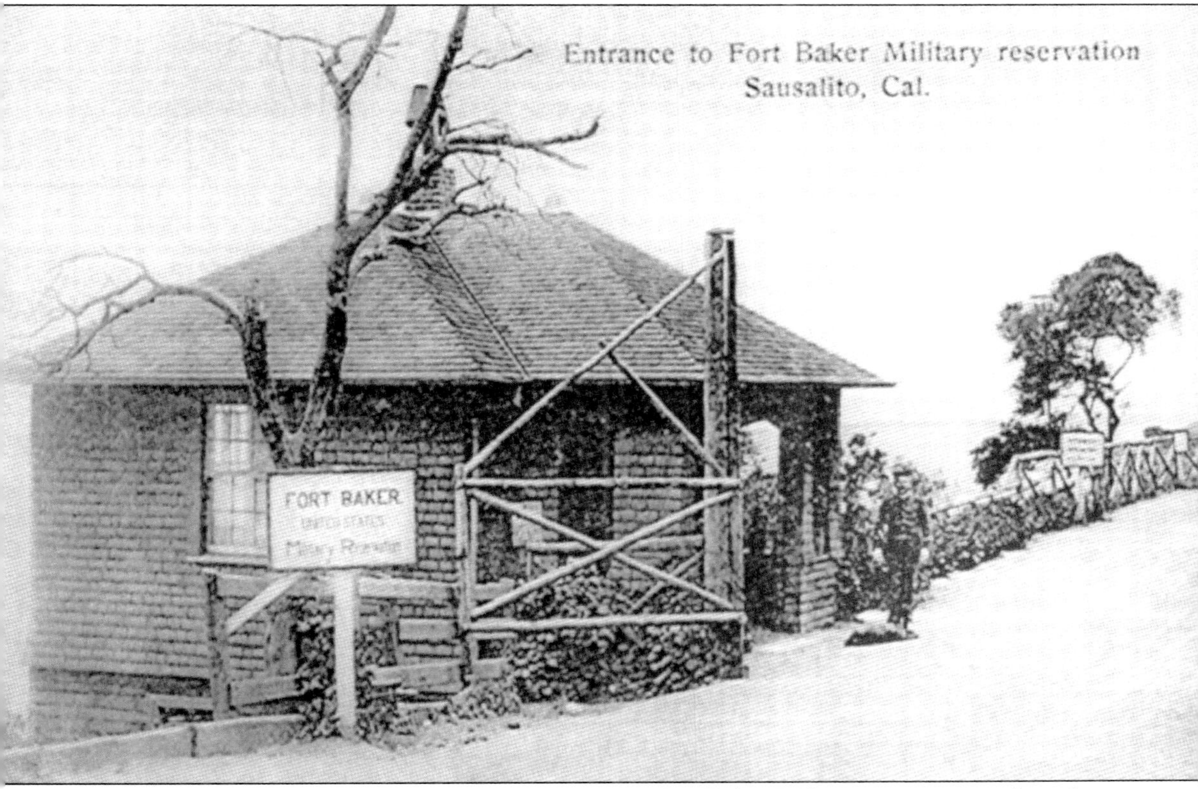

This early-1900s postcard depicts the entrance to "Fort Baker Military reservation, Sausalito, Cal." The sign by the gate reads, "Fort Baker United States Military Reserve." (Photograph by C. H. Becker; courtesy GGNRA Archives, PFbk4.)

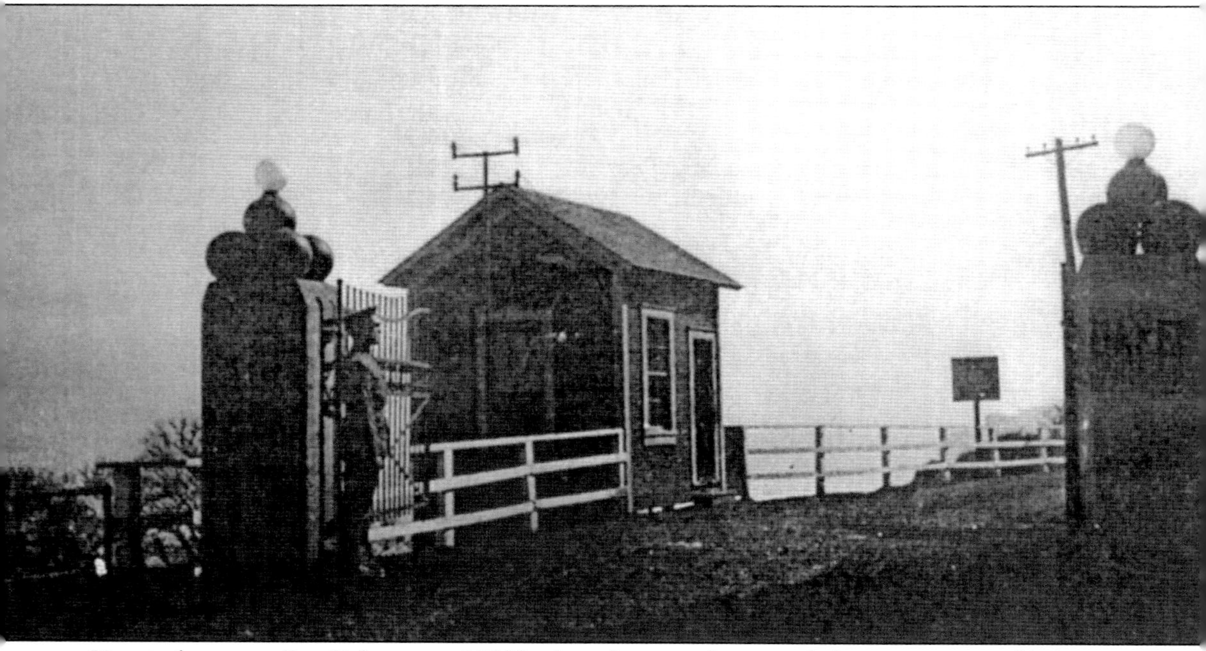

Here is the gate to Fort Baker around 1920, when electricity has provided prominent postal lighting as well as telephone communications to the station. (Courtesy GGNRA Archives, PFbk4.)

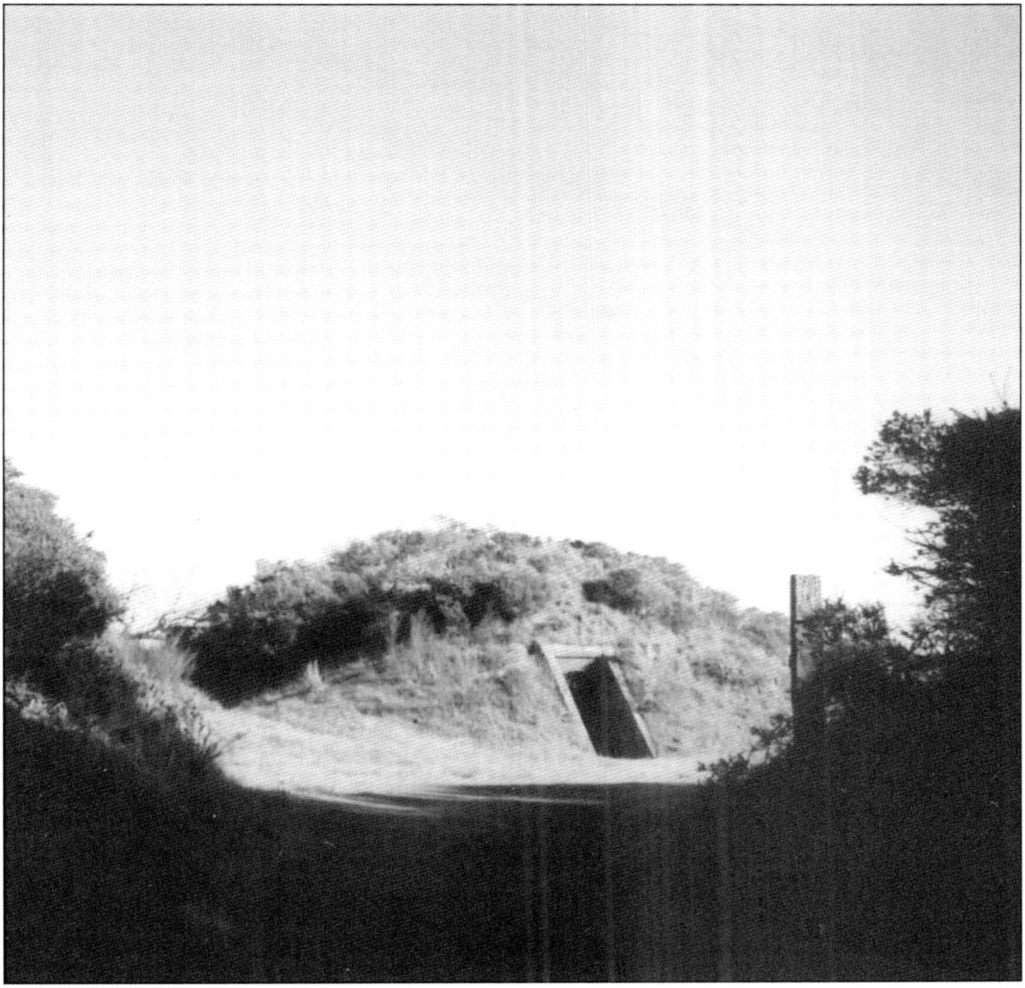

Here is Battery Cavallo at Fort Baker. It was built during the early period (1846–1890) by the Americans with thick brick and stone walls and was designed to be highly camouflaged. (Photograph by Dorothy Gibson.)

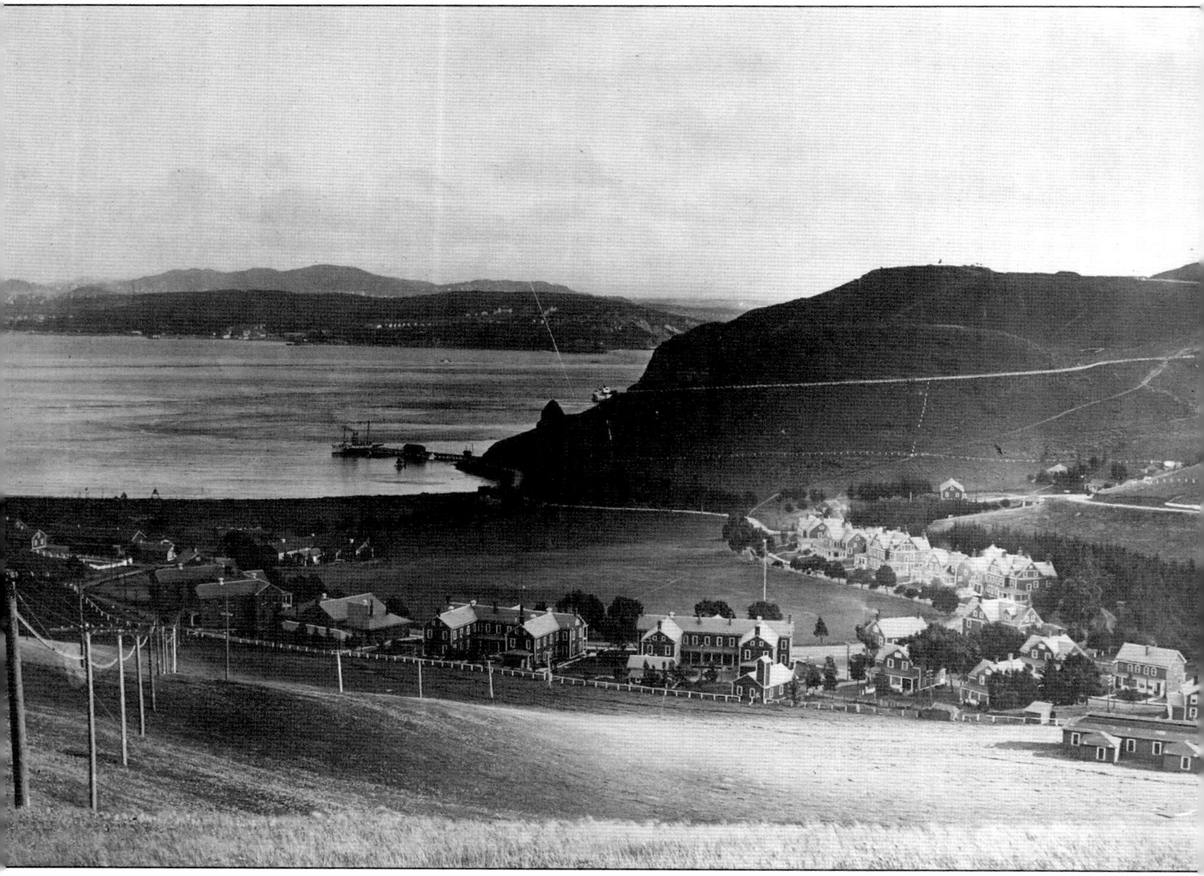

In this c. 1907 view of the Fort Baker parade ground, officer's quarters are on the right and men's barracks on the left as one faces the water. Horseshoe Cove here takes its name from its distinctive shape. Batteries Ridge and Cliff, a little west and above Lime Point, were also built during the early period. Batteries Yates and Duncan, south and north of Cavallo respectively, were built during the more modern period, 1890–1920. (Courtesy Sausalito Historical Society, 81.31a.)

The notation on the back of this photograph reads, "April 1, 1973, Battery Kirby, Ft. Baker." In addition to Cavallo, other batteries were built during the early period at Fort Baker. There were Batteries Ridge, Cliff, and Gravelly, all located further west, Ridge high above Lime Point and Gravelly, as its name suggests, down in Gravelly Cove (also known as Kirby Cove). (Courtesy GGNRA Archives, PFbk5.)

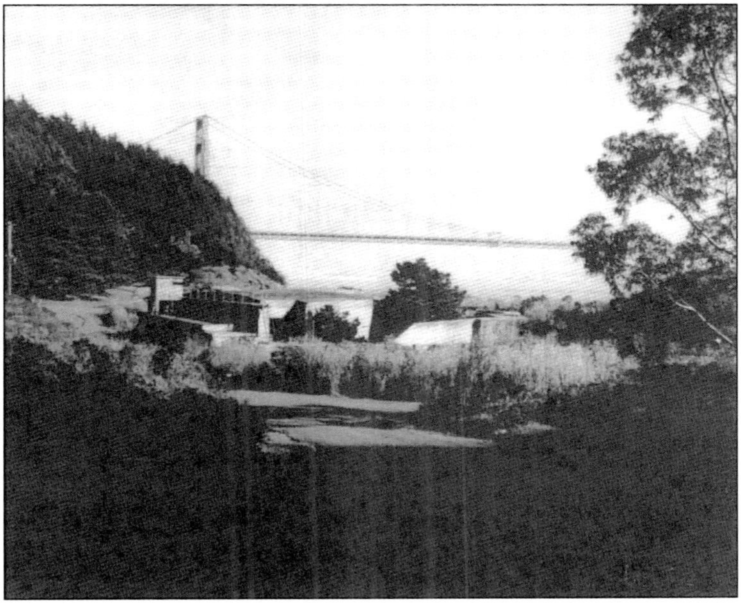

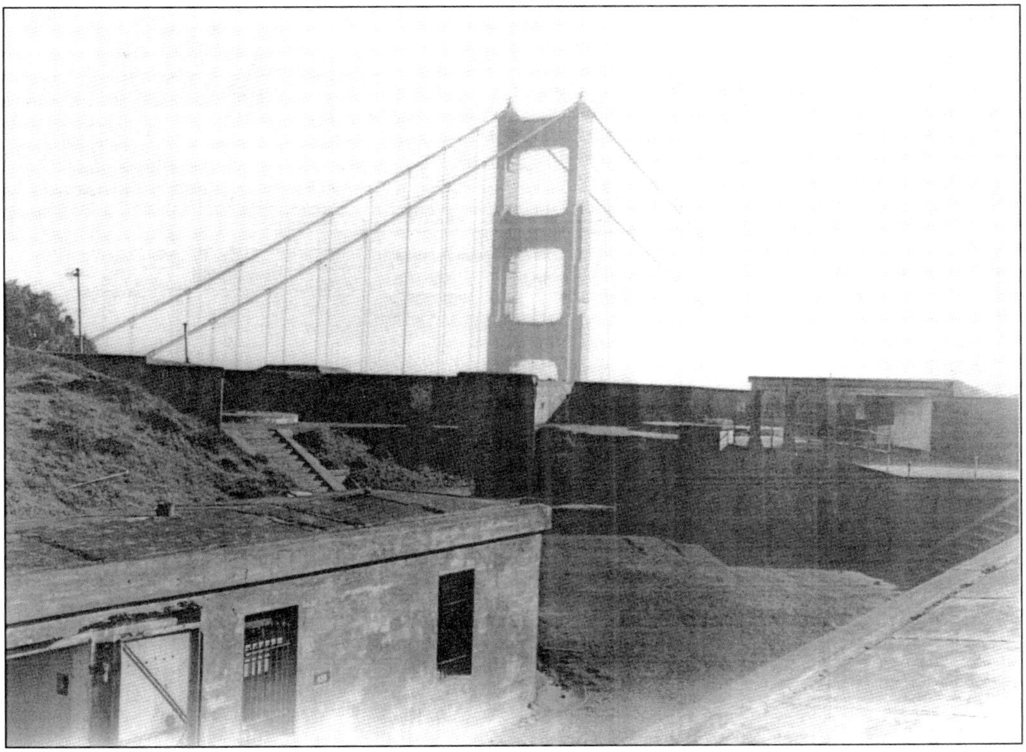

Close to the north tower of the Golden Gate Bridge, Battery Spencer is high above Kirby Cove. Seen here in December 1966, it is one of five batteries built during the "Endicott Period," named for Secretary of War William C. Endicott, who modernized batteries with 12-inch cannons, electricity, and telephones. Other batteries were Yates, Duncan, Wagner, and Kirby. (Courtesy GGNRA Archives, PFbk5.)

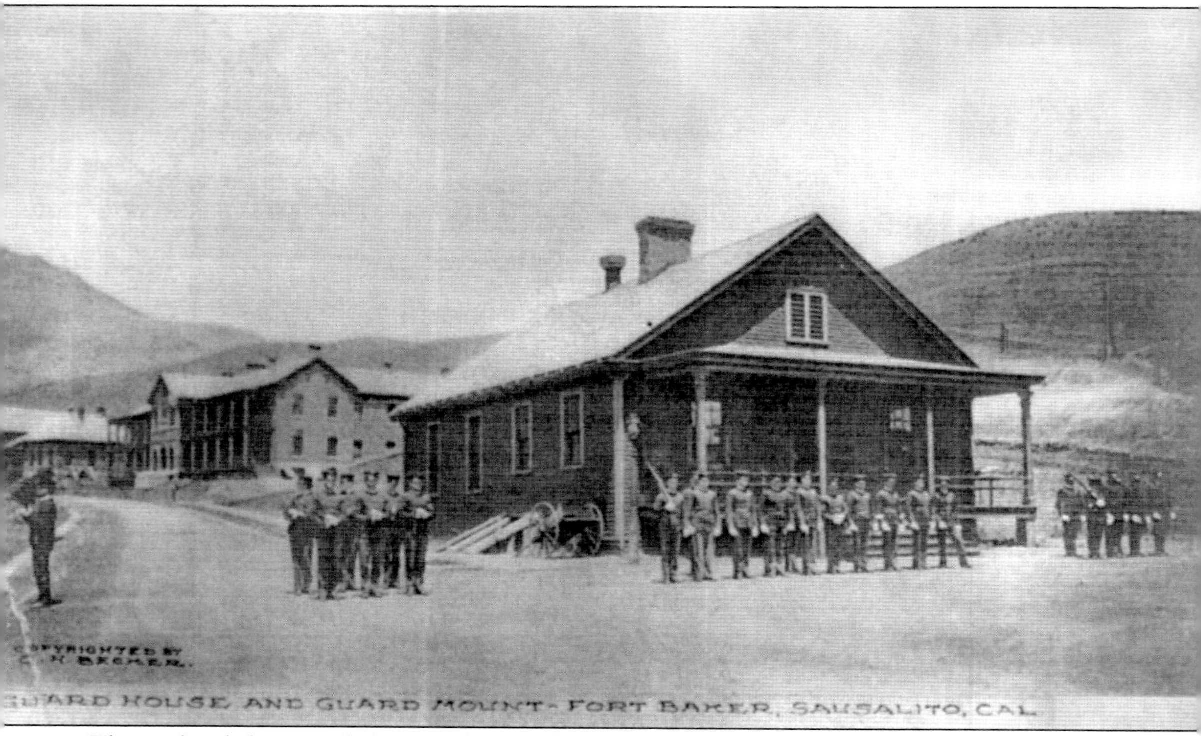

This undated photograph showing the guard house and guard mount at Fort Baker was most likely taken between 1902 and 1918; this was the time frame for the main construction of Fort Baker. The army's engineers filled in the marshland, making 7 additional acres of land by the bay. Built during this period were barracks, a gymnasium, commanding officers' residences, post headquarters, officers' quarters, and a 12-bed hospital. (Courtesy GGNRA Archives, PFbk4; Pamprints Collection.)

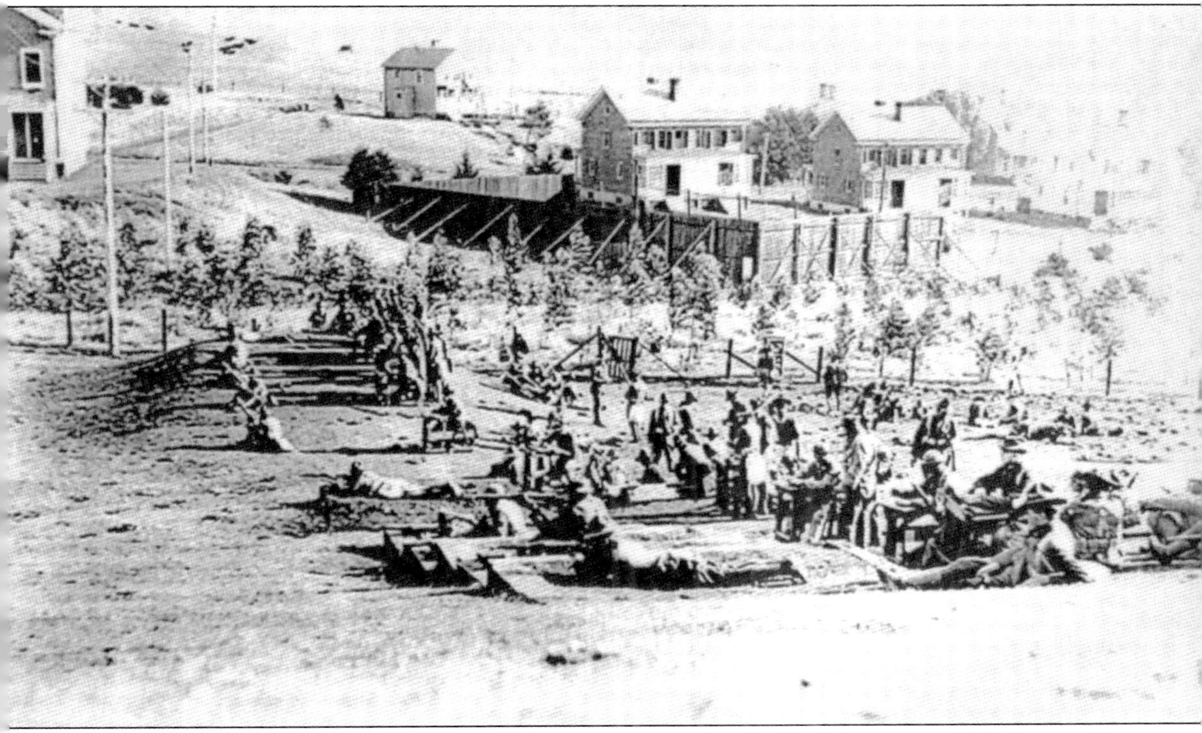

With the additional acreage and the adjacent gymnasium (on the fort's lower east side), the parade grounds had many uses. This photograph shows target practice on a rifle range around 1915. The hospital and the noncommissioned officers' quarters are in the background. (Courtesy GGNRA Archives, PFbk6; Donald A. Thomas Fort Baker Photograph Collection.)

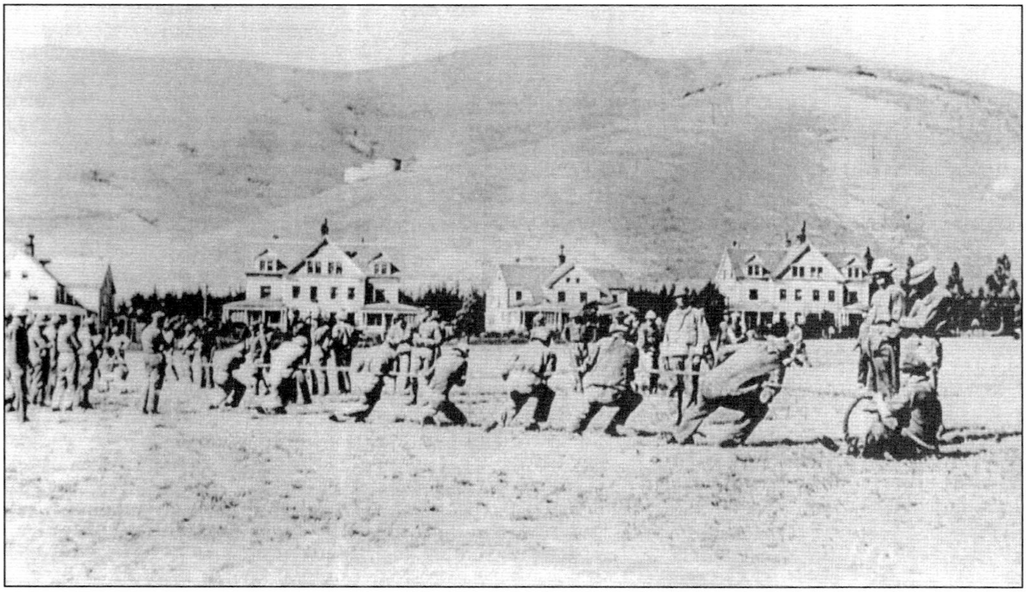

This tug-of-war on the Fort Baker parade ground could have been for fun or for military exercise. While some men stand and watch, others pull as hard as they can on the rope, with an officer, no doubt, standing over. In the background is what appears to be the artillery barracks. They were designed like most of the buildings in the Colonial Revival architectural style: clean simple lines with a minimum of applied decoration. (Courtesy GGNRA Archives, PFbk6; Donald A. Thomas Fort Baker Photograph Collection.)

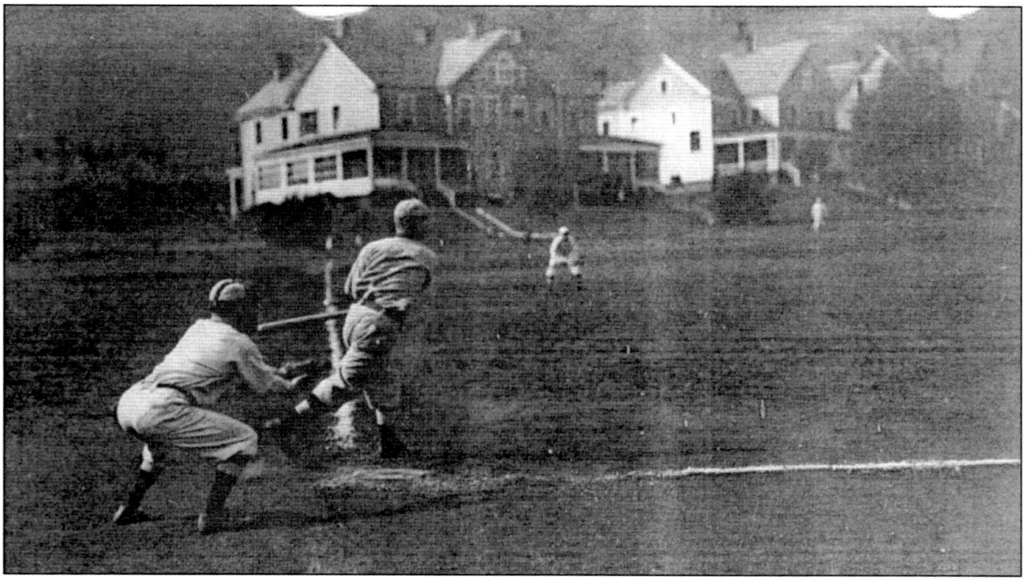

Here is a game of baseball on the parade grounds at Fort Baker around 1915. The buildings were originally painted in dark greens and brown with gray slate roofs. By the 1930s, they were painted to conform with the presidio and other Bay Area forts—white with asphalt shingles. The original front porches were removed in the 1950s. (Courtesy GGNRA Archives, PFbk6; Donald A. Thomas Fort Baker Photograph Collection.)

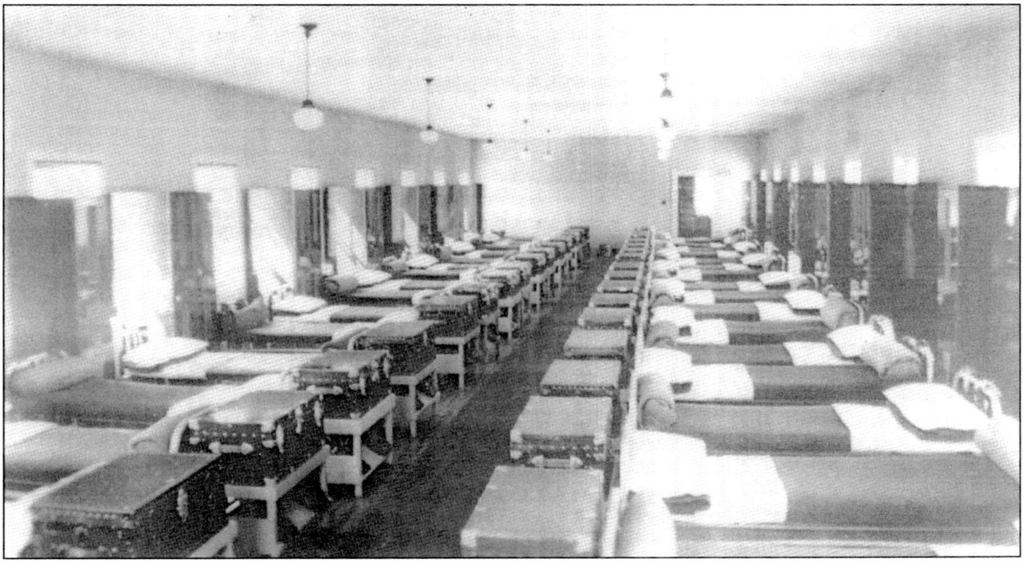

This interior view of the Fort Baker barracks shows that by the early 1900s, the U.S. Army had begun to develop healthier, cleaner accommodations for its soldiers than it had previously. Fort Baker had clean, modern barracks that were comparatively spacious with windows, ventilation, running hot and cold water, showers, toilets, electricity, real beds, and mattresses. (Courtesy GGNRA Archives, PFbk4.)

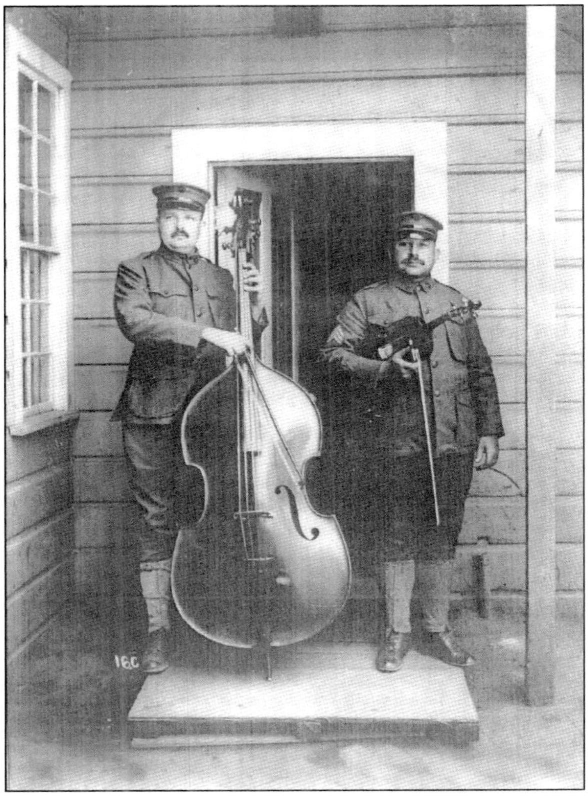

This photograph has an inscription reading, "Musicians thought to be Ft. Baker, possibly Ft. MacDowell," but there is no date. The dress seems to suggest the early 1900s. In addition to a more modern environment, there was an attempt to make life more pleasant, including music. (Courtesy GGNRA Archives, PFbk6.)

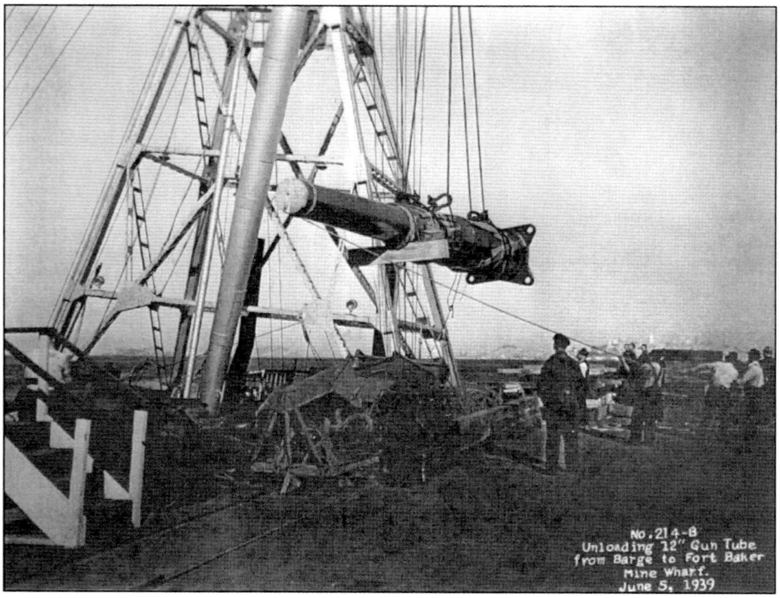

This image shows the unloading of a 12-inch gun tube from a barge to the Fort Baker Mine Wharf on June 5, 1939. These high-powered rifle gun tubes were slated for Batteries Duncan, Yates, Spencer, Wagner, and Kirby in Fort Baker. (Courtesy GGNRA Archives, PFbk4.)

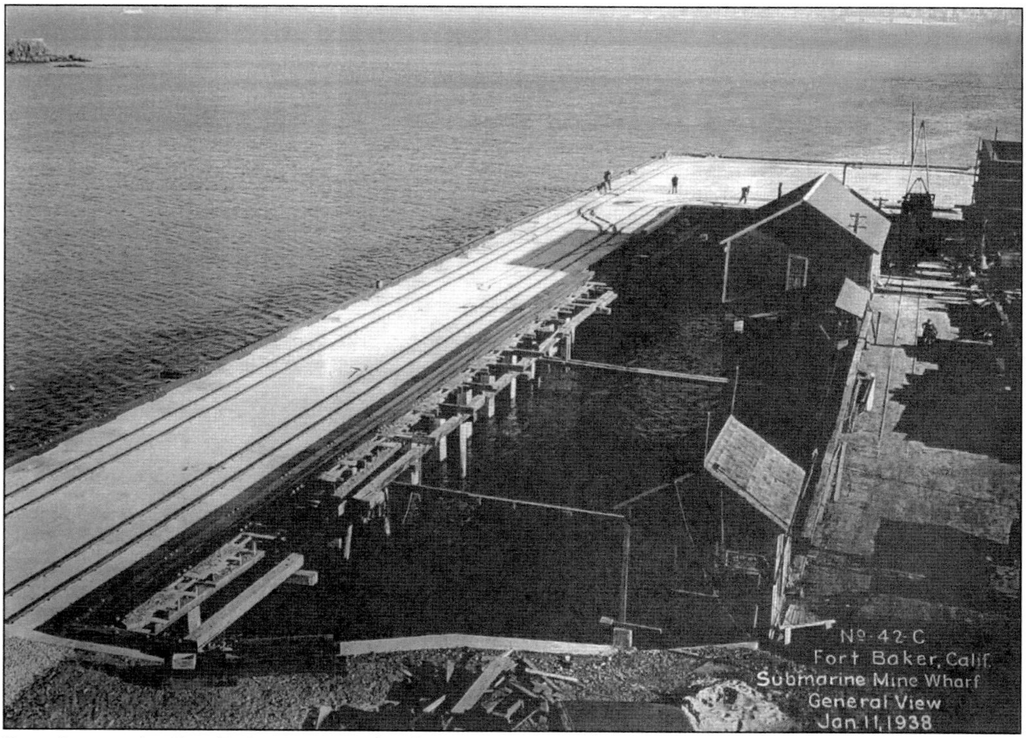

Seen here is the Fort Baker Mine Wharf at Fort Baker on January 11, 1938. Built at Horseshoe Cove abutting the 1903 Quartermaster Supply Wharf, Buildings 410 and 411 were where ammunition was stored. Building 12 had mine-loading rooms where soldiers loaded explosive charges into the mines. Building 409 was the powerhouse, and Building 70 was the mine cable storage building. On the harbor, soldiers manned mine planters, large ships with powerful cranes and hoists to raise and lower the mines. (Courtesy GGNRA Archives, PFbk4.)

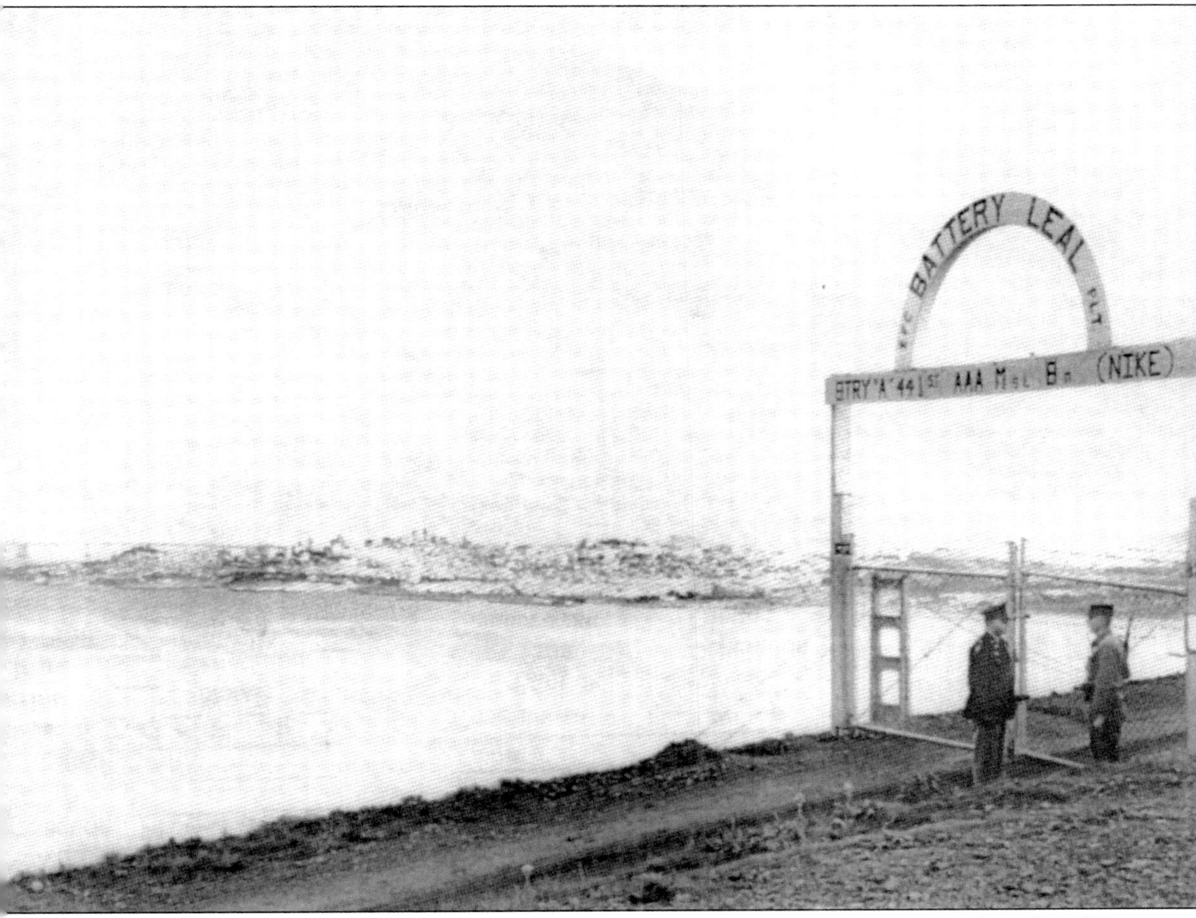

In 1956, Capt. George P. Leal (left), commander of A Battery, inspects a guard at the 1FC Area at Fort Baker. Also pictured is Pvt. James DeSavio of Los Angeles. (Courtesy GGNRA Archives, PFbk5.)

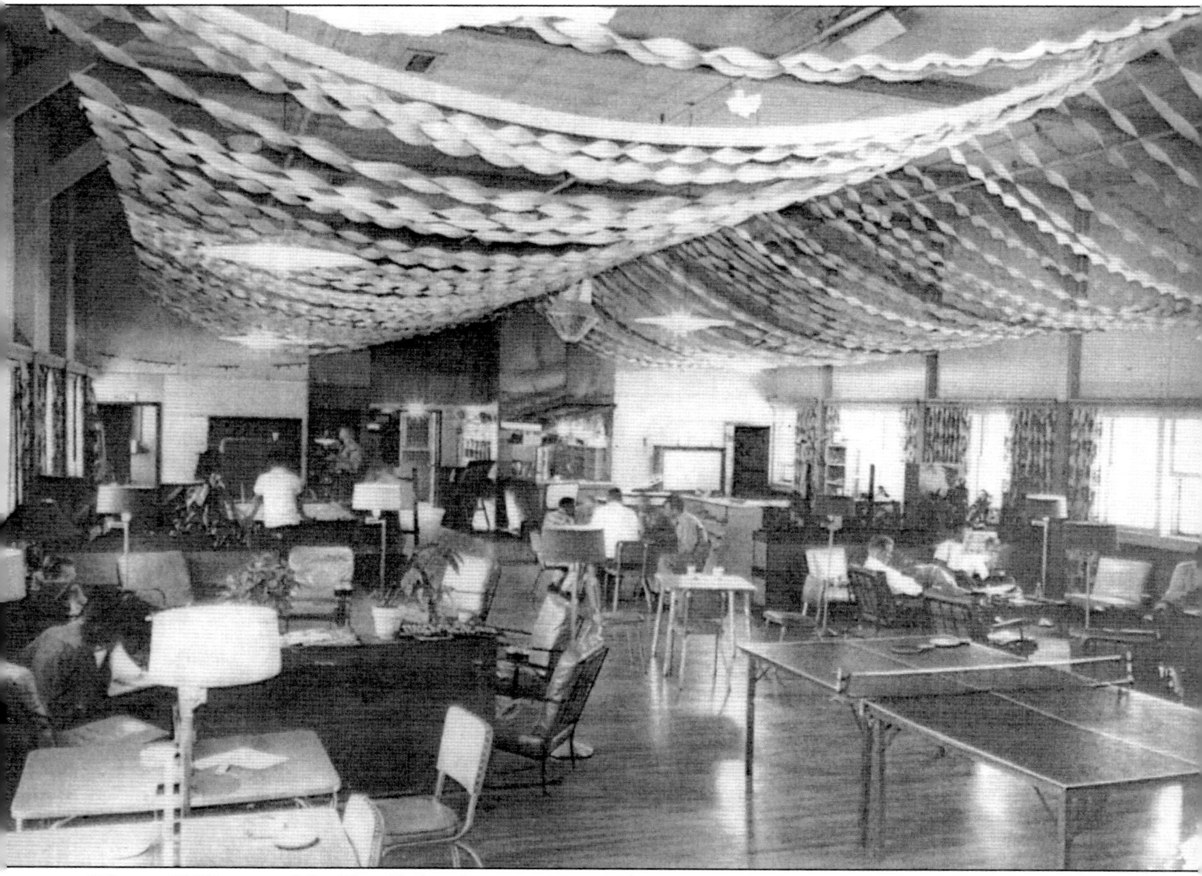

This c. 1957 view of the Fort Baker Service Center shows a very comfortable, well-equipped center. All modern conveniences are present, such as tables with lamps and chairs for eating, conversing, reading, or playing games. Note the festive ceiling. (Courtesy GGNRA Archives, PFbk6.)

The notation on this c. 1908 map reads in part, "Military Reservation, Forts Baker and Barry, showing point of beginning at rock south of 'Old Sausalito' 300 yards offshore from there at low water mark, to and around Pt. Bonita and Pacific Ocean to Rodeo Lagoon and return." (Courtesy GGNRA Archives, 32456f.)

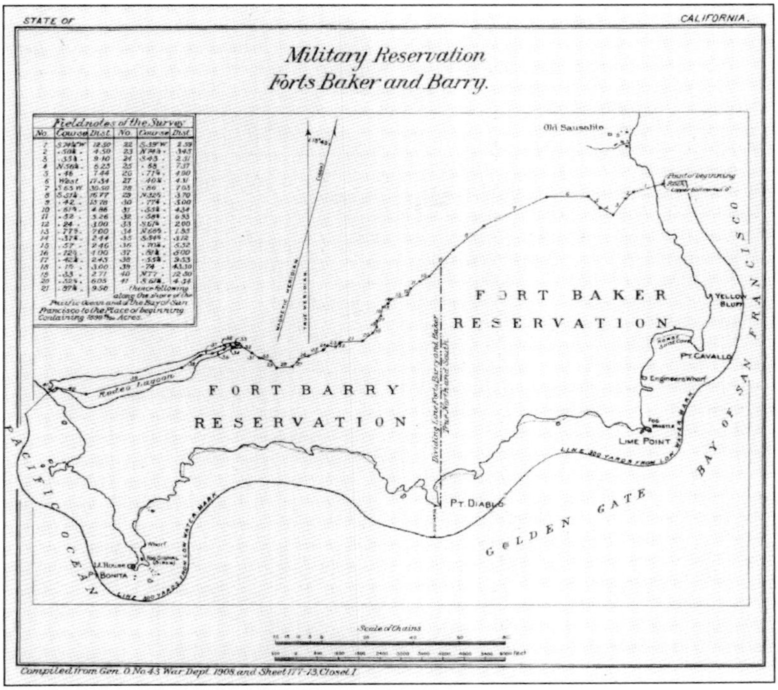

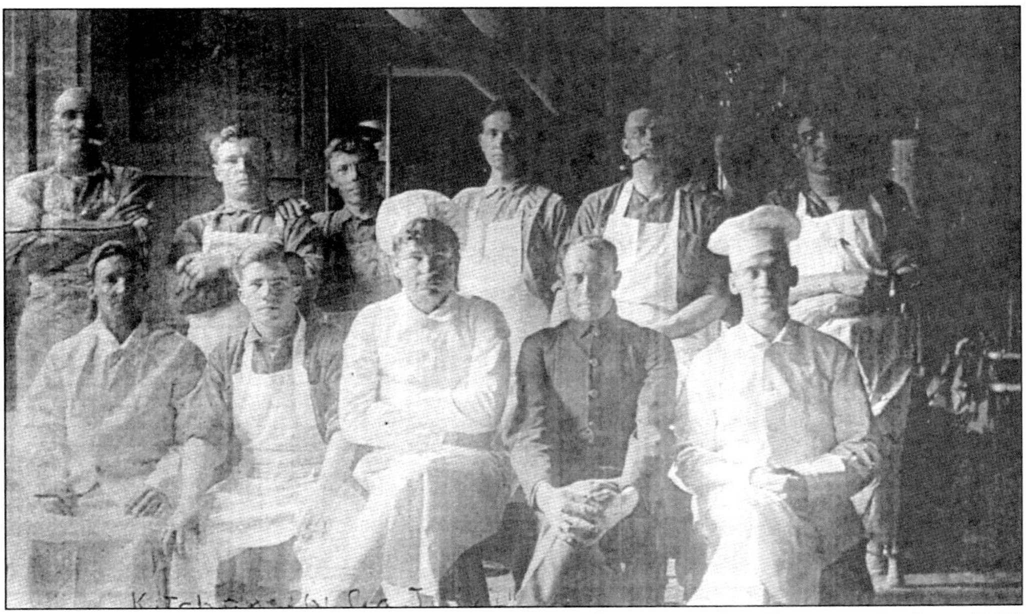

This postcard reads, "Fort Barry Kitchen, 161st Co., July 4, 1911." Fort Barry was built in 1905. Like Forts Baker and Cronkite, it was in the jurisdiction of the Harbor Defense of San Francisco. A complete community, Fort Barry, like Fort Baker, had service facilities, a chapel, and a hospital. Fort Barry is named for Brig. Gen. William Farquahar Barry (1818–1879). He was a veteran of both the Civil and Mexican-American Wars. (Courtesy GGNRA Archives, PFbk7.)

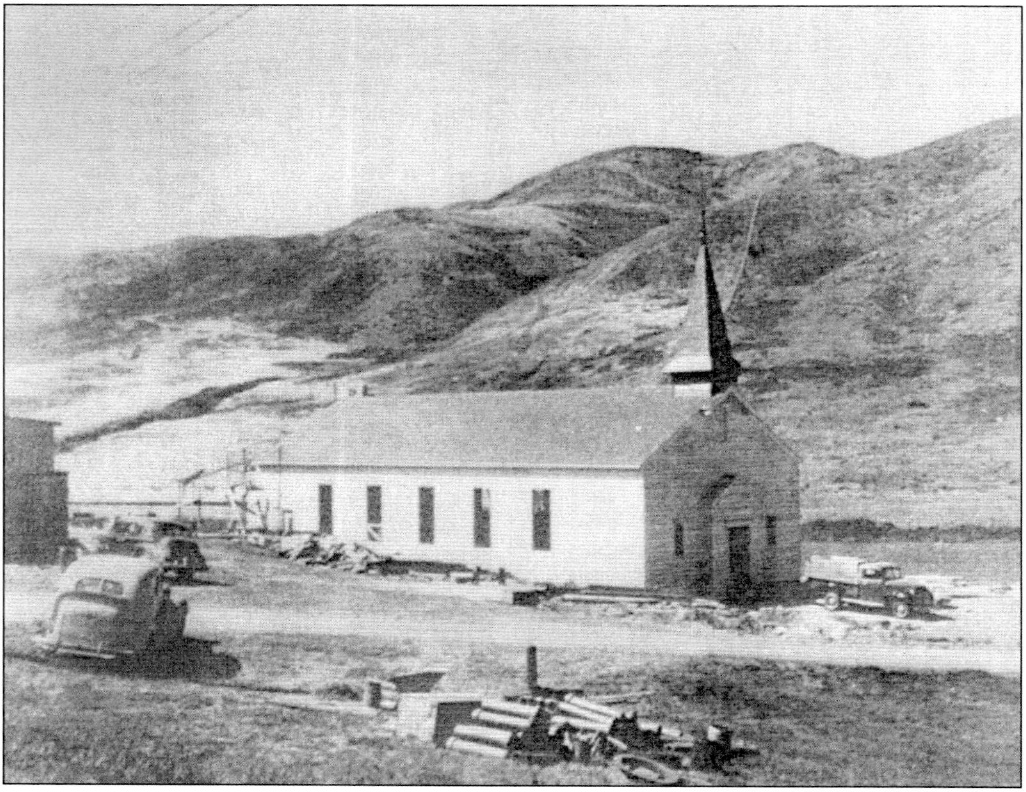

This image shows the chapel at Fort Barry in 1941. On the lower south slope of Rodeo Valley, the chapel is just above the lagoon. The post exchange and gymnasium are to the left. (Courtesy GGNRA Archives, PFbr4.)

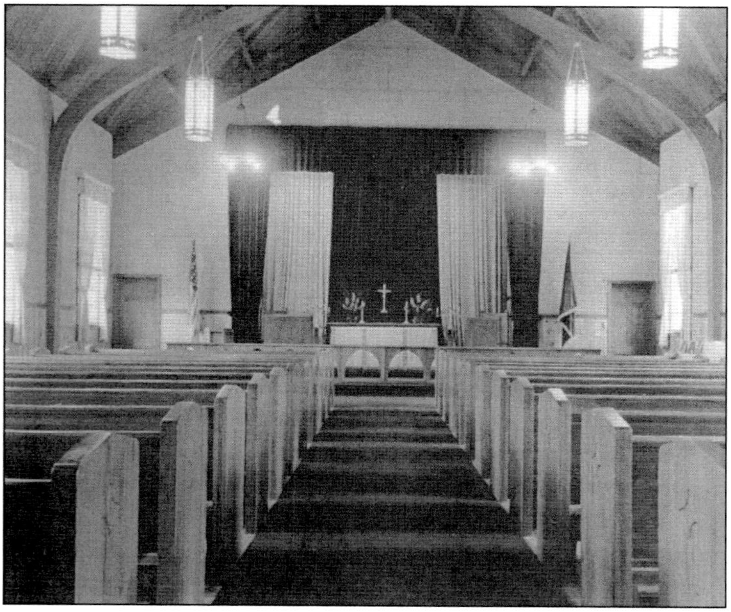

This is the interior of Fort Barry's chapel; note the crucifix at the altar. Although ostensibly nondenominational, it was used in a Christian manner. (Courtesy GGNRA Archives, PFbr4.)

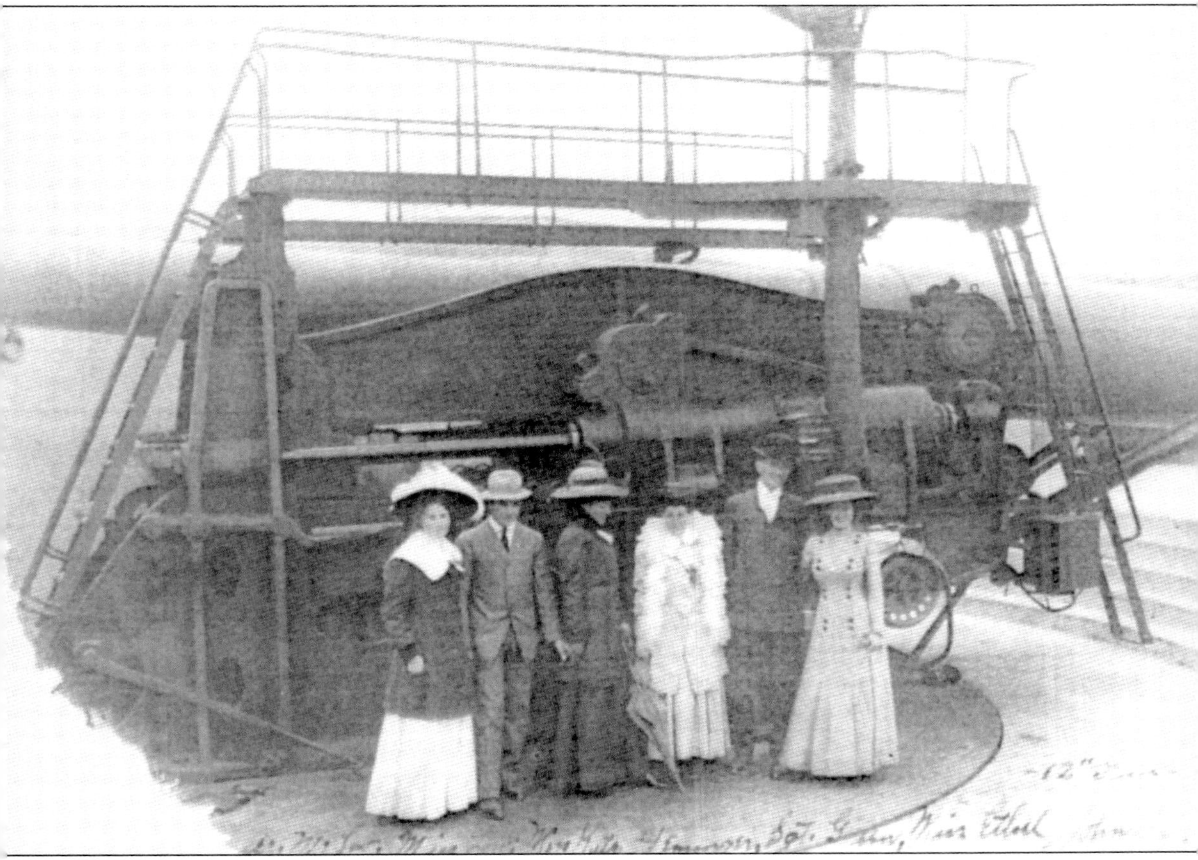

Pictured here around 1908 at Battery Mendell are, from left to right, unidentified, "Mr. Low, Miss Low, Kate H., Sgt. Green, Miss Ethel Johnson." These are Fort Barry soldiers on their day off with lady friends. Battery Mendell is atop Bird Island on the south end of Rodeo Beach. (Courtesy GGNRA Archives, PFbr5.)

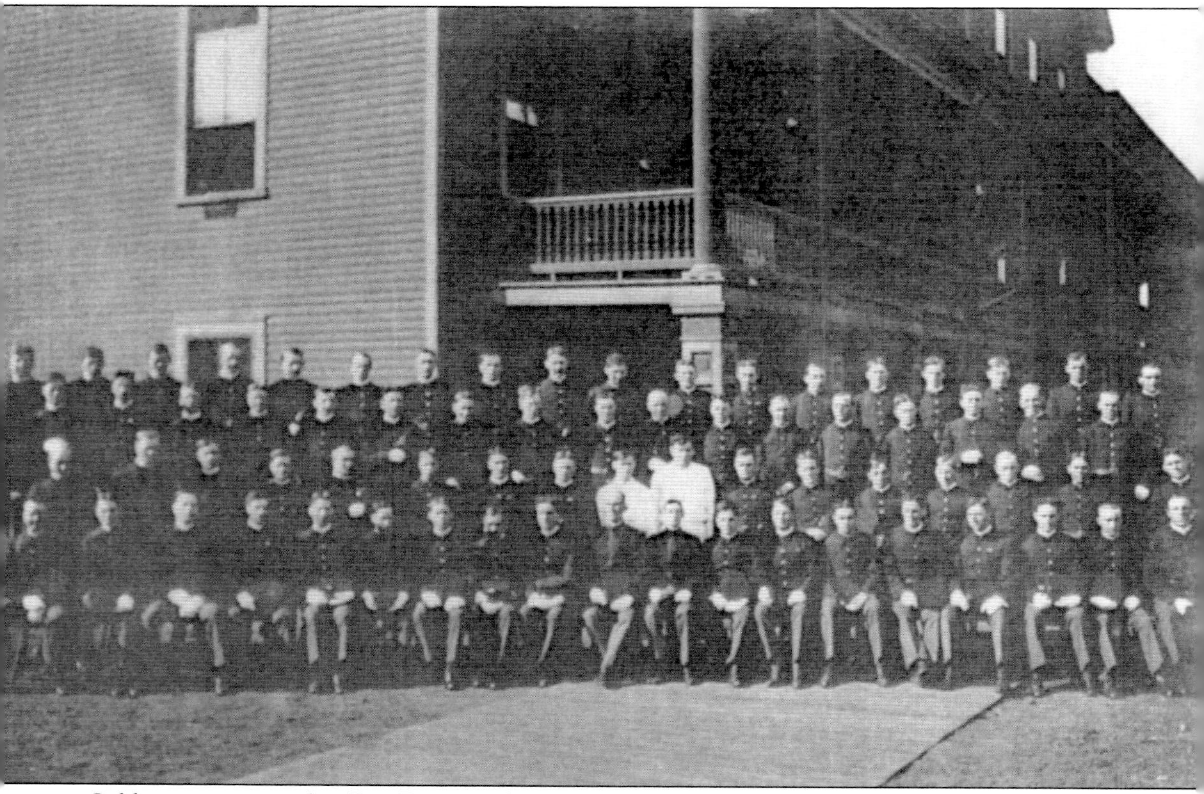

Soldiers are pictured at Fort Barry in this c. 1908 image, formally lined up, spanking neat and clean with hands on knees, and seated behind the post headquarters building. The two in white are most likely hospital employees. (Photograph by Ralph Durland; courtesy GGNRA Archives, PFbr5.)

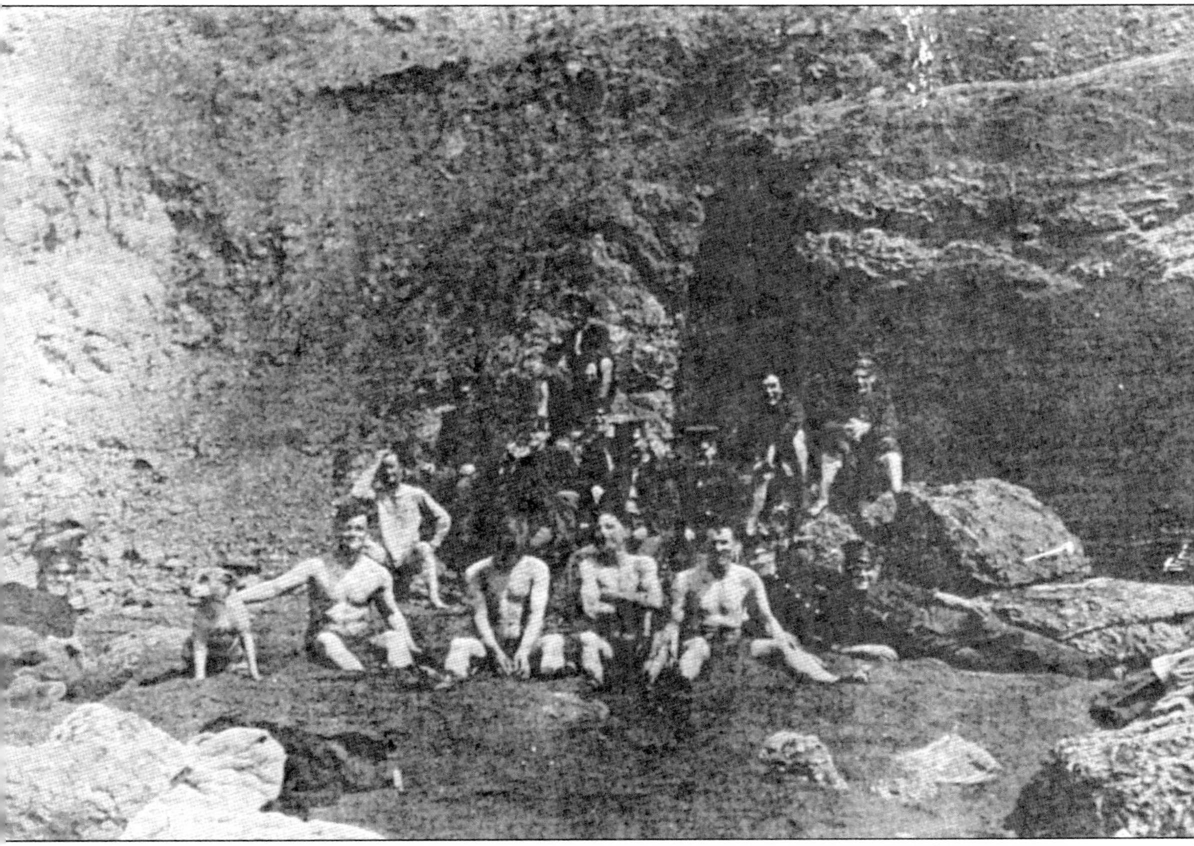

In this *c.* 1910 image of Rodeo Beach, seated on the flatter rocks against the cliff, the men are in shorts with clothes strewn about, and one pats a friendly dog to the left. Rodeo Beach was also called Carnelian Beach, as there were many colored pebbles, including carnelians. The name is now seldom used. As people have collected them, they are now very rare. (Courtesy GGNRA Archives, PFbk8.)

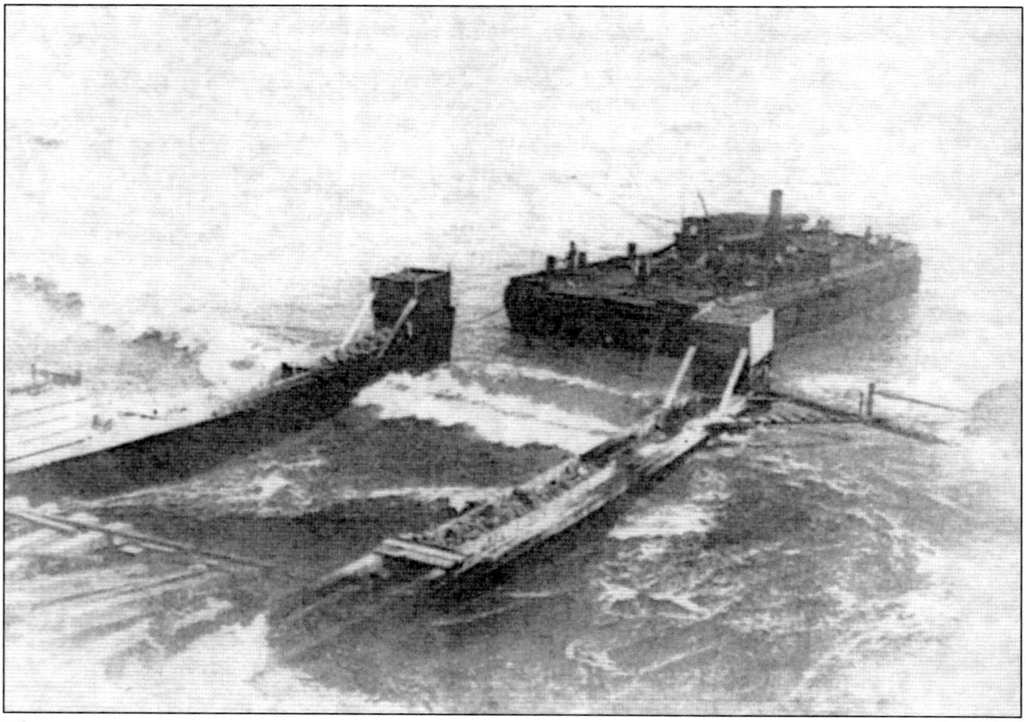

This *c.* 1902 image of Battery Mendell shows a method of landing guns on the beach. The U.S. Army Corps of Engineers used a specially designed barge for transporting the big guns, carriages, and heavy material to the Bonita Cove Wharf. Battery Mendell is above the cove on the ocean side of Point Bonita. (Courtesy GGNRA Archives, PFbr5; Griswold Collection.)

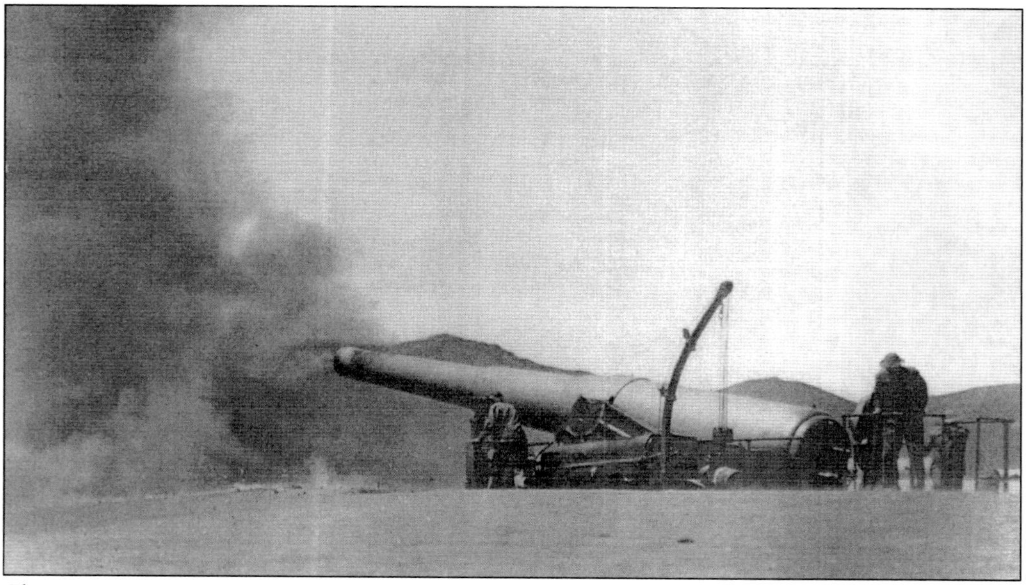

This post-1915 image shows the base ring for a 12-inch mortar at Battery Alexander, Fort Barry. (Courtesy GGNRA Archives, PFbr4; Griswold Collection.)

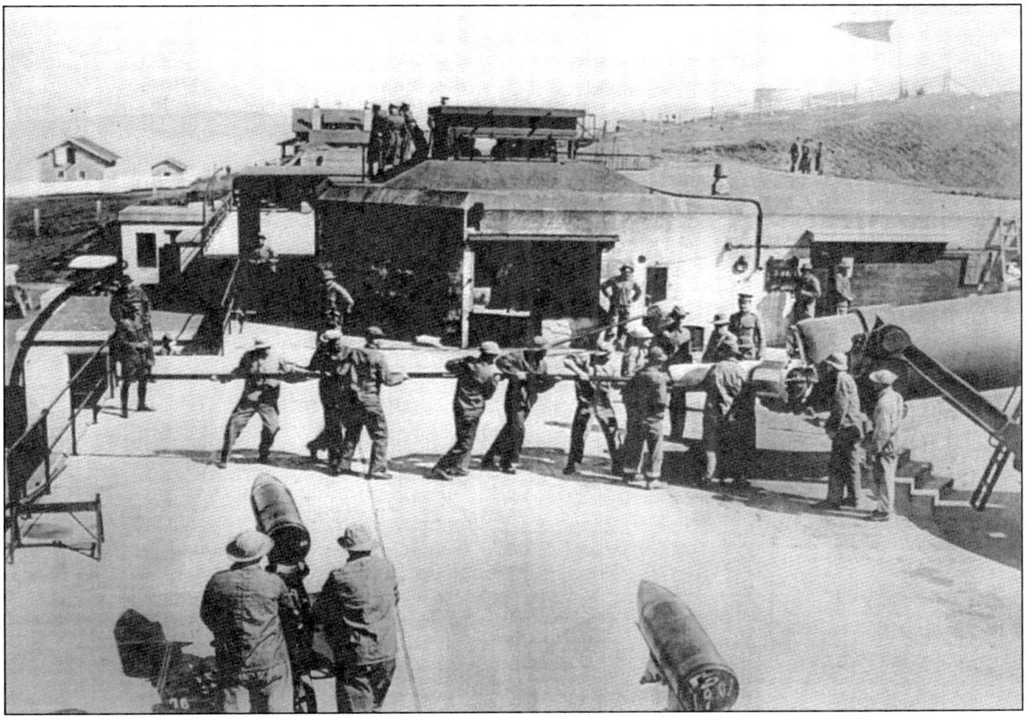

A 12-inch disappearing gun is seen here on April 20, 1921, at Battery Mendell in Fort Barry. These guns were widely used in coastal batteries for a time but were complex mechanisms—the recoil of the gun helped propel it backwards into its protective housing, and it would swing out again with the help of a counterweight system. (Courtesy GGNRA Archives, PFbr5.)

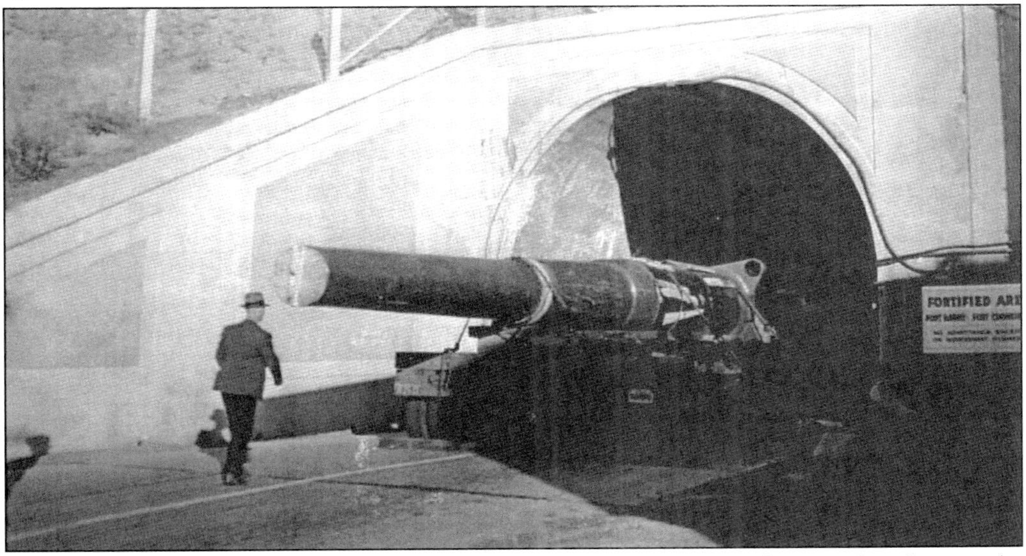

This June 6, 1939, photograph from the U.S. Army Corps of Engineers shows a 12-inch gun tube for Battery Wallace emerging from the Fort Barry tunnel on June 6, 1939. The U.S. Army Corps of Engineers built the narrow tunnel between Forts Baker and Barry. It is still in use. (Courtesy GGNRA Archives, PFbr5.)

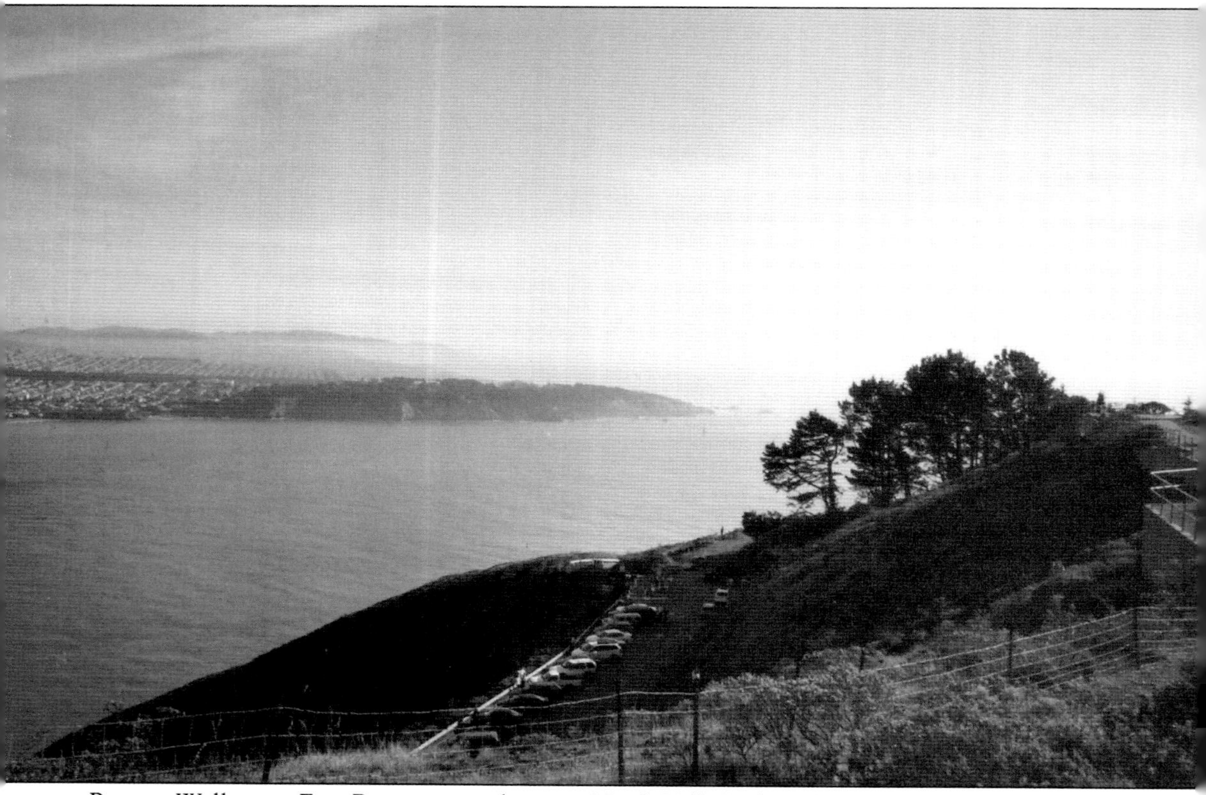

Battery Wallace at Fort Barry is seen here on Hawk Hill. Built early in the post–World War I period, the seacoast guns were casemate under thick concrete shields. After World War I, the 16-inch gun fired 1-ton projectiles for 25 miles, intending to keep the newest battleships out of striking range from any invading forces. San Francisco's Land's End with Fort Miley is seen on the opposite side. (Photograph by Dorothy Gibson.)

Looking happy and proud, Sgt. Edward Larson is standing behind the Fort Barry hospital in this 1941 image. (Courtesy GGNRA Archives, PFbr8; Ed Larson Collection.)

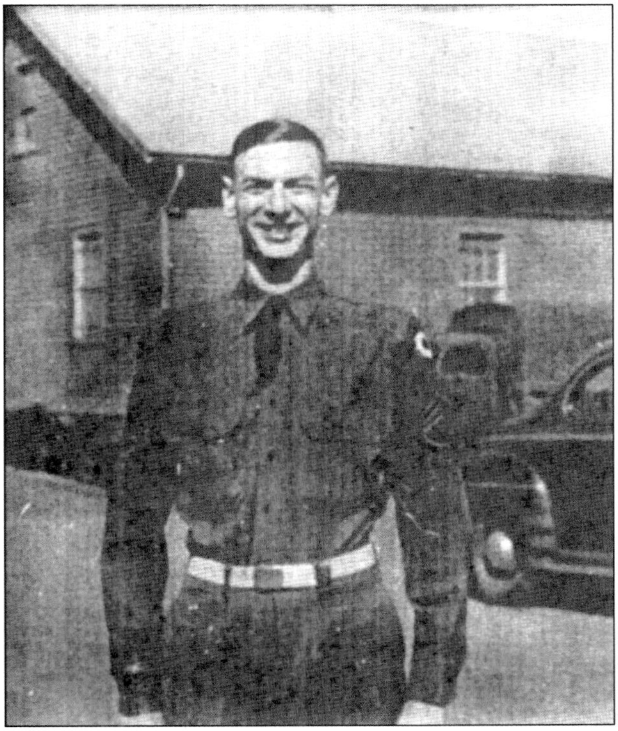

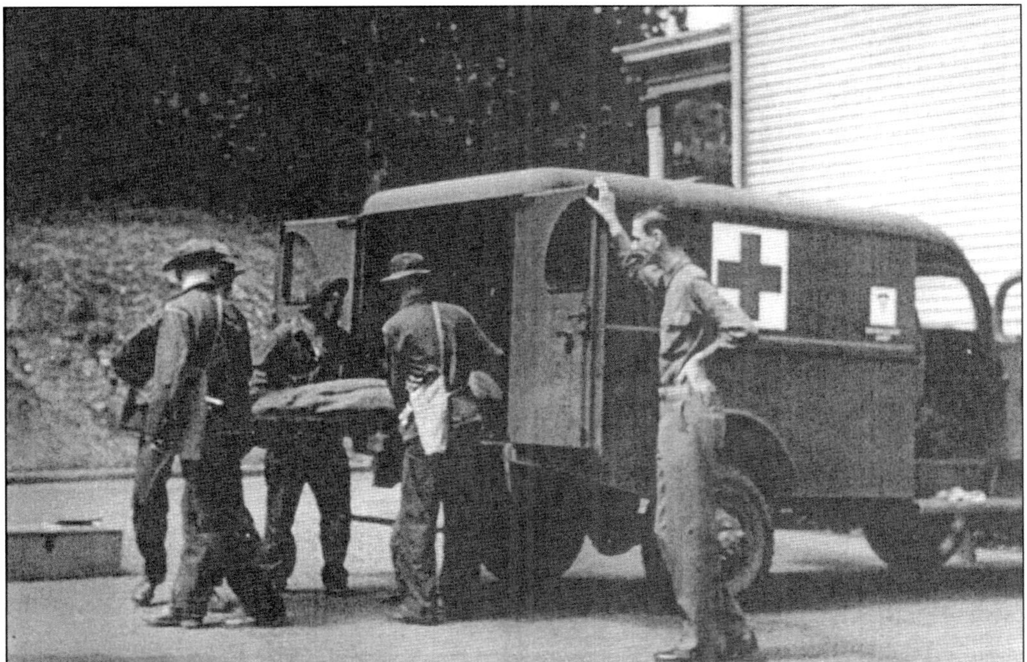

The back of the photograph reads "Sgt. Ed Larson litter drill outside Fort Barry dispensary 1941." The ambulance has been pulled up to the flattened parking area next to the hospital. The trees behind were planted as a windbreak. (Courtesy GGNRA Archives, PFbr7; Ed Larson Collection.)

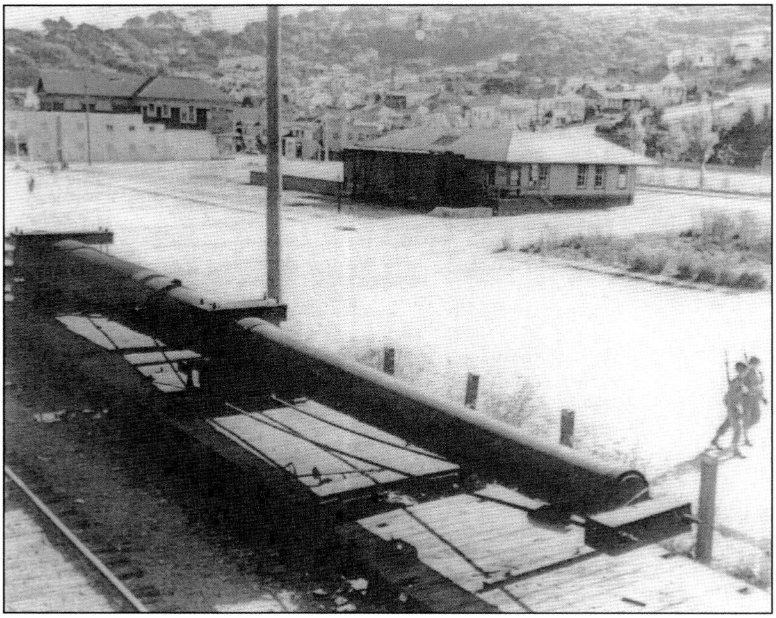

This *c.* 1943 photograph shows 16-inch gun tubes for Battery No. 129 en route in Sausalito, near today's Litho and Caledonia/ Bridgeway Streets. Note the two soldiers with rifles guarding the cargo. (Courtesy GGNRA Archives, PFbr4; TASC Collection.)

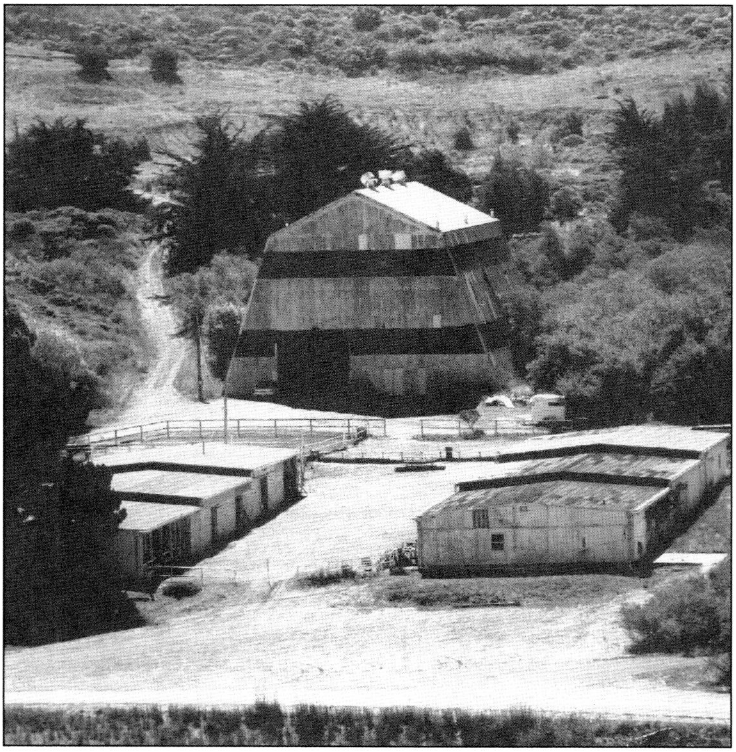

Fort Baker's balloon hangar and motor vehicle sheds have a long and varied history. The hangar was completed in 1921 and in 1943 was converted to motor pool use. In 1944, a portion of the vehicle shed was converted to paint shed, and in 1953, the hangar was converted to antiaircraft artillery maintenance facility. In 1966, the Presidio Riding Club received a permit to use the old vehicle shed and hangar for riding stables. (Courtesy GGNRA.)

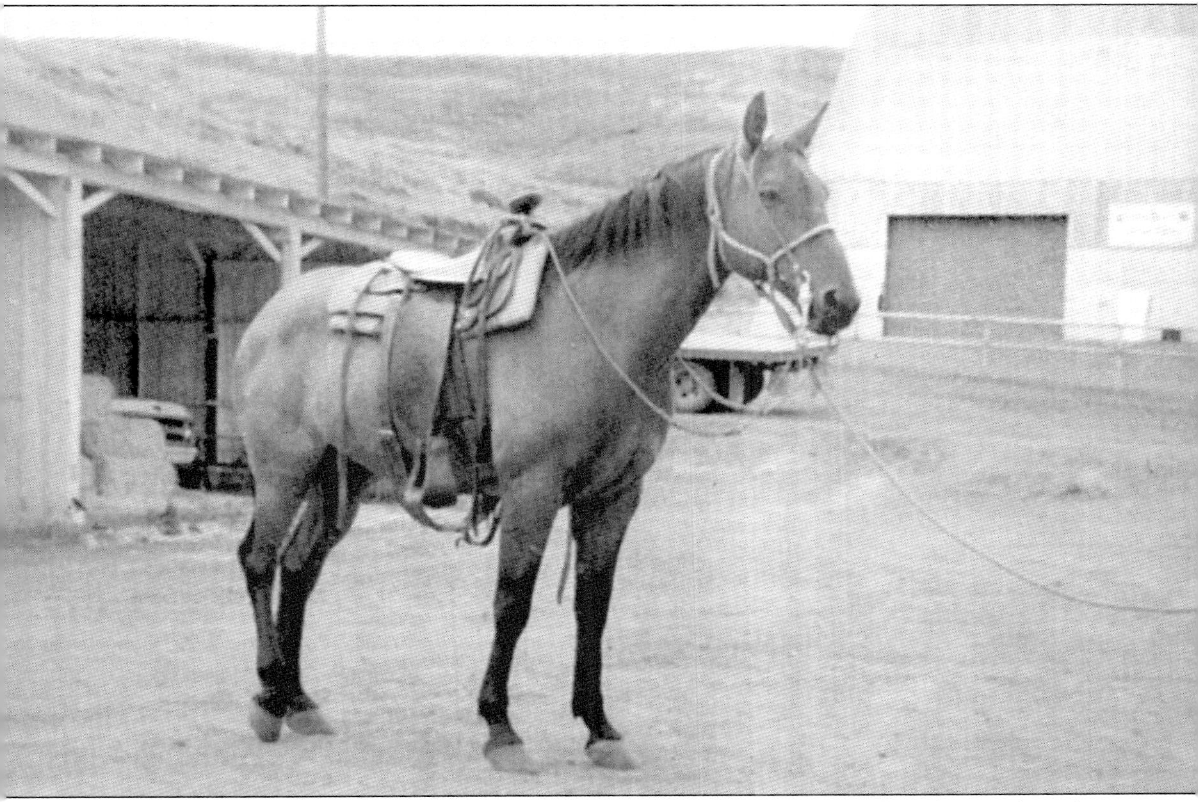

The Presidio Riding Club had four trail bosses who were army personnel, and several civilian personnel who were in charge of feeding and grooming the horses. This is Amigo; his owner was a member of the military police battalion. (Courtesy Linda Pfeiffer.)

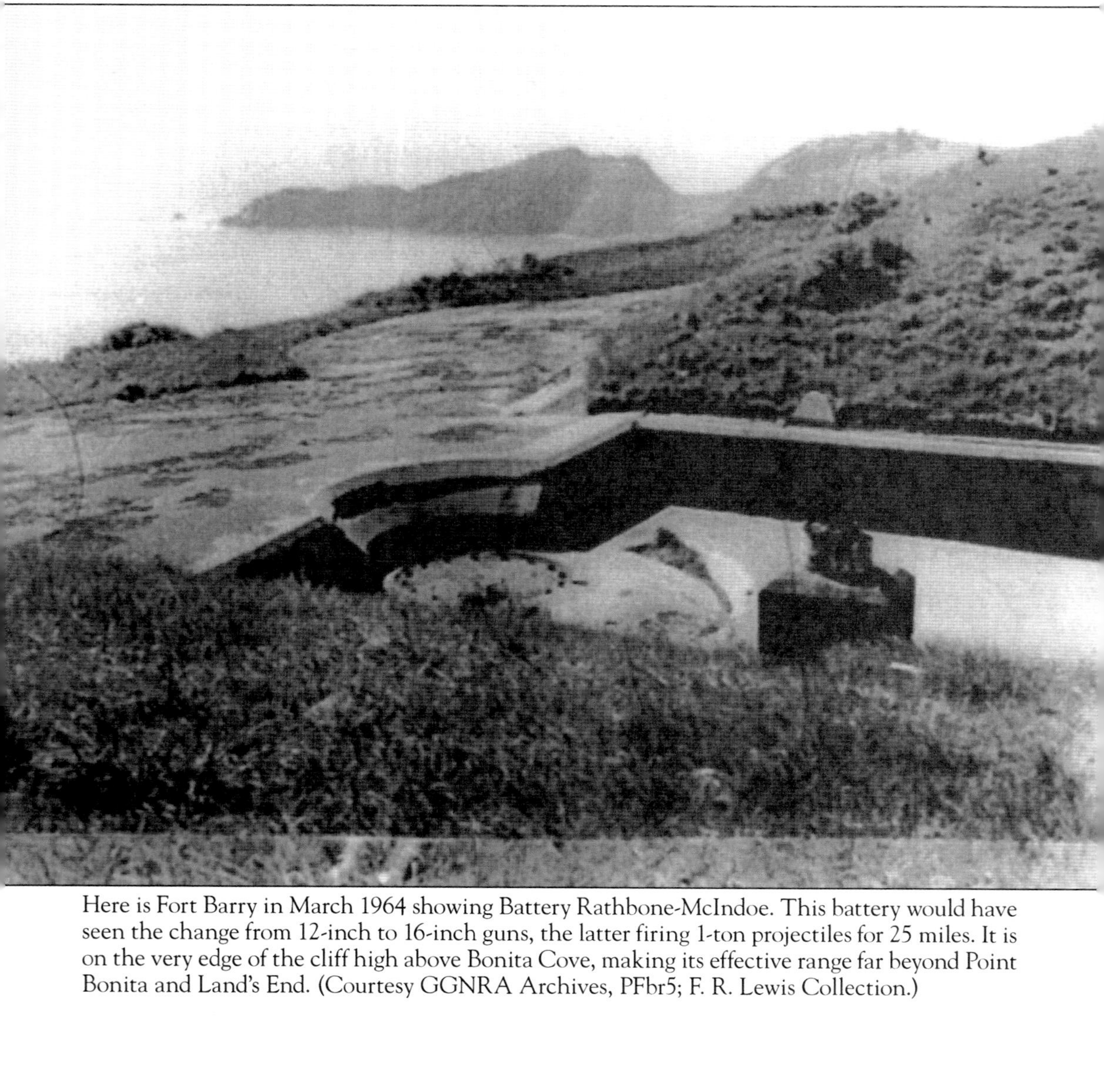

Here is Fort Barry in March 1964 showing Battery Rathbone-McIndoe. This battery would have seen the change from 12-inch to 16-inch guns, the latter firing 1-ton projectiles for 25 miles. It is on the very edge of the cliff high above Bonita Cove, making its effective range far beyond Point Bonita and Land's End. (Courtesy GGNRA Archives, PFbr5; F. R. Lewis Collection.)

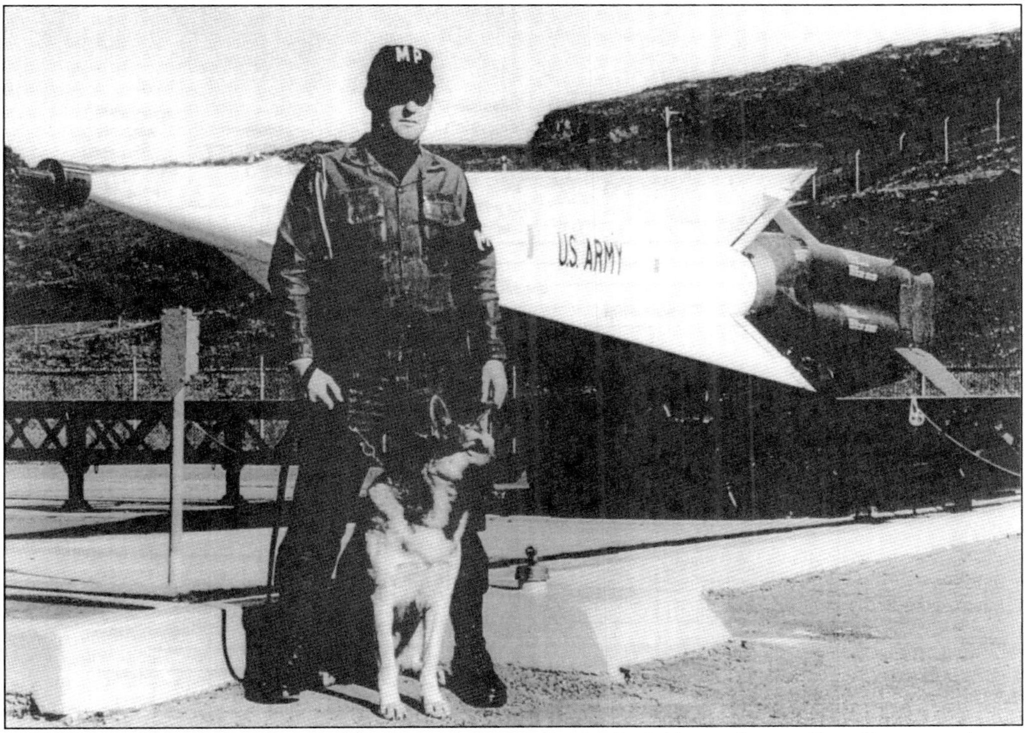

An unidentified sergeant sits with a guard dog in front of a Nike rocket at Fort Barry in this c. 1968 photograph. After World War II, the threat of attack shifted from naval to the air. From 1954 to 1974, in the midst of the cold war era, such missiles were placed in several locations around southern Marin County. (Courtesy GGNRA Archives, PFbr7; Chuck Oysen Nike photograph collection.)

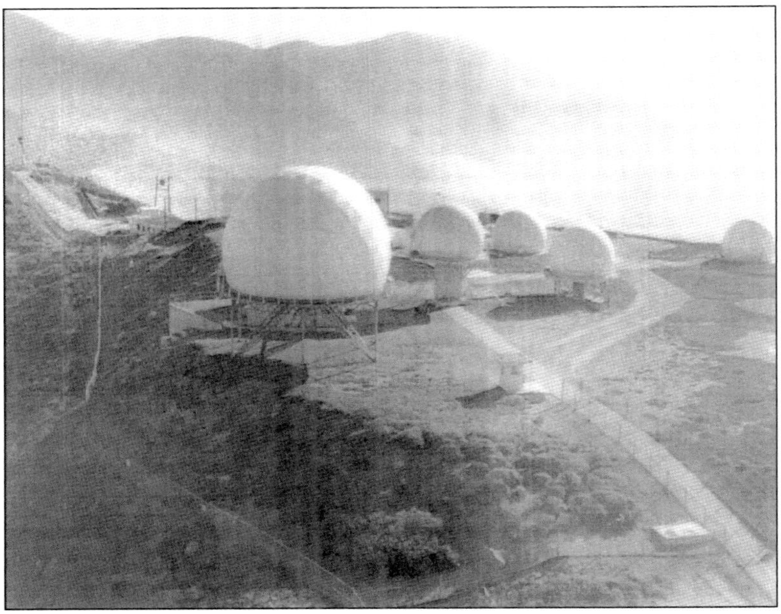

This aerial view of the Nike site on Wolf Ridge at Fort Cronkite is from January 16, 1967. The launcher site is at Fort Barry, which is adjacent to Fort Cronkite south of the lagoon. (Courtesy GGNRA Archives, PFbr6.)

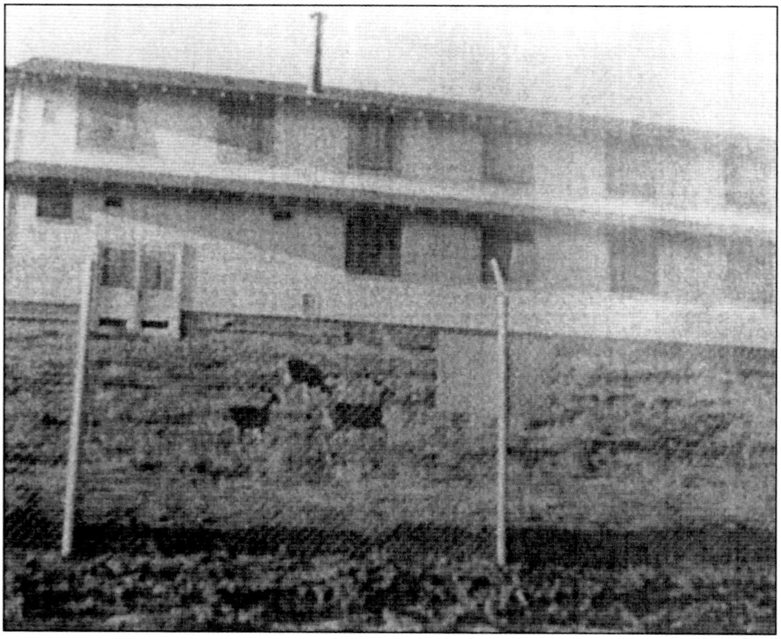

The area around this Nike site at Fort Barry, shown in October 1966, has been fenced. Was it maybe to keep the deer out? (Courtesy GGNRA Archives, PFbr6.)

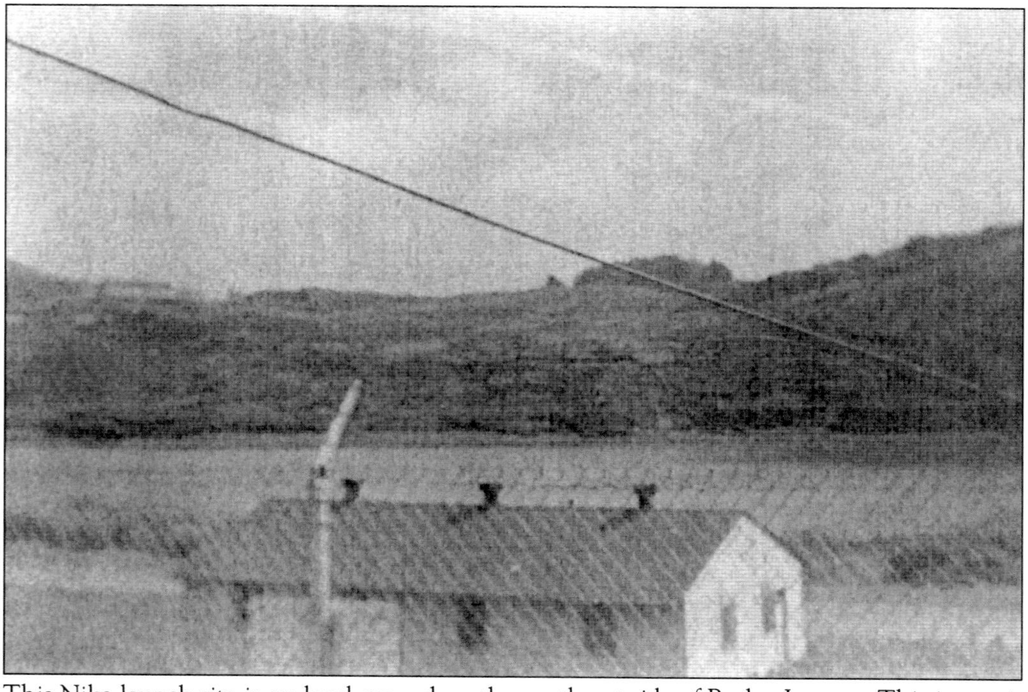

This Nike launch site is on level ground on the northeast side of Rodeo Lagoon. This image is also from October 1966. (Courtesy GGNRA Archives, PFbr6.)

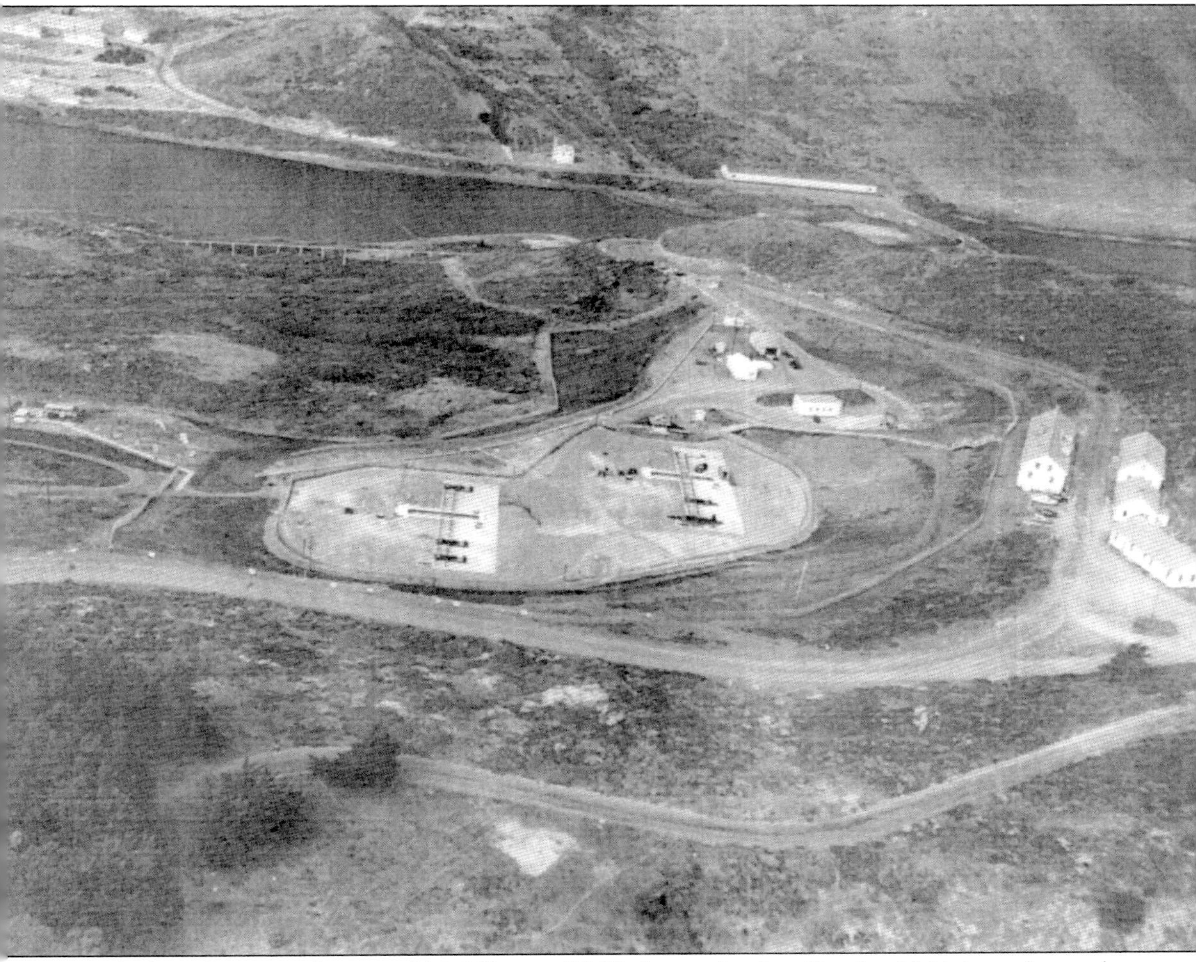

The launcher area of western U.S. Nike site SF-88, depicted in late October 1964, is on the south side of Rodeo Lagoon, upgrade from the service area buildings off Conzelman Road. Fort Cronkite is at far left opposite. (Courtesy GGNRA Archives, PFbr6.)

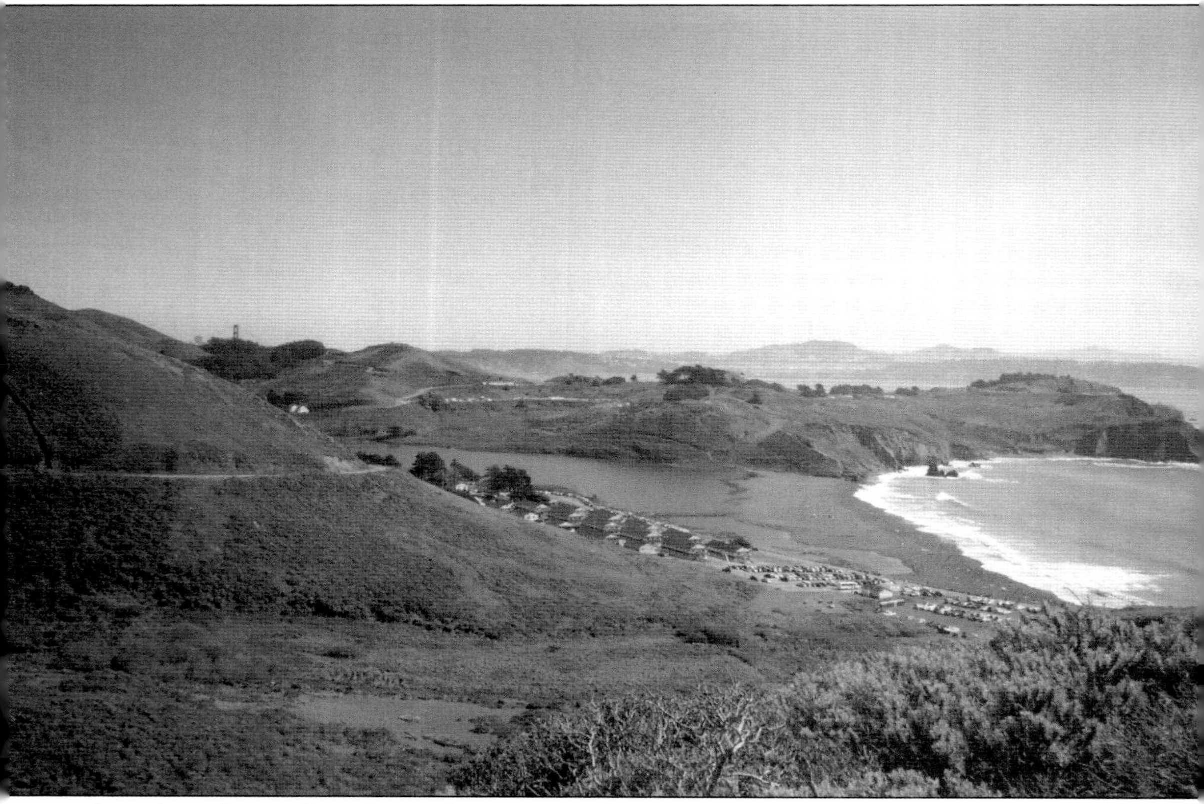

Seen from the north in this modern view on the roadway leading to the Coastal Trail, Point Bonita is to the far right. The service buildings are tucked against the north edge of Rodeo Beach and lagoon. Fort Cronkite was the third and last fort to be built in the headlands. It was established in 1939, when the U.S. government acquired land north to Tennessee Point, beyond Tennessee Cove and Tennessee Valley Beach. The beach area was originally part of a dairy ranch operated by Louis Gioli. Local residents called the beach "Jolly's," as his Italian-Swiss name sounded like that. The fort is named for Maj. Gen. Adelbert Cronkite (1861–1937), a career officer who was a division commander and a corps commander during World War I. (Photograph by Dorothy Gibson.)

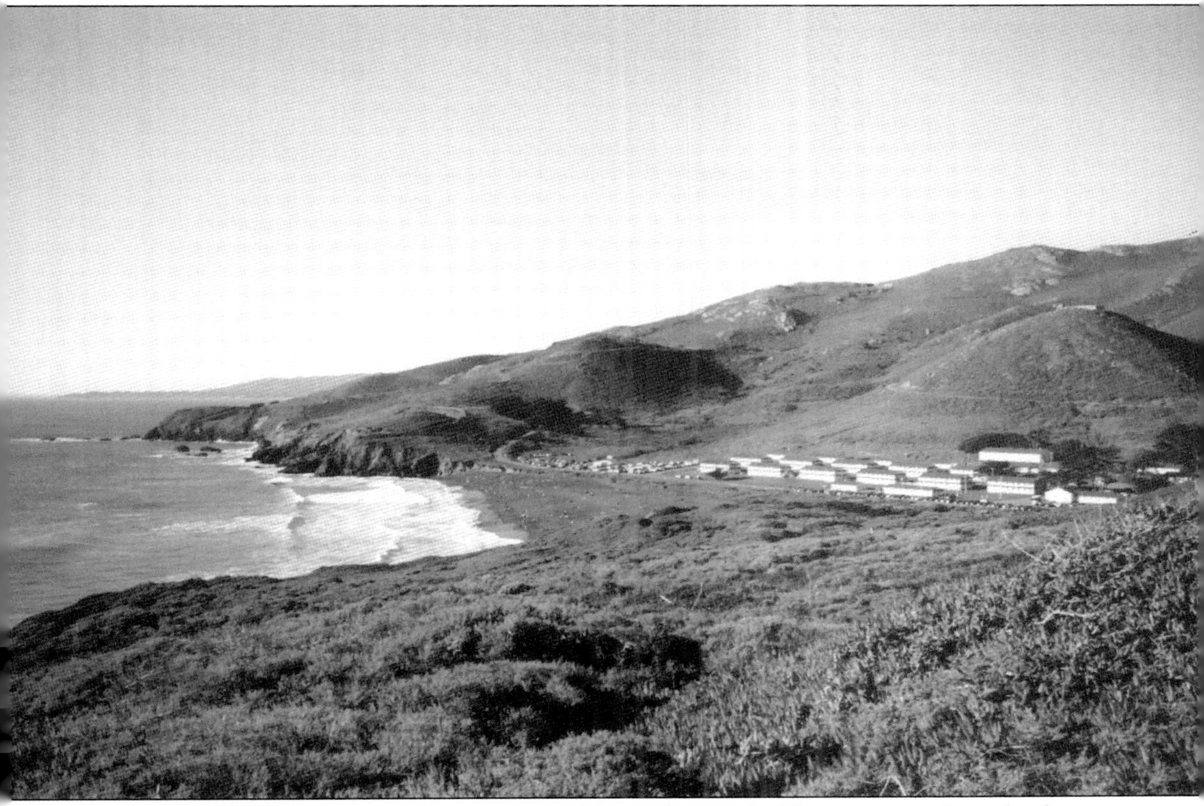

Looking north is Fort Cronkite, as viewed from the south. There is a roadway leading to the Coastal Trail. This is the base of Wolf Ridge, at the top of which is Battery Townsley. (Photograph by Dorothy Gibson.)

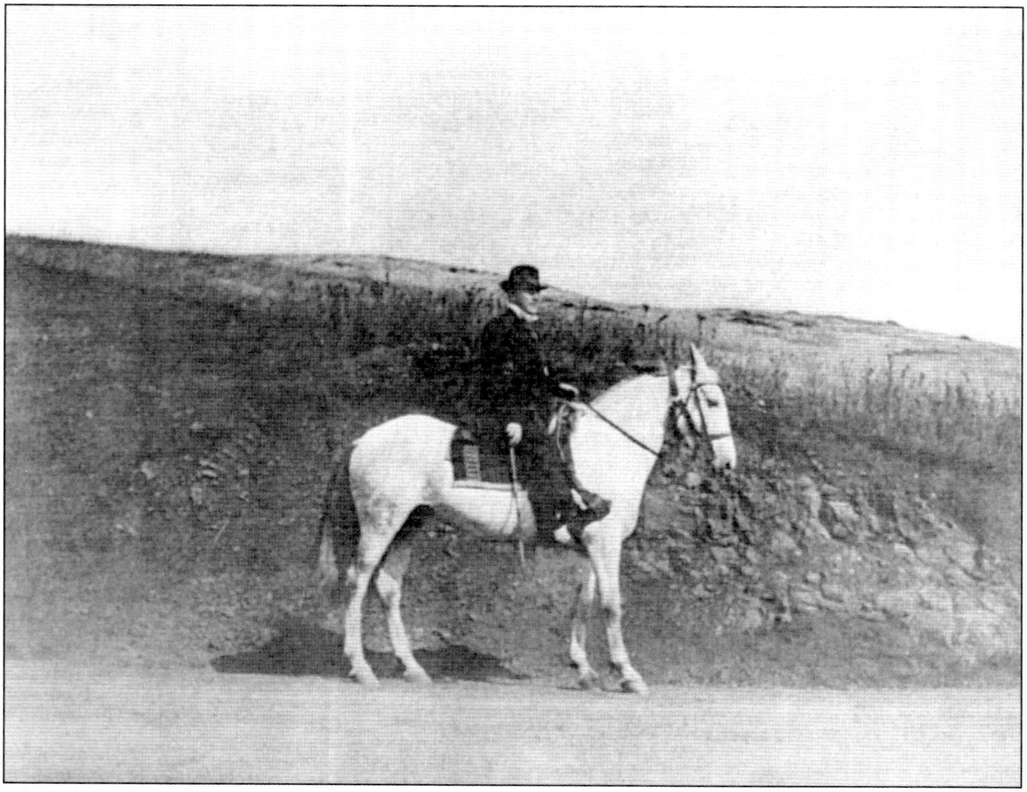

This undated image shows a slice of military life that is somewhat appealing. These two look as if they are enjoying the scenery along the pleasant walk (or ride) from Fort Barry to Fort Cronkite. (Courtesy GGNRA Archives, PFBBC.)

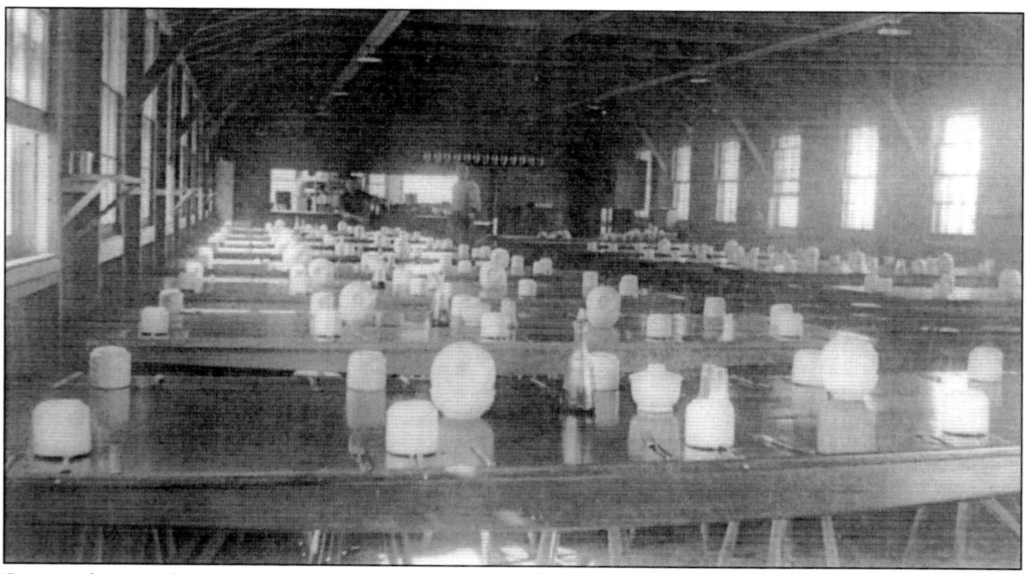

Spic and span, the Fort Cronkite mess hall awaits diners in this undated photograph. As were the other two forts, Cronkite was a full-service community. (Courtesy GGNRA Archives, PFbk4.)

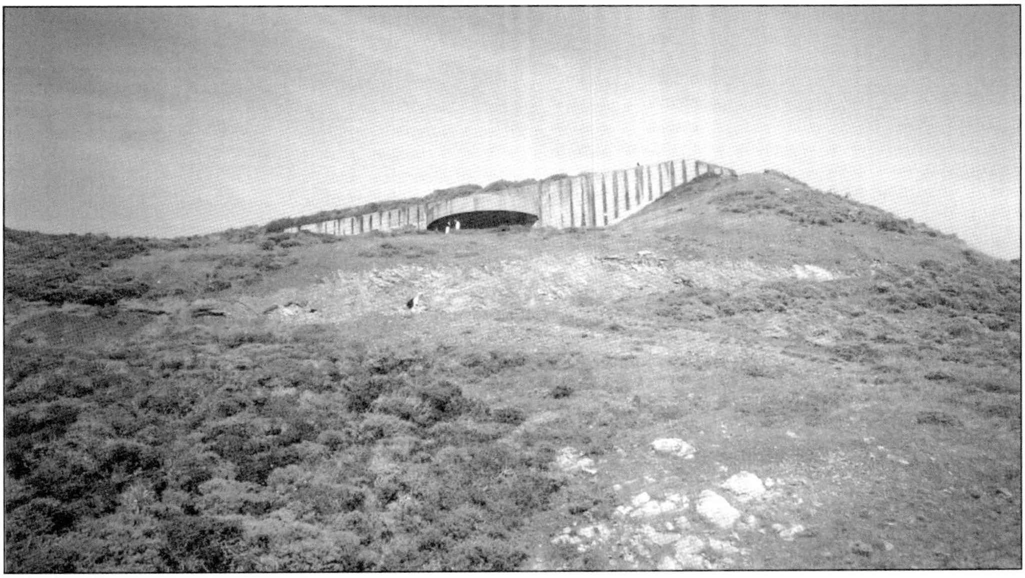

Battery Townsley was built above the Pacific Ocean on the side of the hill leading to Wolf Ridge. The Coastal Trail goes past it—seemingly an open invitation to explore the headland's vast open spaces. (Photograph by Dorothy Gibson.)

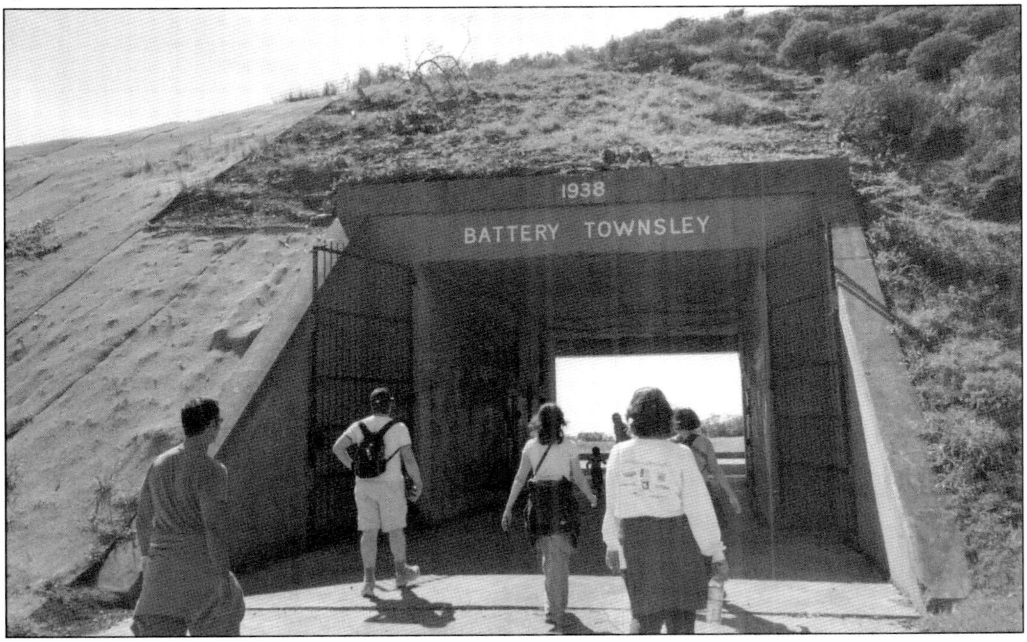

Further up the grade to Wolf Ridge is Aircraft Battery No. 1. Both Battery Townsley and Battery No. 1 were built during the post–World War I/World War II years with the 16-inch guns and upgraded for the cold war. SF-88, the radar counterpart to SF-88 launcher at Fort Barry, was built on the ridge. Battery Townsley was named for Maj. Gen. Clarence Page Townsley, who was a superintendent at West Point Military Academy. Battery Townsley operated from 1954 until 1974, when it was transferred to its present guardian, the National Park Service. (Photograph by Dorothy Gibson.)

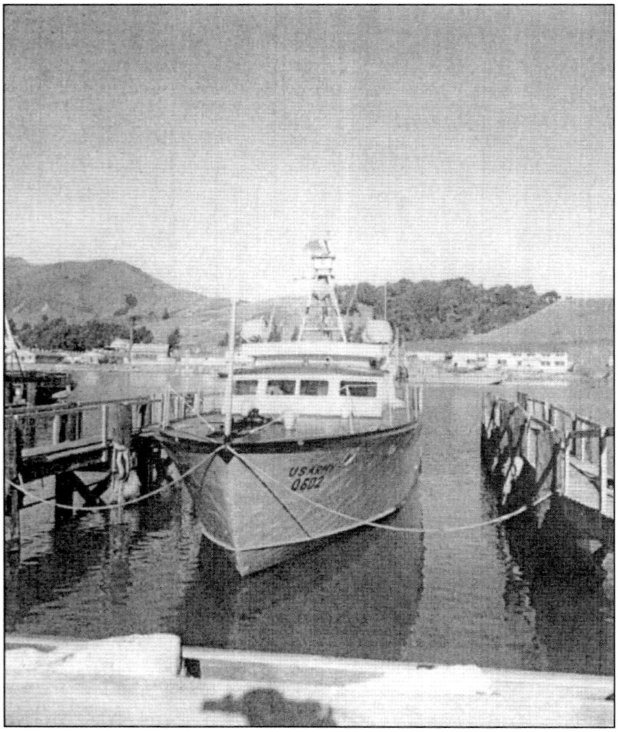

Army Boat 602, used for tests at Forts Baker and Cronkite, is shown here in December 1953 docked at Fort Baker's Horseshoe Bay. (Courtesy GGNRA Archives, PFBBC.)

This U.S. Army Corps of Engineers photograph from the 1930s shows a cement pour at the Fort Baker Mine Wharf. The mine field was from Point Bonita to San Francisco's Land's End. (Courtesy GGNRA Archives, PFbk4.)

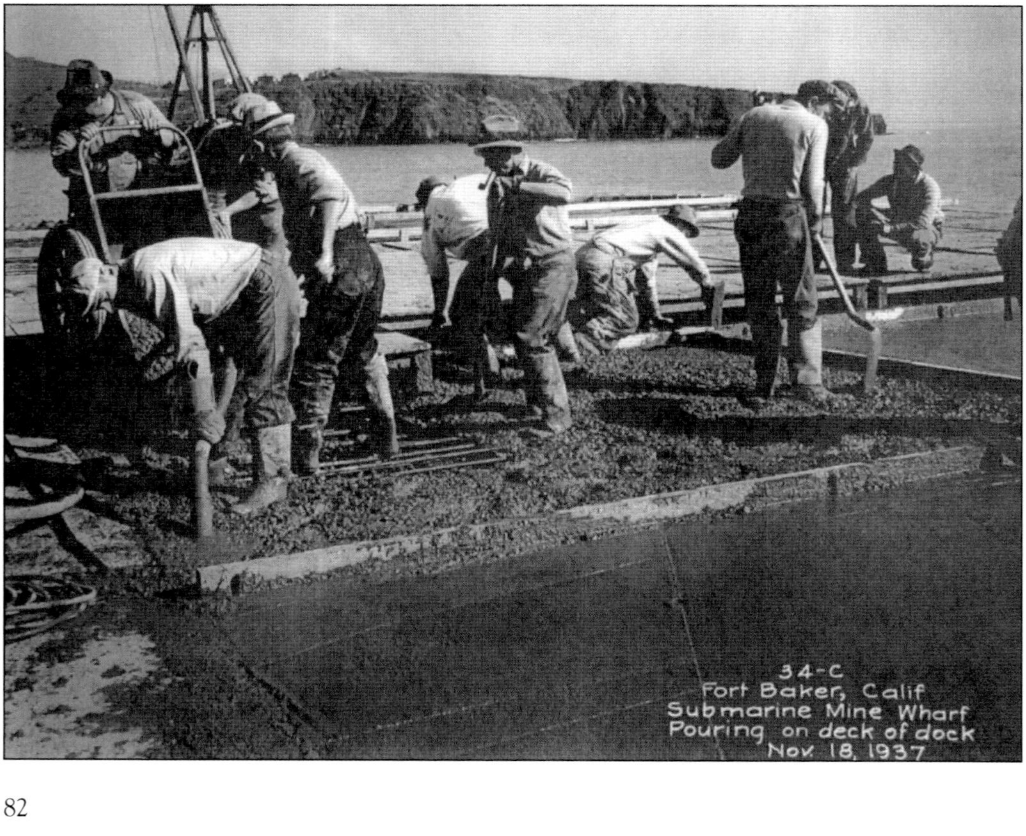

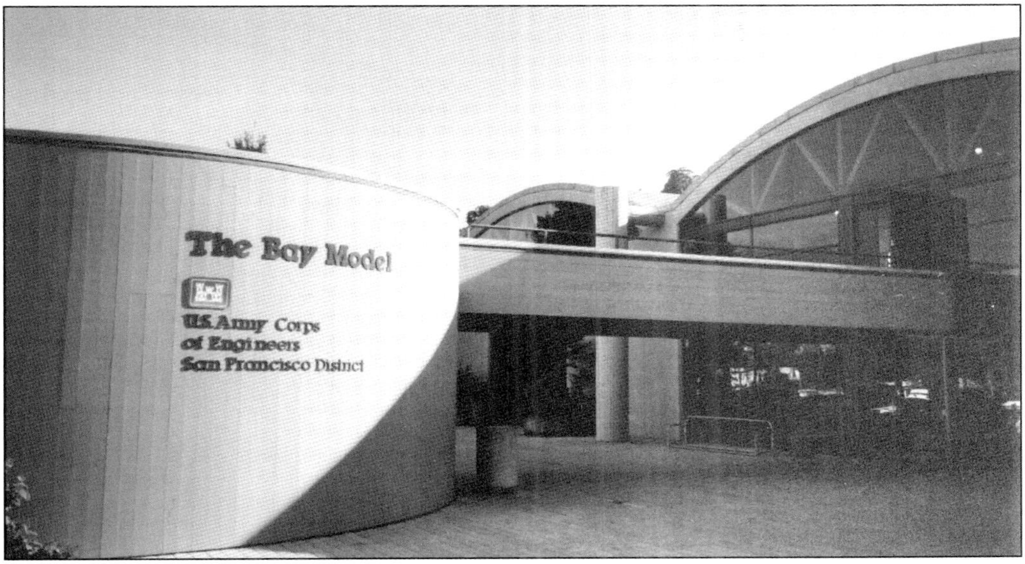

Sausalito's "Bay Model," as it is familiarly called, is a real model of waterways through the San Francisco Bay region and the Sacramento/San Joaquin Delta. It is large enough to walk around and see how the water moves throughout the area. It was built in 1957 by the U.S. Army Corps of Engineers as a scientific tool to test the impact of proposed changes to the bay and related waterways. An educational facility, it is open to the public. Exhibits show the watershed from the Sierra Nevada mountains to the San Francisco Bay. (Photograph by Dorothy Gibson.)

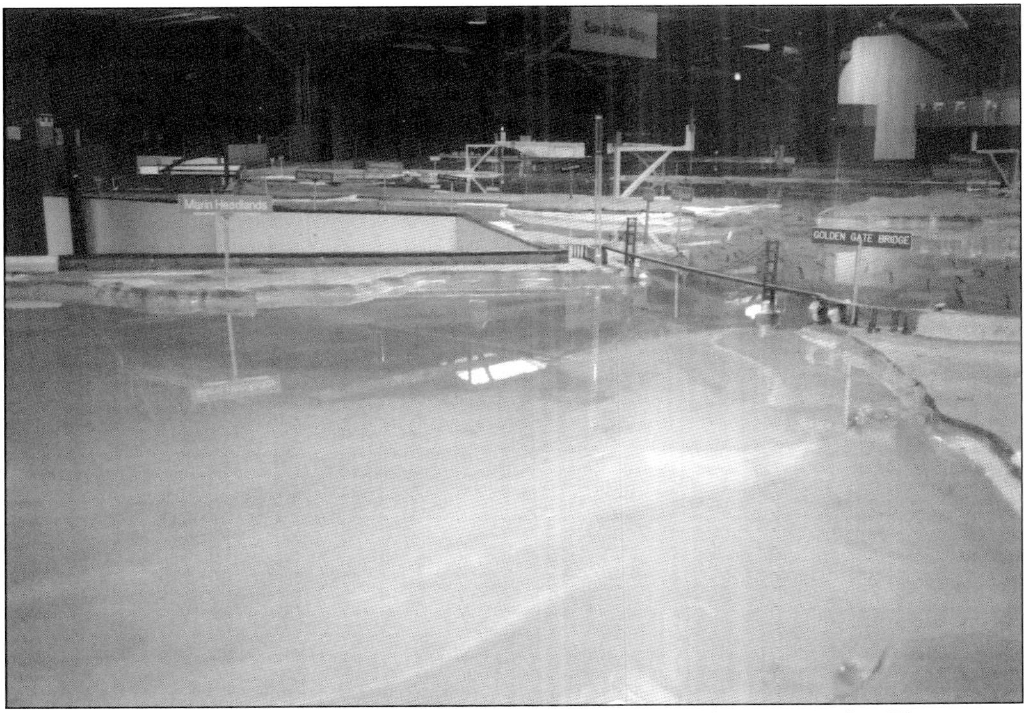

Note the headland's internationally known major sentinel, the Golden Gate Bridge. The majestic bridge was completed in 1937. (Photograph by Dorothy Gibson.)

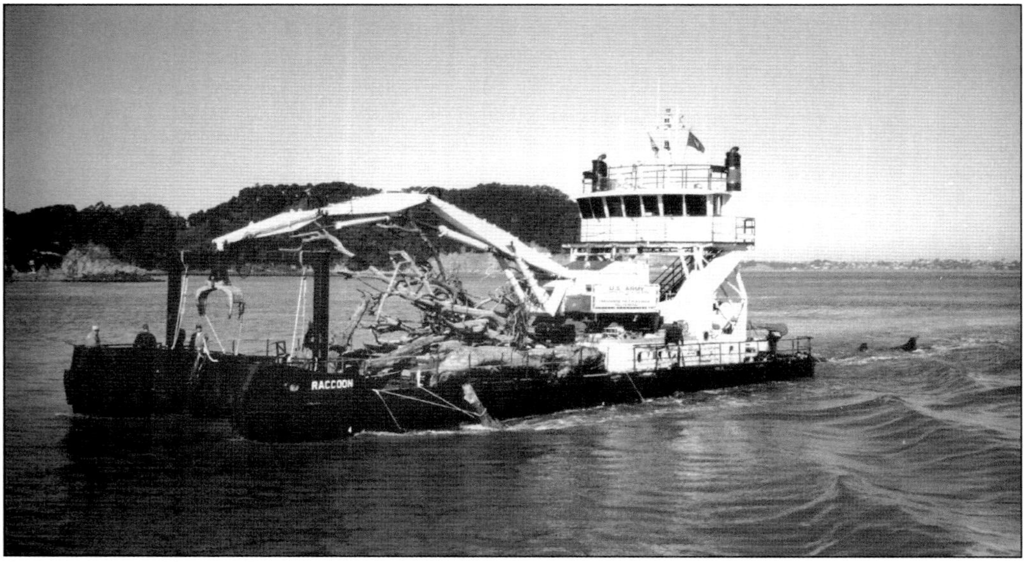

On a continual basis, the U.S. Army Corps of Engineers at the Bay Model location gather litter from the bay, cleaning the channels for the ships that go in an out and ridding the waterways of potentially dangerous debris. It is hauled in for disposal and/or recycling. (Courtesy San Francisco Bay Model, U.S. Army Corps of Engineers, Sausalito.)

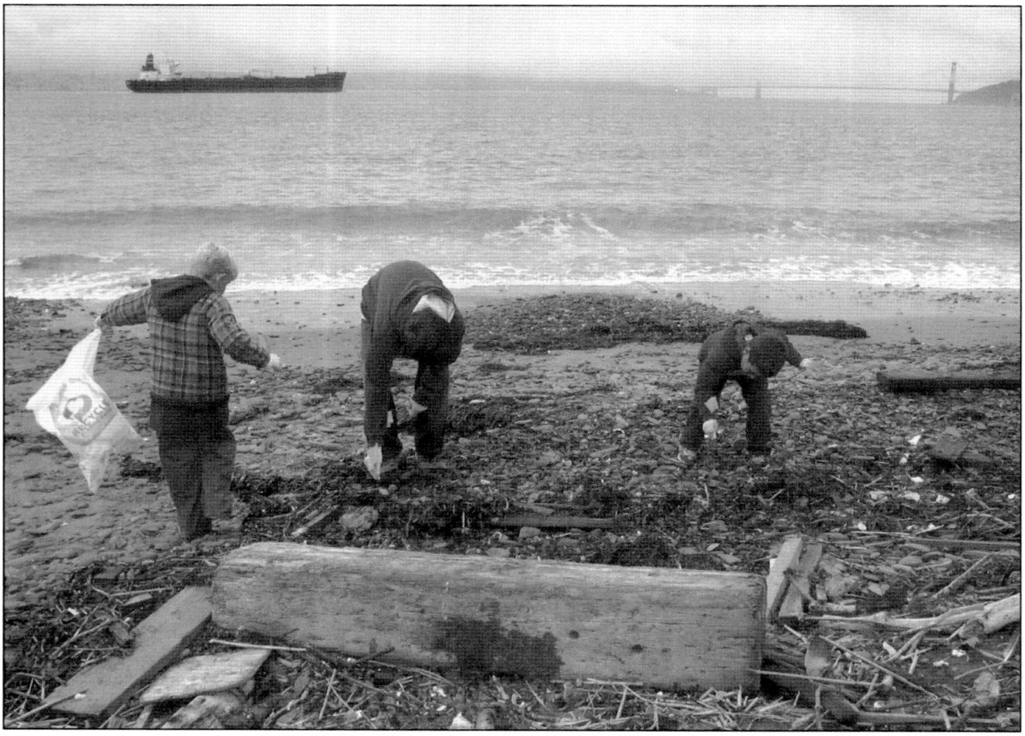

Another of the U.S. Army Corps of Engineers' services for the public is the annual Coastal Cleanup. The Bay Model contingent assumes responsibility for all of Marin County, including Angel Island. (Courtesy San Francisco Bay Model, U.S. Army Corps of Engineers, Sausalito.)

Six

Saucito, Saucelito, Sausalito

It was "Saucito" on an early map, "Saucelito" by those who came and went, and "Sausalito" by Capt. William A. Richardson, who held the land grant for the southern peninsula from the base of Mount Tamalpais to the Golden Gate and named it Rancho Sausalito. The Spanish name translates to "little place of willows." Following Lt. Juan Manuel de Ayala's discovery of the San Francisco Bay in 1775, the early explorers and commercial ships found refuge in the little bay northwest of the Golden Gate. There was water and wood; whales, fish, shellfish, and animals for food; and hide and blubber for trade. It came to be called Whaler's Cove. Later it was called Hurricane Gulch or Old Town. Richardson began his cattle ranch here. Then the family moved north to the next valley, to be called New Town or Turney Valley after a subsequent owner. Although leading an active life as rancher, captain of the San Francisco Port, surveyor, and owner of commercial ships, Richardson experienced great losses and before his death deeded most of his land. The southern portion, the 1,700-acre Lime Point Tract, was later sold to the U.S. government to fortify the Golden Gate. The new Fort Baker defined Sausalito's southern boundary. The Hill at Sausalito's Point, high above the water, became the preferred residence of the English who moved over from San Francisco. Along the water's edge settled the boat builders, craftsmen, and their families: Portuguese, Italian, French, German, Scotch, Irish, and Scandinavian. Over time, people settled the next two valleys, Spring and Nevada, and moved up higher on the ridges between, to be called Hannon and Pine Hill. During World War II, Sausalito was tapped for the building of Liberty ships. Workers were recruited from all over the country, and housing was built on a mass scale, creating a new little Marin City. When the war ended, the area was abruptly vacated, although many stayed in Marin City. Marinship lay fallow. There followed a wave of new people (artists, philosophers, and poets) to the north, living mostly on houseboats. This was followed in the 1960s by the Free Speech Movement—college students rebelling against the impersonalization of authority. This led to the flower power period and a migration of young people to Sausalito. Very creative, they found and made homes in and around the structures of Marinship. That is, until it was rezoned in the 1970s for waterfront industrial and commercial use.

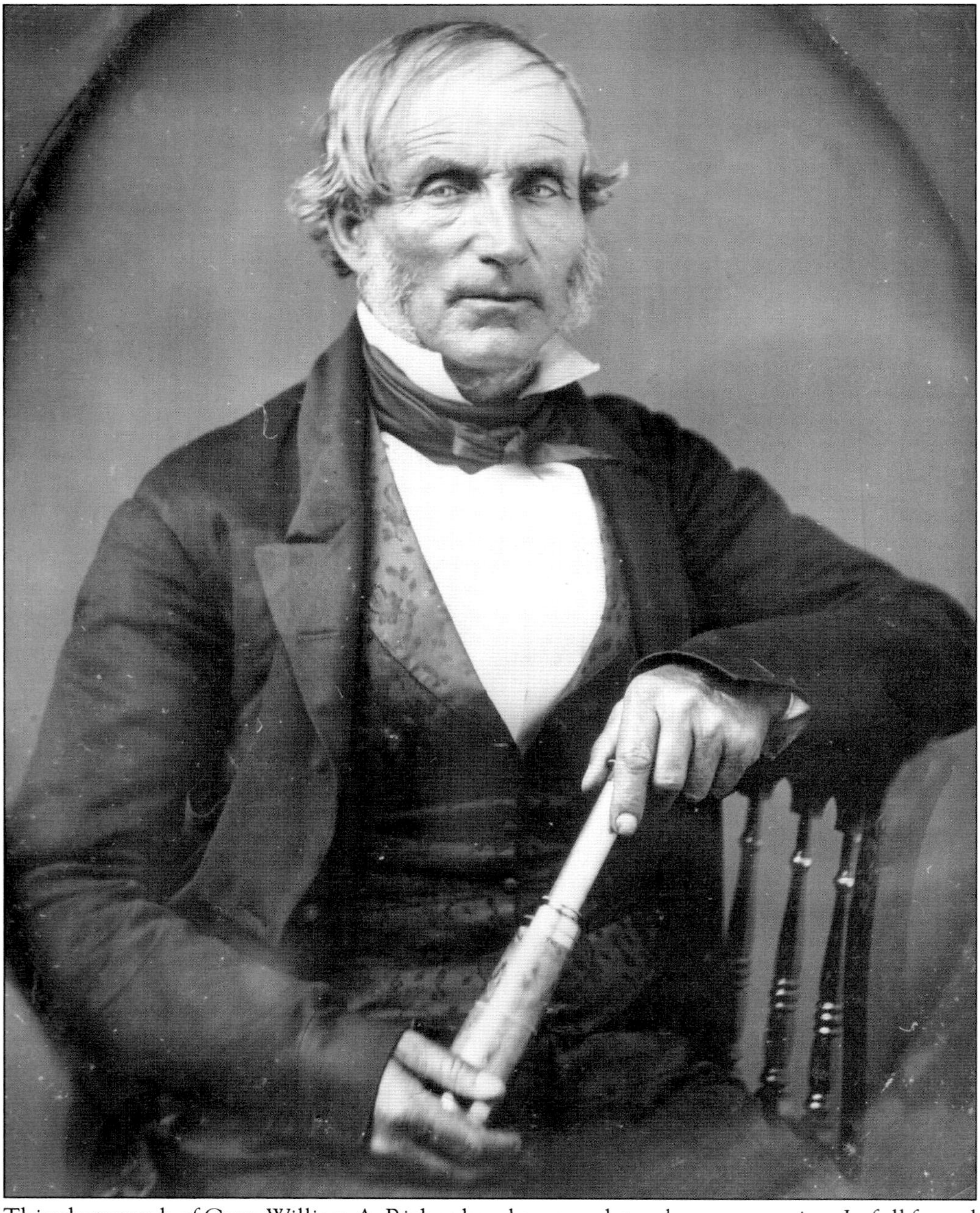

This photograph of Capt. William A. Richardson bears no date, place, or occasion. In full formal dress, seated with spyglass, his hair is thin and graying and his blue eyes tired. Born in London, England, on August 27, 1795, he was a sailor at 12 years old—a cabin boy on merchant ships. In 1820, he sailed as first officer on the whaler *Orion*, landing at San Francisco Bay's Presidio on August 2, 1822. (Courtesy Sausalito Historical Society, 78-68a.)

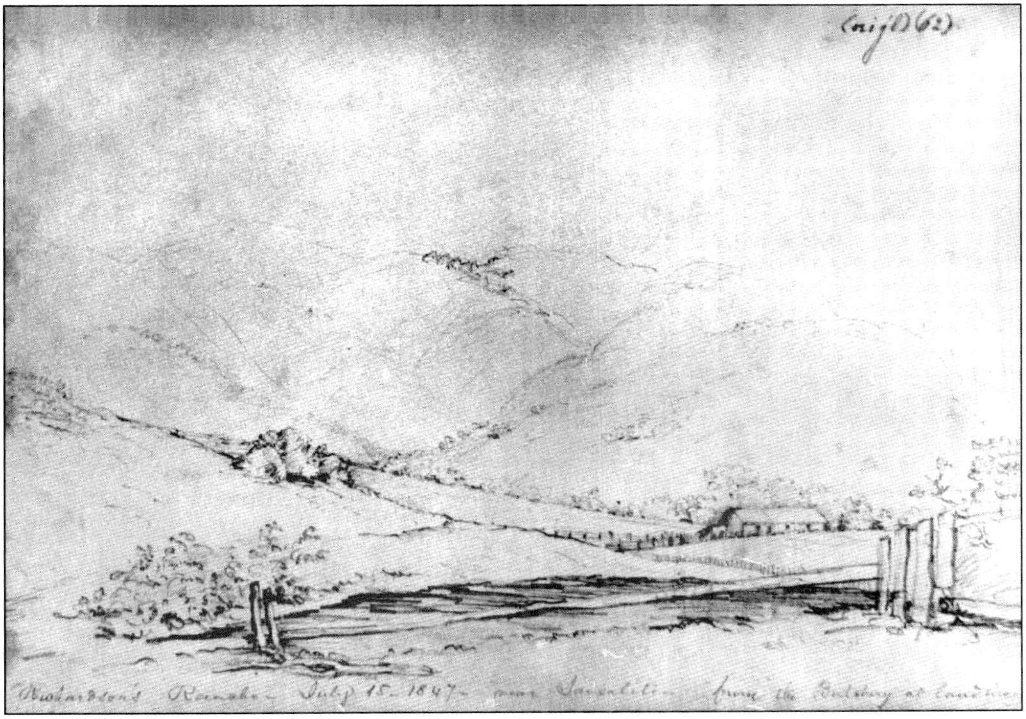

Here is a depiction of Richardson's rancho near Sausalito on July 15, 1847. (Courtesy Sausalito Historical Society, 95-135d.)

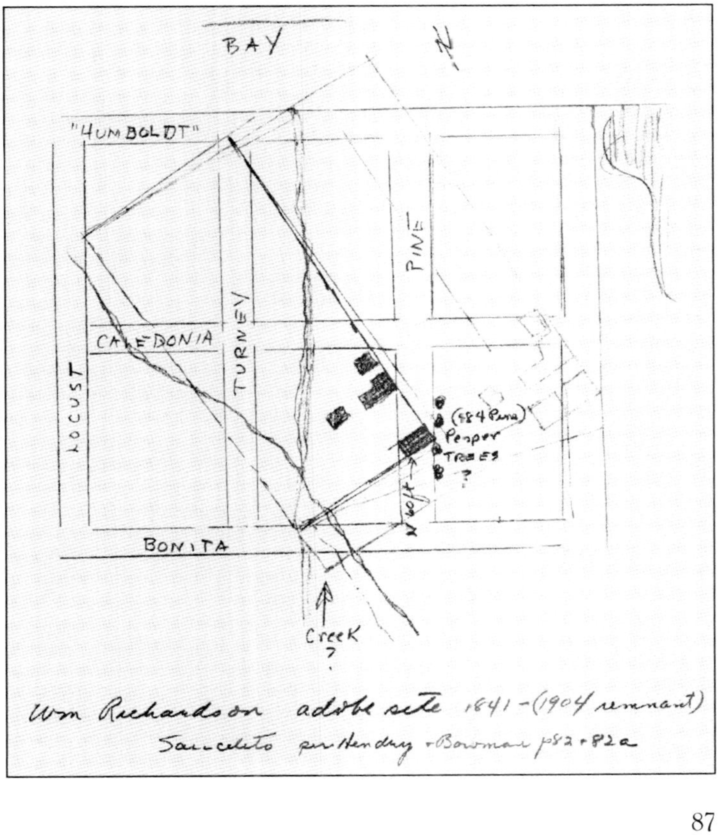

This map shows "William Richardson's adobe site 1841—(1904 remnant)." (Courtesy Sausalito Historical Society, 93-562.)

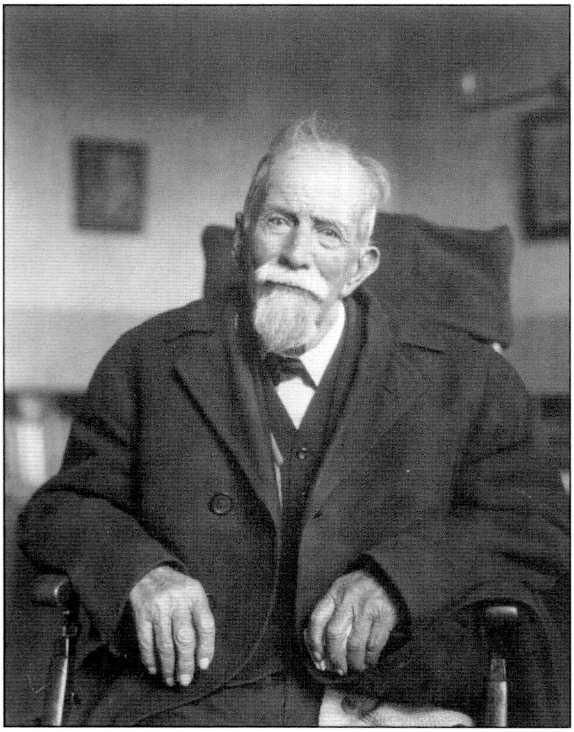

Stephen Richardson had, by 1847, taken over management of Rancho Sausalito. He had 2,800 cattle and 300 horses. After the family lost the land, he continued to live in Marin County. In 1870, he married and had four children. His mother lived with him. He dictated his memories in "The Days of the Dons: Reminiscences of California's Oldest Son," which was published in the *San Francisco Bulletin* in 1918. He lived to be 93 years old and is buried in Mount Olivet Cemetery in San Rafael. (Courtesy California Historical Society, N-24887.)

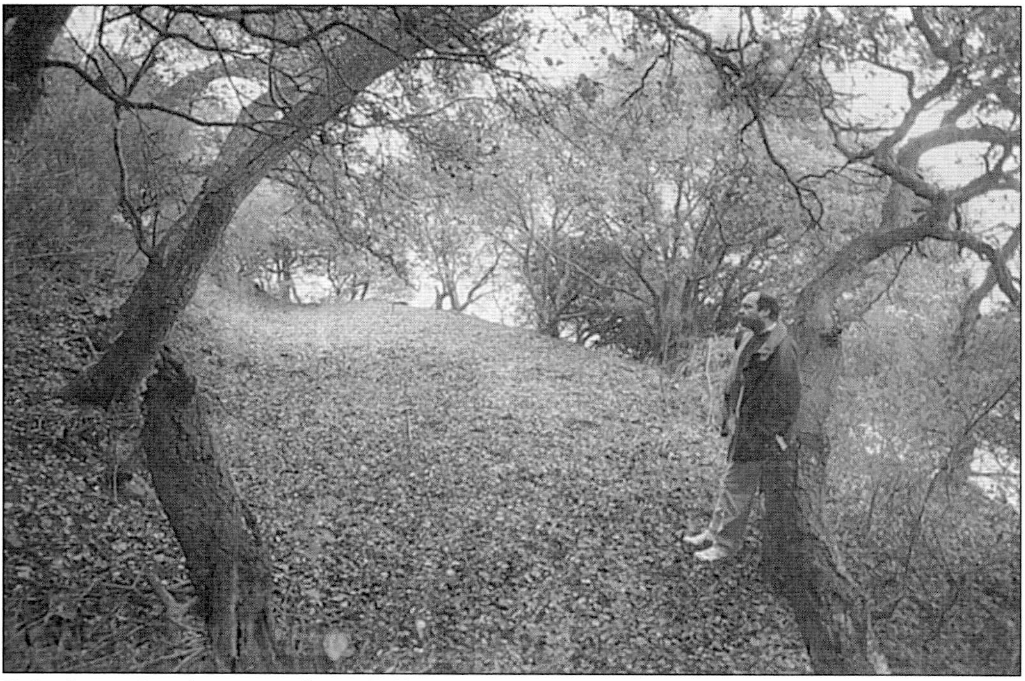

Tide Gauge Beach, near Yellow Bluff, was a spot for burials, including sailors' graves from the 1850s. This unidentified man is marking the spot. (Photograph by Martin Limek; courtesy Sausalito Historical Society.)

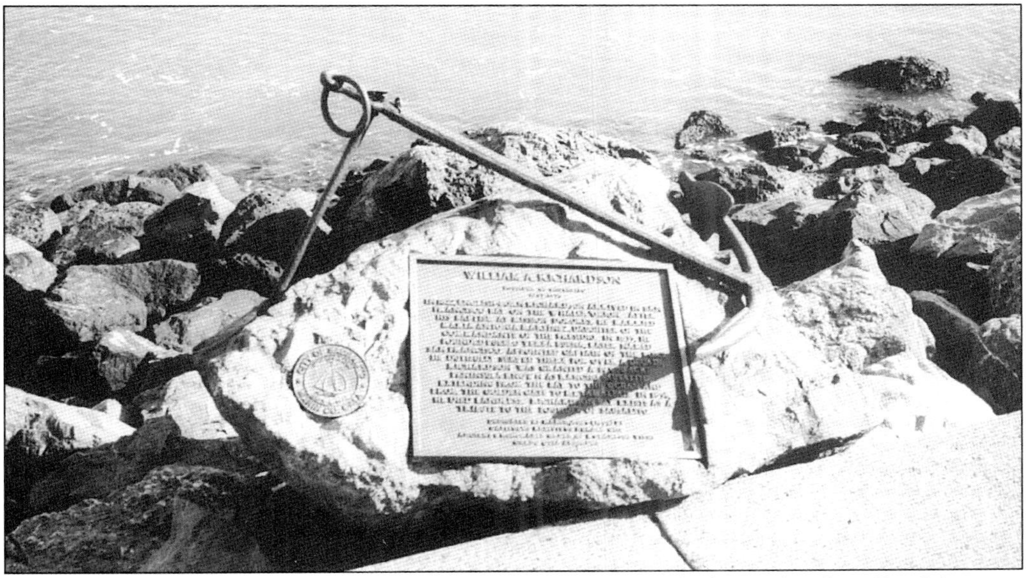

In April 1999, the organization E Clampus Vitus, together with the Richardson Bay Maritime Association, the Sausalito Historical Society, and the City of Sausalito, honored the memory of Capt. William Richardson with a plaque on the bay-side walkway of Gabrielson Park in the center of the city. Phil Frank, historical society board member, emceed a celebration with a parade. Members of the Richardson family attended, including three- and four-generation granddaughters and grandsons of the founder of Sausalito. (Photograph by Dorothy Gibson.)

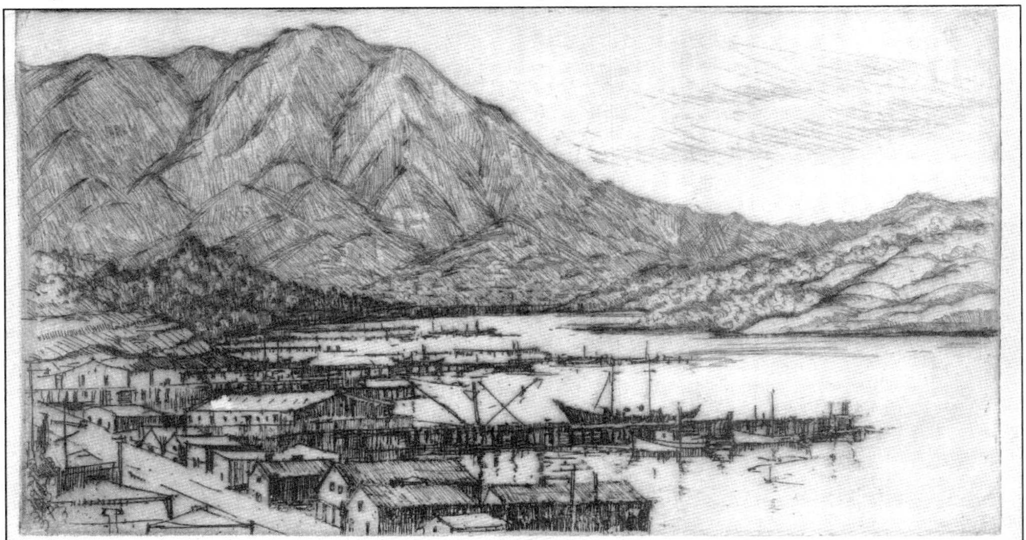

This is New Town, also known as Turney Valley, before the railroads, somewhere between 1840 and 1880. In the background is Mount Tamalpais's East Peak. The young, developing city of Mill Valley is tucked in back to the left of upper Richardson Bay. Activity is water-oriented: shipbuilding and repair and both private and commercial fishing. The new little public school and the Methodist church would soon be side by side on Hannon's Hill. The main street would be today's Caledonia Street. (Courtesy Gibson collection.)

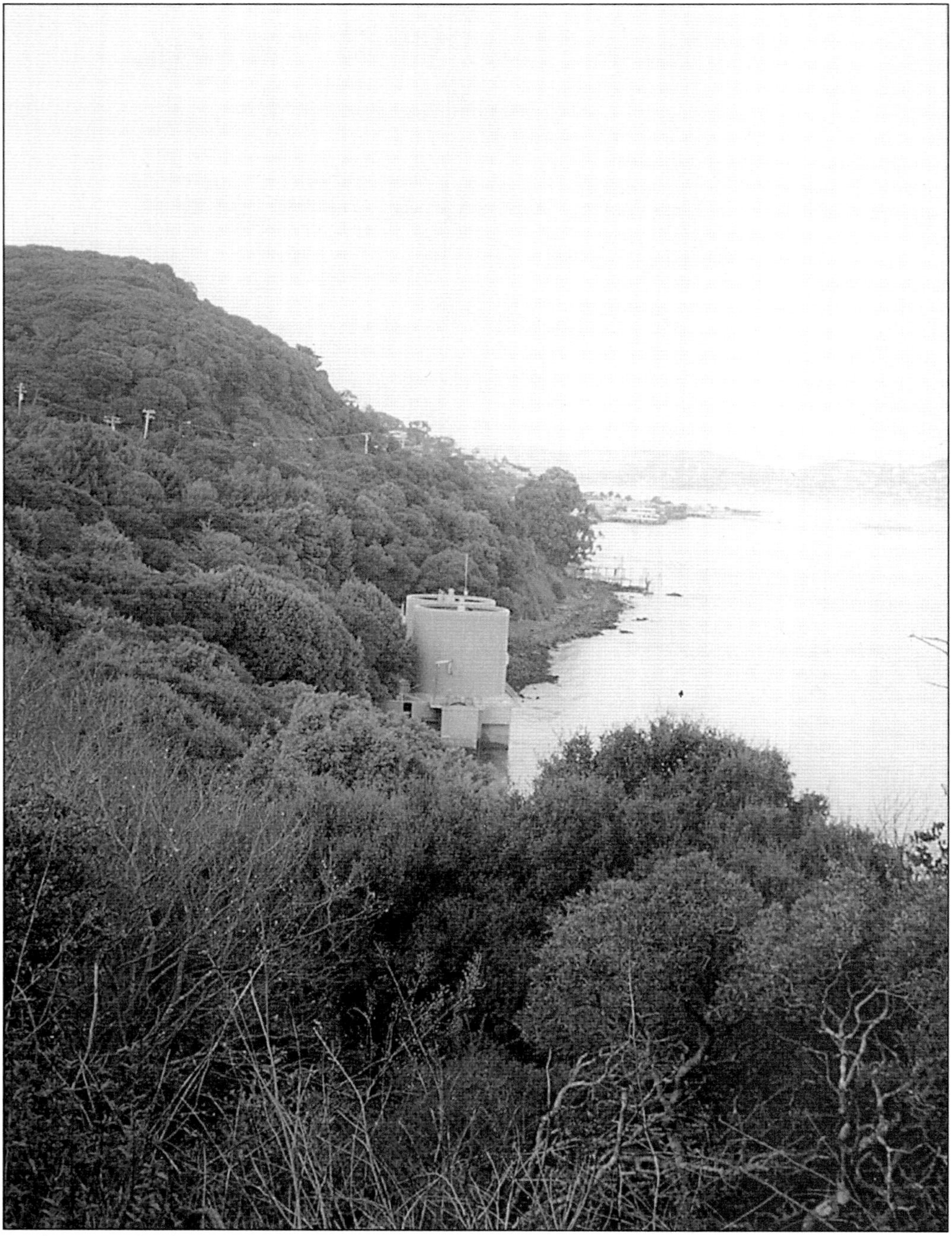

Looking north, this is the area from Yellow Bluff to Tide Gauge Beach (the little point past the sewage plant). (Photograph by Dorothy Gibson.)

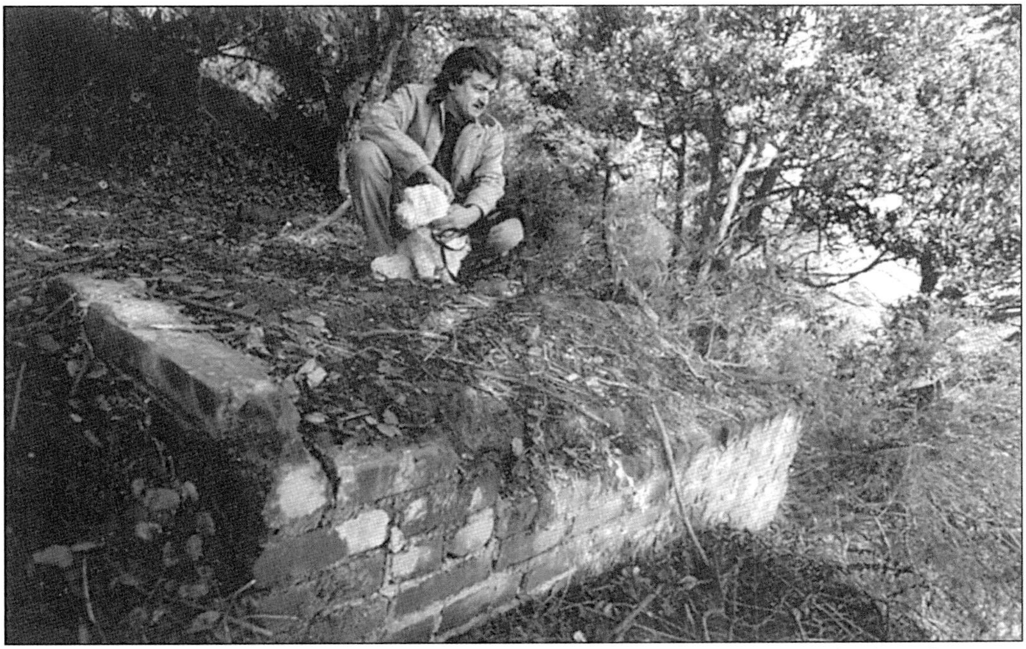

Phil Frank, then president of the Sausalito Historical Society, inspects the burial area at the Sausalito/Fort Baker boundary. Note the brick frame of a grave site. (Courtesy Sausalito Historical Society.)

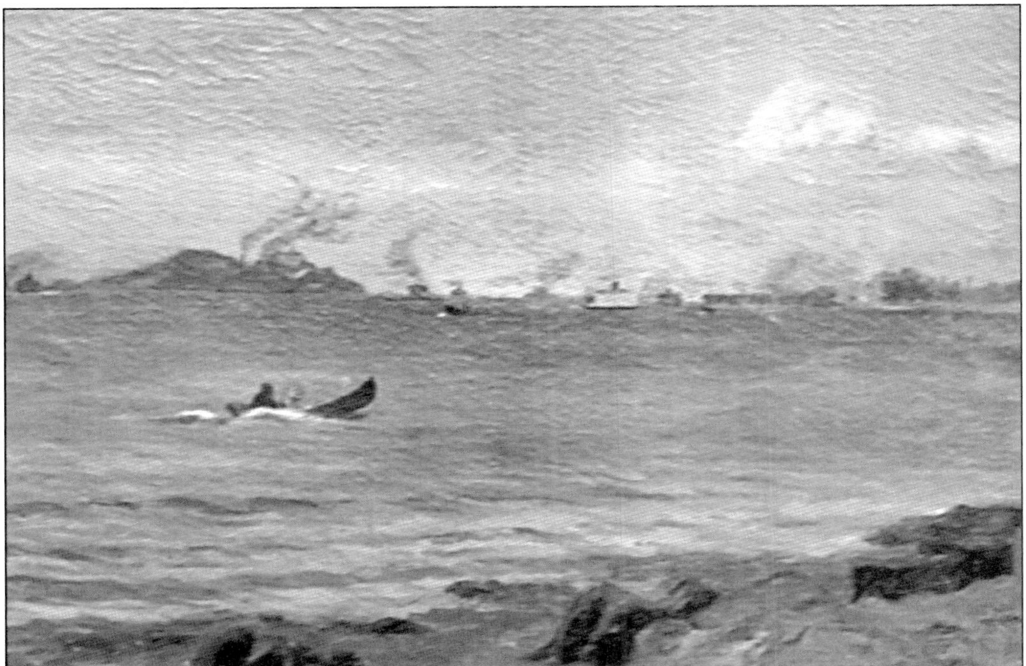

This untitled painting is probably of Tide Gauge Beach on the Sausalito/Fort Baker boundary. Smoke coming from the numerous boats and the painting style suggest the early 20th century. (Courtesy Allan and Carol Hayes.)

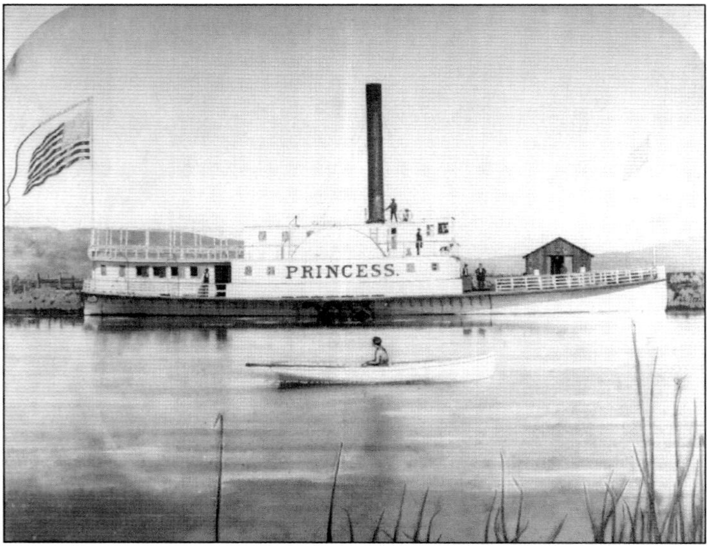

Pictured is the *Princess*, the first ferry to serve passengers from Sausalito to San Francisco from the Sausalito Point/Princess Street dock. It began on a Sunday in 1868 and ran for seven years before being replaced. The chief engineer was Thomas Wosser, whose family of eight sons and six daughters lived across Pine Street from Capt. William Richardson's family. Mabel Wosser (a daughter) tended the town's library. (Courtesy Sausalito Historical Society, 75-98.)

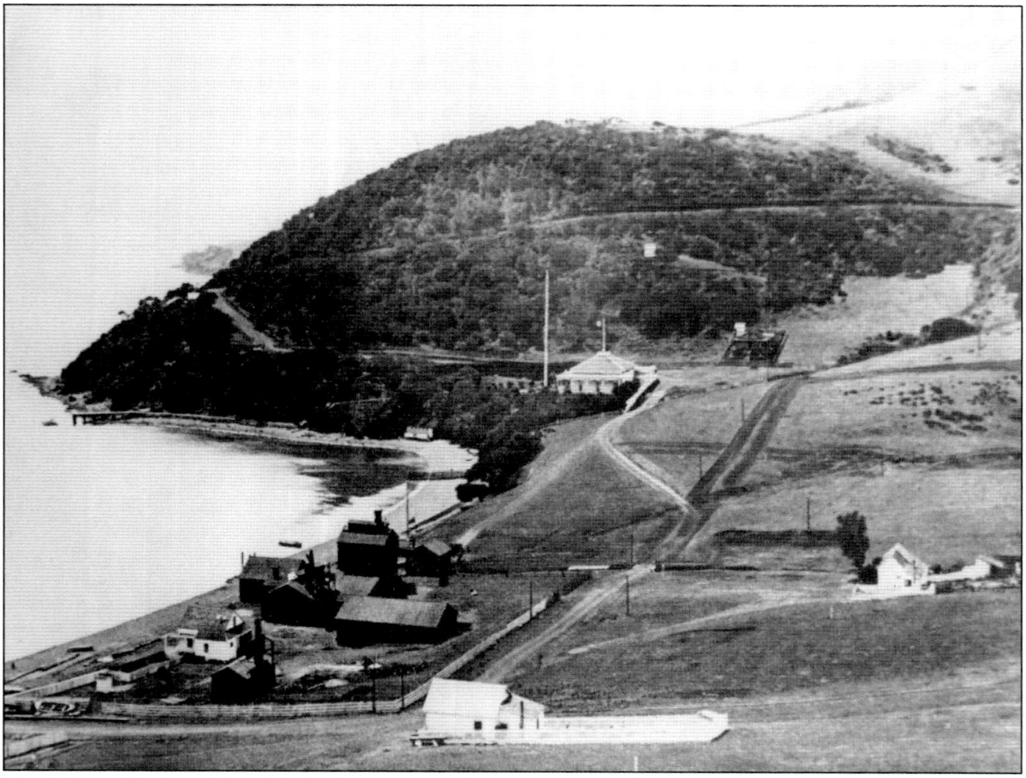

This 1882 photograph of Old Town (also known as Whaler's Cove and Hurricane Gulch) shows a vast undeveloped area. The Pacific Yacht Club's flagpole is at center with "Captain Storey's 1850 home below," as noted on the photograph. The manganese smelting plant is the lower large building, where the creek runs to the bay—the streambed will run parallel to the future Main Street. The early Emmon's Map (1851) had laid out the town like an old Spanish grid: north/south and east/west with alleys between each. (Courtesy Sausalito Historical Society, 95-135c.)

This historic house is characteristic of those built on the Hill (the hill that descends to form Sausalito Point) by the British who came in the late 1800s—two stories, a peaked roof, and a front porch with pillars. (Courtesy Sausalito Historical Society, 86-11.)

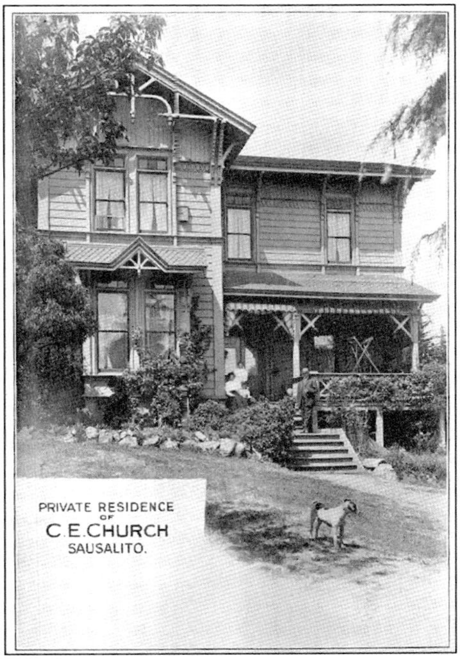

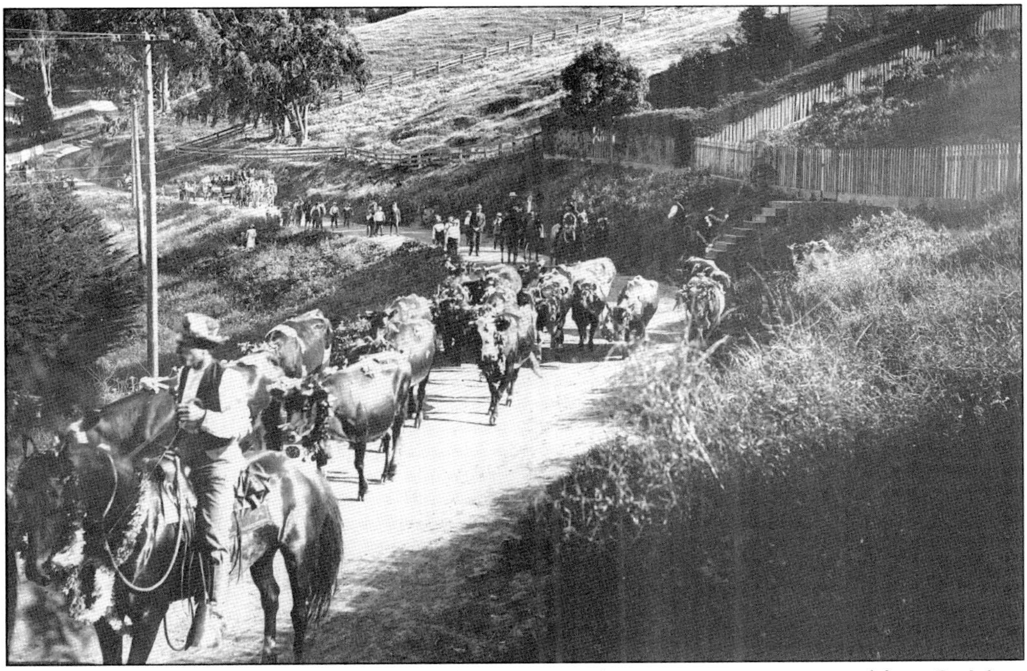

The Festival of the Holy Ghost is the annual Portuguese *chamarita* procession to and from St. Mary Star of the Sea Roman Catholic Church. It celebrates Pentecostal Sunday, the end of the two-year famine in Portugal when Queen Isabella's prayers to the Holy Ghost were answered. A mass is held, a queen is crowned with a white dove, and the priest blesses the cows. The procession then proceeds to the hall for the feast of beef, broth, bread, and wine. (Courtesy Sausalito Historical Society, 75-502a.)

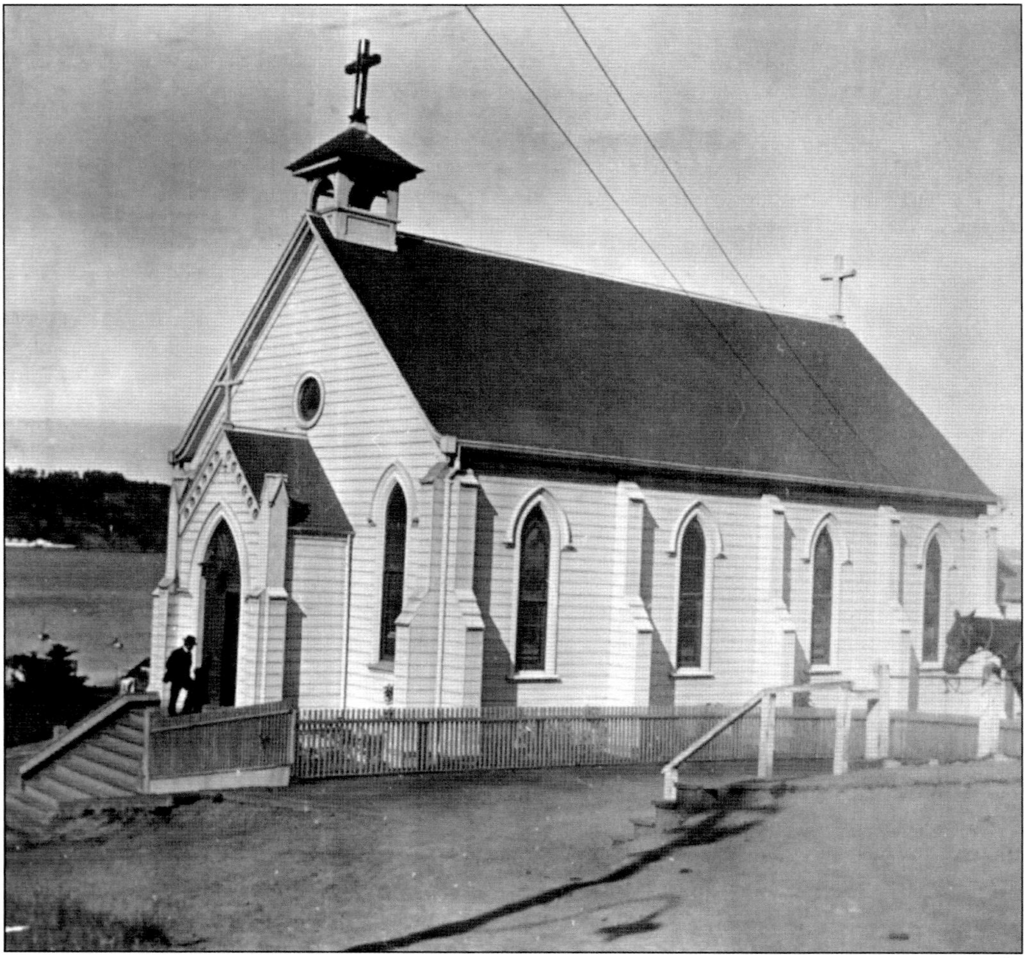

In this photograph of St. Mary Star of the Sea, the Roman Catholic church at Bonita and Litho Streets, a man enters through the open door with his horse tied in back. (Courtesy Sausalito Historical Society, 75-1392.)

Before today's highly mechanized cleaners, there were simpler machines like this two-horse-drawn street pickup sweeper on the streets of Sausalito. (Courtesy Sausalito Historical Society.)

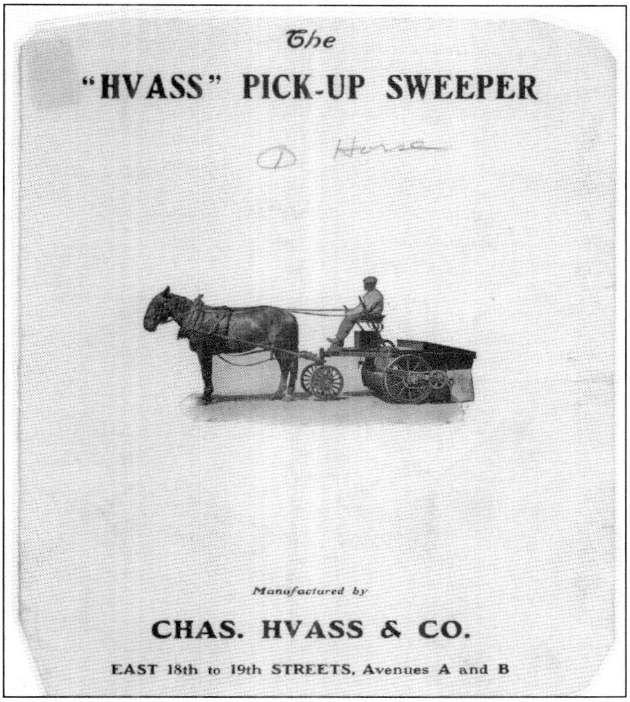

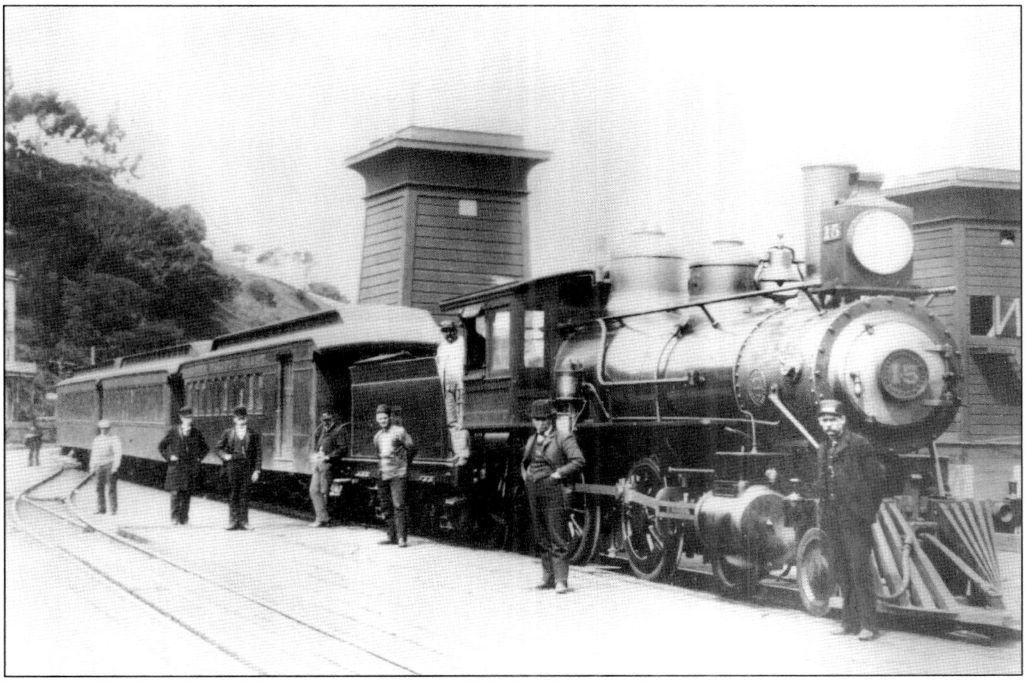

After the transcontinental railroad was completed, the connection was made to Sausalito, the terminus at the Golden Gate. Here is the North Pacific Coast passenger train with crew. Built in 1891, it is narrow-gauge railroad. This 1893 photograph is at Sausalito's terminal. (Courtesy Sausalito Historical Society, 84-113.)

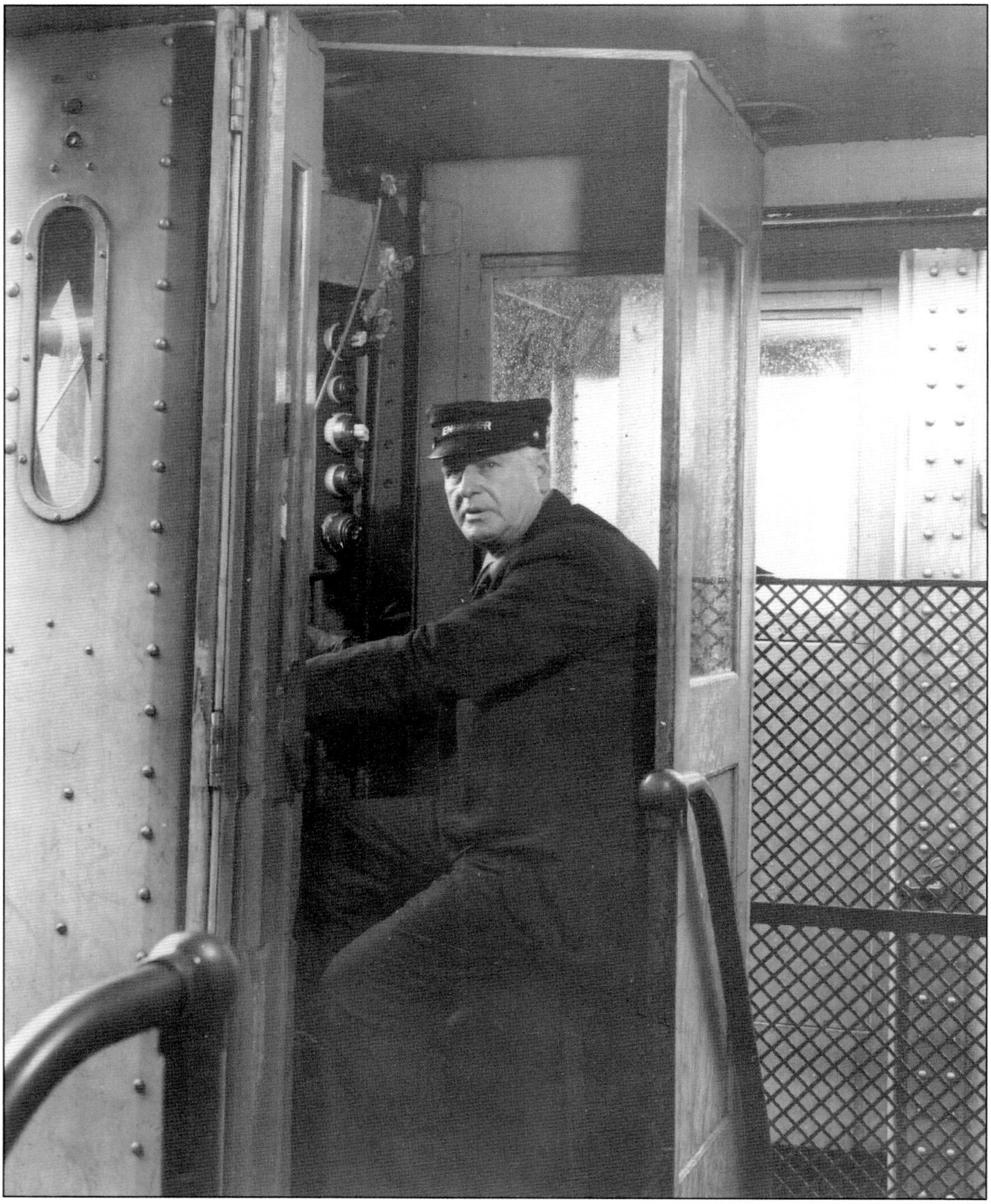

Will Ritchie hired out as a locomotive fireman on the North Pacific Coast narrow-gauge railroad in 1896 and was promoted to engineer in 1899. He continued when it became the North Shore Railroad and with its successor, the Northwestern Pacific. He was an engineer on the electric train for 38 years. He is shown in the motorman's compartment of the Mill Valley train while in the Sausalito depot. The year is 1941, and in a few weeks, the electric system will cease. Mignone Truette Connor's husband, Roy, was also an engineer. In her oral history, she tells of Roy having a special signal for her as he pulled out of the station. (Courtesy Sausalito Historical Society, 84-148; photograph from George H. Harlan Jr. Collection, Ted Wurn Estate, courtesy of Ted Wurn.)

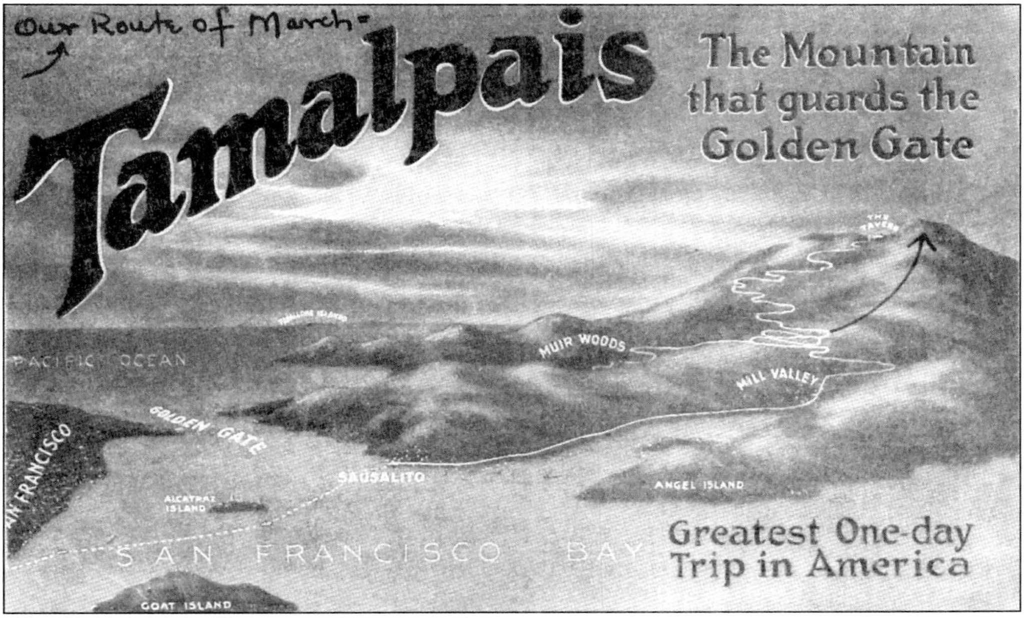

San Francisco's population grew rapidly after the Civil War, Gold Rush, and the transcontinental railroad, and this growth brought increasing numbers of people to Marin County for recreation. Trails were developed on Mount Tamalpais along with a wagon road to the top in 1884. This postcard, the front and back seen above and at right, promotes the Mount Tamalpais Scenic Railway, built in 1896. It carried people to the top of East Peak, where there was a summit tavern (hotel and restaurant). It took 281 curves and one double bowknot loop to get to the top. Some of the cars were open, some closed. There was a spur to the Muir Woods Redwood Canyon. When the automobile became affordable, it replaced the scenic railroad. The electric train connection from Sausalito to Mill Valley met the train to go up "Mt. Tam." It was very popular to take photographs and to stop at various levels for refreshment. Souvenirs like this card were mailed all over the world. (Courtesy California Historical Society.)

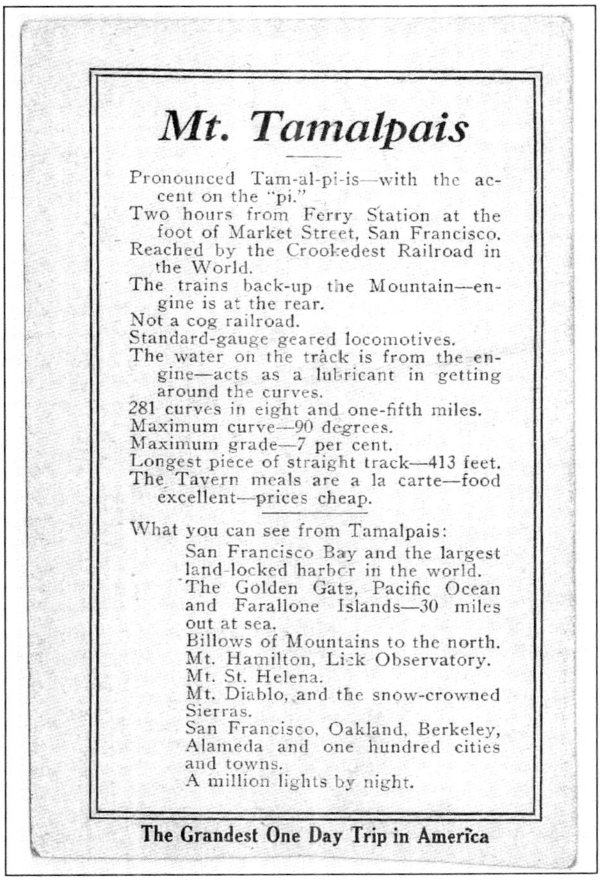

Mt. Tamalpais

Pronounced Tam-al-pi-is—with the accent on the "pi."
Two hours from Ferry Station at the foot of Market Street, San Francisco.
Reached by the Crookedest Railroad in the World.
The trains back-up the Mountain—engine is at the rear.
Not a cog railroad.
Standard-gauge geared locomotives.
The water on the track is from the engine—acts as a lubricant in getting around the curves.
281 curves in eight and one-fifth miles.
Maximum curve—90 degrees.
Maximum grade—7 per cent.
Longest piece of straight track—413 feet.
The Tavern meals are a la carte—food excellent—prices cheap.

What you can see from Tamalpais:
San Francisco Bay and the largest land-locked harbor in the world.
The Golden Gate, Pacific Ocean and Farallone Islands—30 miles out at sea.
Billows of Mountains to the north.
Mt. Hamilton, Lick Observatory.
Mt. St. Helena.
Mt. Diablo, and the snow-crowned Sierras.
San Francisco, Oakland, Berkeley, Alameda and one hundred cities and towns.
A million lights by night.

The Grandest One Day Trip in America

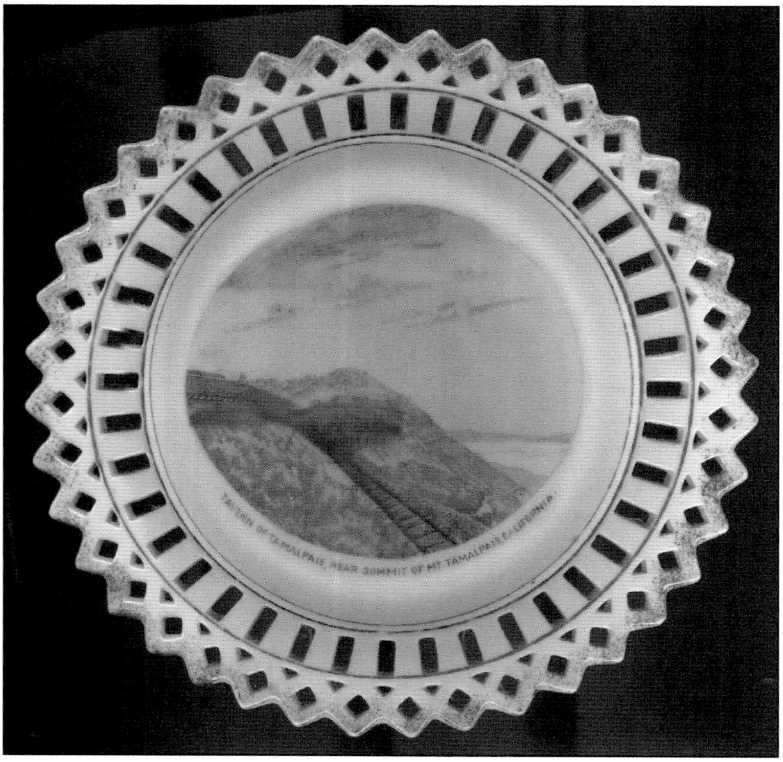

This 19th-century souvenir plate depicts the Tavern of Tamalpais near the summit of Mount Tamalpais. (Courtesy Allan and Carol Hayes.)

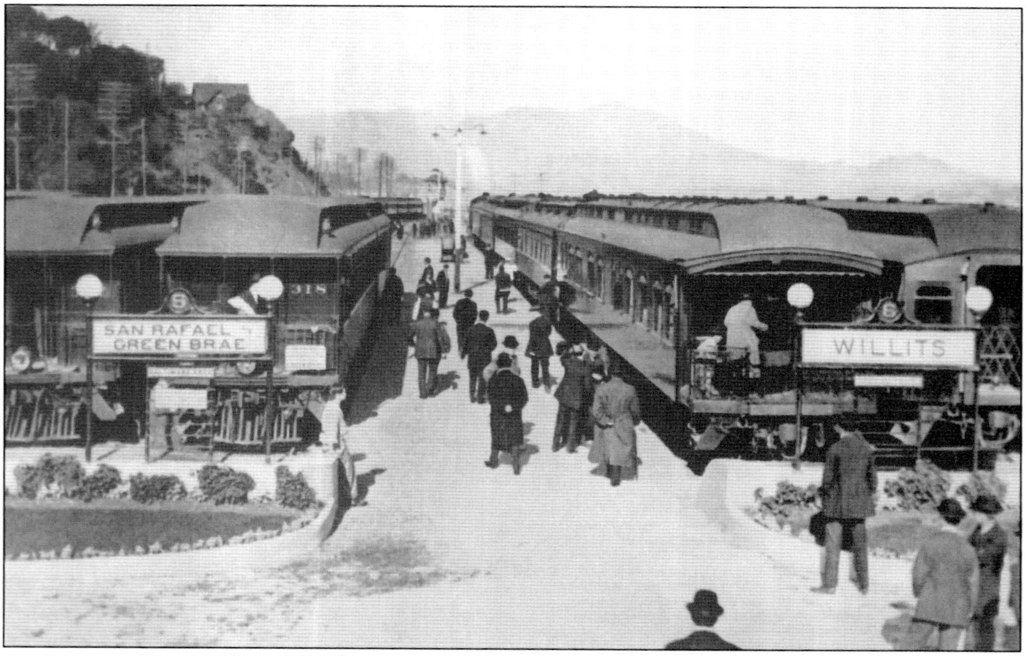

At the train depot in Sausalito, destinations such as San Rafael/Greenbrae or Willits are displayed at the head of each line. Mount Tamalpais is prominent in the background. This photograph is from October 1914. (Courtesy Sausalito Historical Society, 2005-10.)

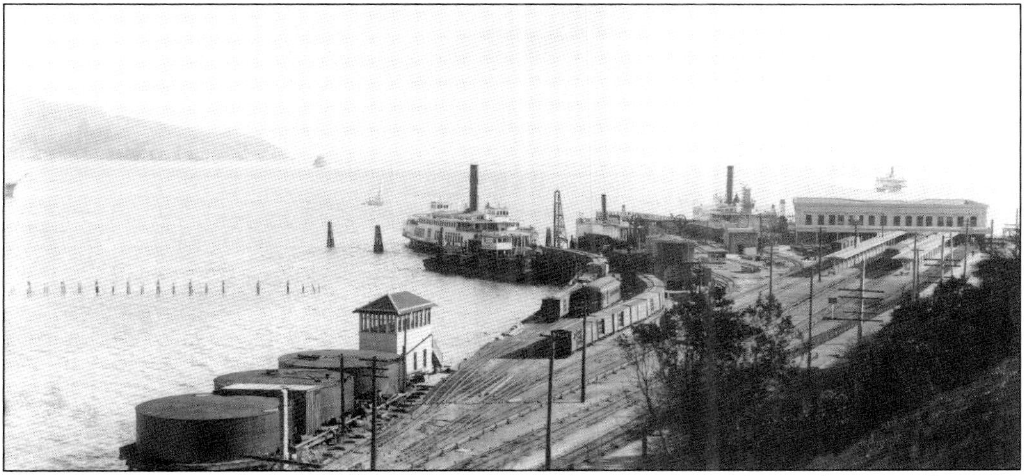

The train and ferry terminal on Princess Street in downtown Sausalito is shown in this 1903 photograph. The triangular area in front of the long building would be the future park, the land being given to the city by the Northwestern Pacific specifically for this purpose. (Courtesy Sausalito Historical Society 78-196.)

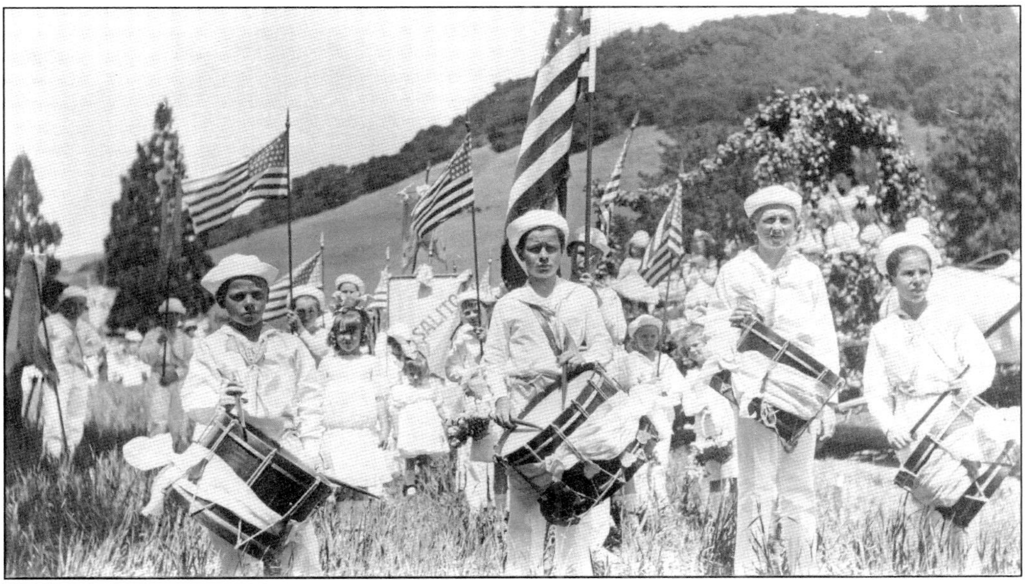

The flag bearers and drummers in this Maypole dance on May 1, 1914, are readying for a trip to San Francisco and the Panama-Pacific International Exposition, which celebrated the opening of the Panama Canal. (Courtesy Sausalito Historical Society, 76-561.)

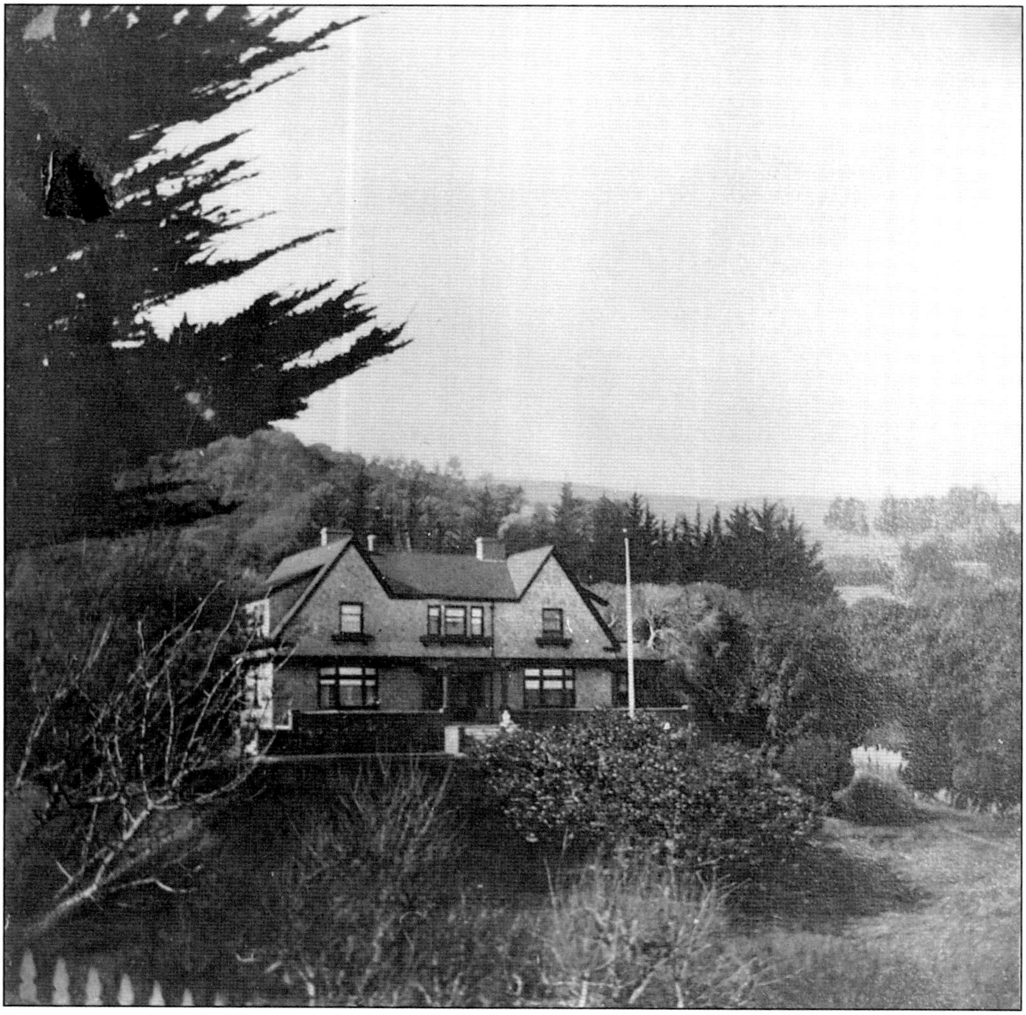

In 1849, Obadiah Livermore, who came to be known as "Colonel," came to San Francisco. Born in western New York, he had gone to New Orleans, then to Mexico, and back to New Orleans again. Seeking his fortune in the West, he became associated with a real estate firm and later developed his own business selling many estates and properties. Between 1878 and 1886, he purchased three adjoining properties north of Sausalito proper. He called it Gilead, recalling the mountain between the Dead Sea and the Sea of Galilee. Meaning "heap of witness," the name recalls the covenant between Labah and Joseph, when they heaped stones as a sign. Gilead is 3,596 feet high, Tamalpais in 2,604.

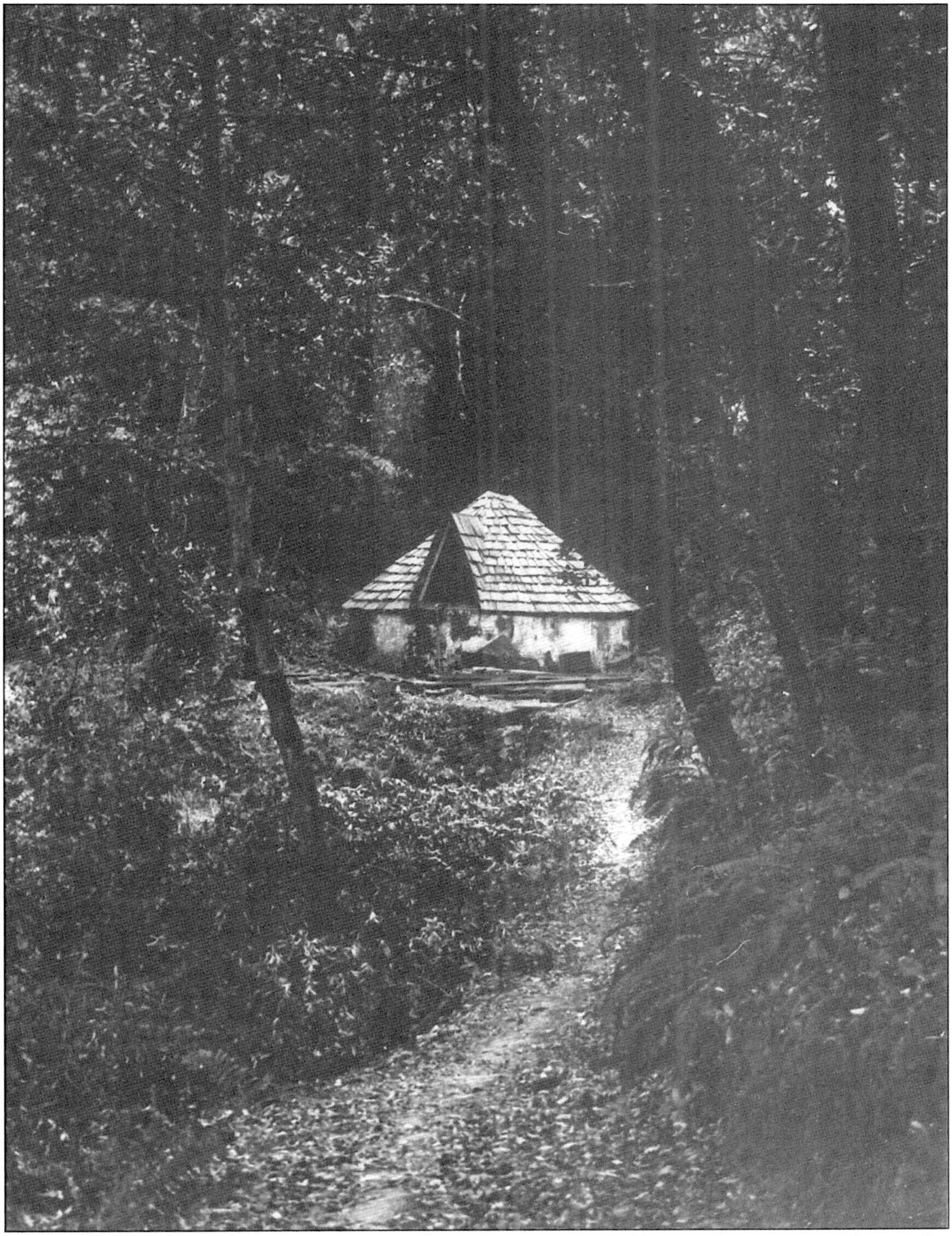

The house at Gilead was built on an old Native American shell mound on 30 acres facing the bay. A large spring was in the back. There were also stables, a barn, and outbuildings. A world traveler, Obadiah Livermore planted exotic fruits, vegetables, trees, and statuary around the estate. It caught fire at the time of the 1906 San Francisco earthquake. In 1907, following Livermore's death, Charles Walter Burgess purchased the property. It remained in the family until the 1990s. Currently it is a private school. (Courtesy Sausalito Historical Society, 77-365a and 77-365b.)

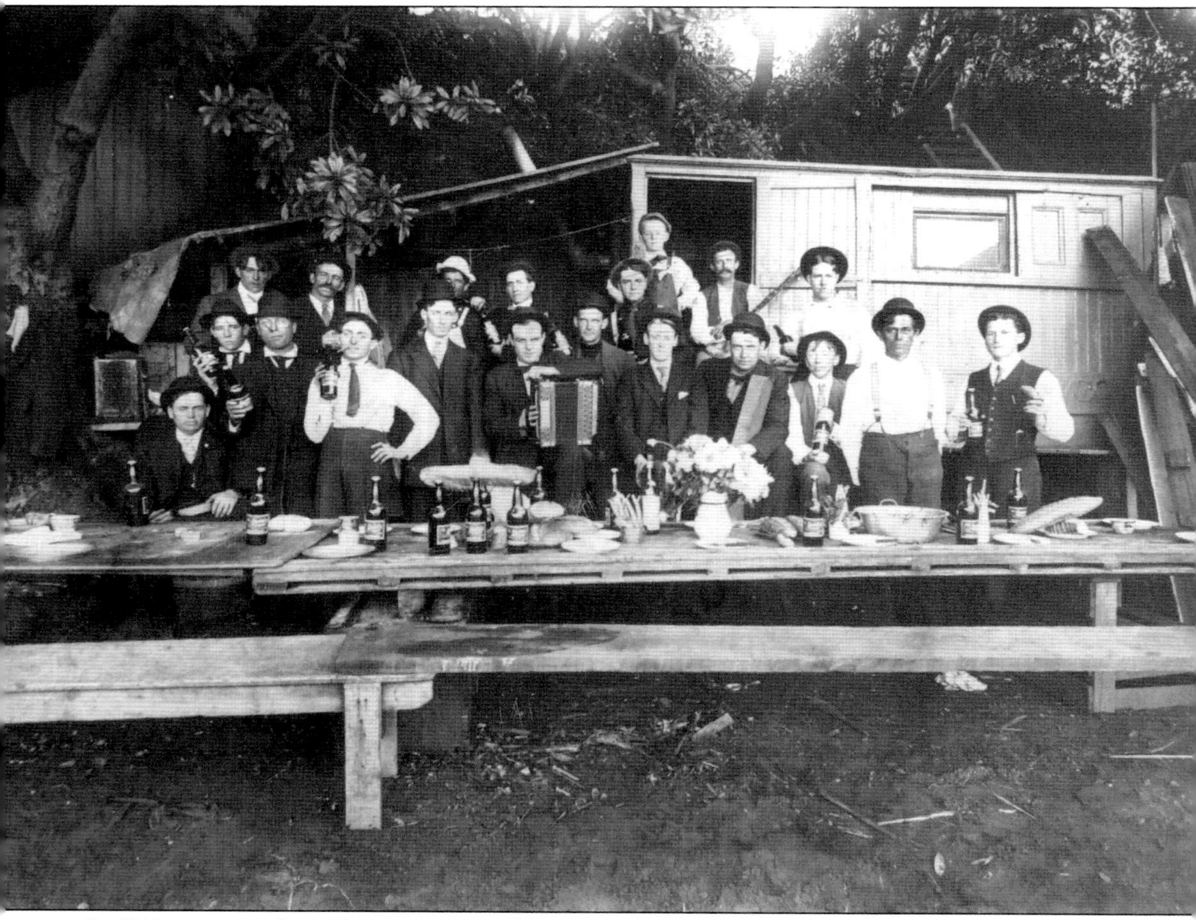

In 1910, a group of men have a party with an accordion in Wildwood Glen at the center of New Town. Tucked back into the valley, this was the broadest and the deepest of the gulches coming off Wolfback Ridge. Along the ridge is Alta Road, which descends to Waldo Point, meeting the county road to Mill Valley. William Richardson was first buried in Wildwood Glen. (Courtesy Sausalito Historical Society, 85-11.)

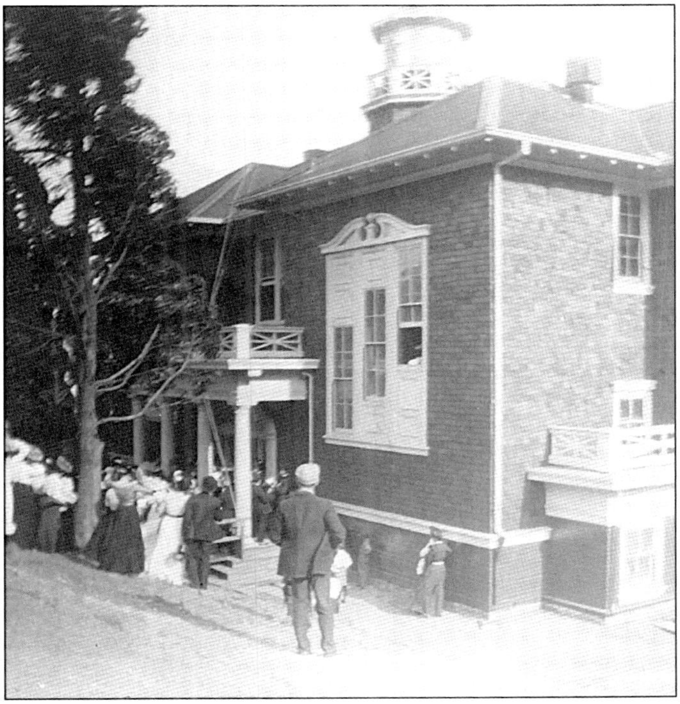

South View School was built in 1905; the school did indeed have a sweeping view of the San Francisco Bay. Old-timers in oral histories recall with glee how after school they would slide down the hill on boards and race to the beach—not the commercial one but to the one with the path between the Spreckels's two-story Victorian and General Dickinson's house at Alexander and South Streets. A formation called Square Rocks was used as a tidal gauge by fishing boats. (Courtesy Sausalito Historical Society, 75-970.)

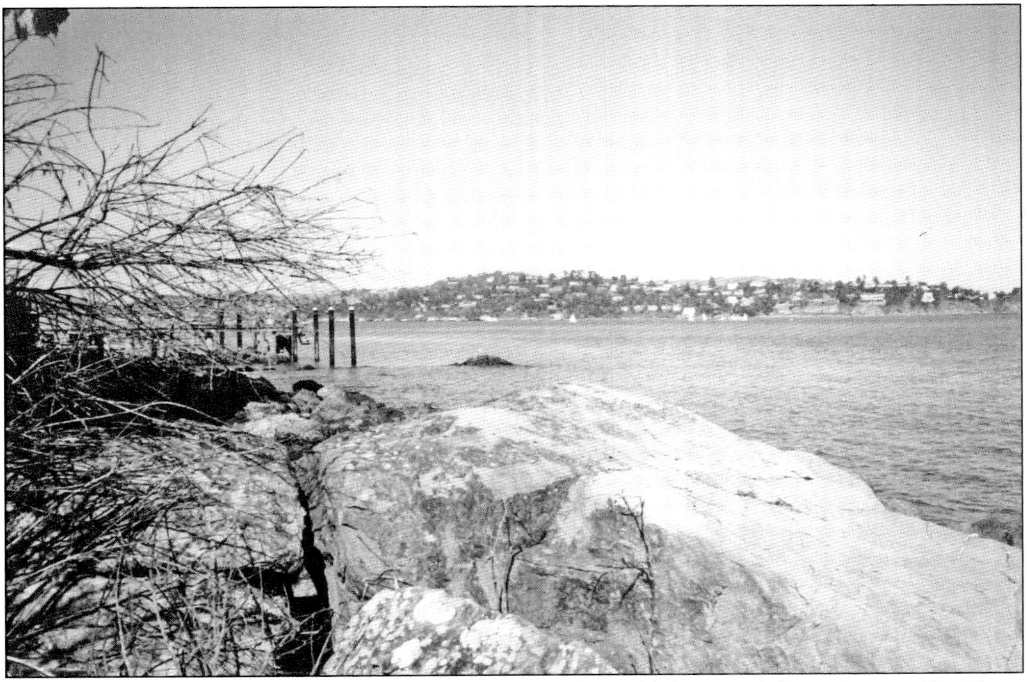

Here is the same area today—the old pilings are rotting but still there, and the rock is visible. There is still a way down to the shore, but it now starts in a driveway to two properties. The tidal-gauge rock can be lined up with one at Alexander Street and one on top of the ridge called "Appetite Hill," the Sausalito/military reservation boundary. (Photograph by Dorothy Gibson.)

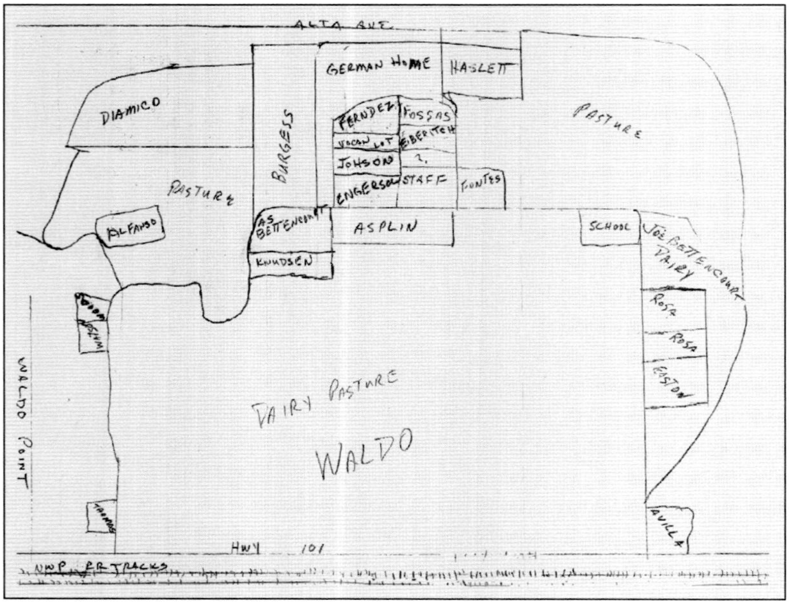

This is Waldo at Waldo Point in the north end of Richardson Bay. Waldo station is by the railroad tracks, and Waldo Grade is the slope that descends from Alta Road (at the top, behind Burgess). The time of property ownership shown on the map would be after 1907 because of the railroad line. (Map drawn by and courtesy of Konrad Knutson.)

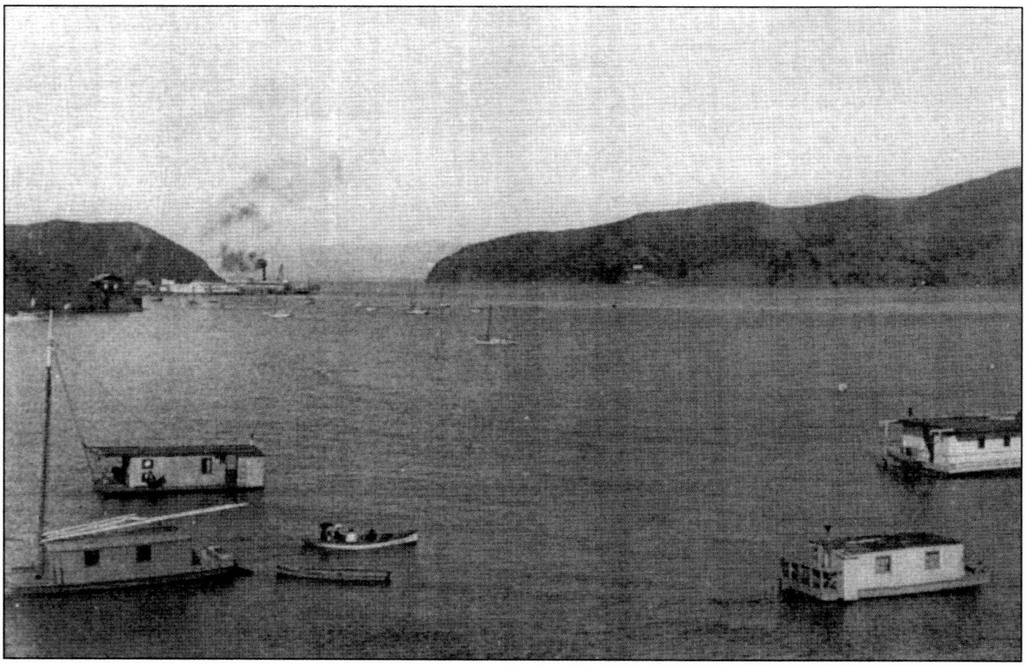

This 1898 photograph was taken from Belvedere looking through Raccoon Strait (the strait between Angel Island and Belvedere). Two ferry steamers are shown: the *James M. Donahue* to the left and *Tiburon* at the right. Note the four houseboats at front. They were very practical for living and working in the area. Their popularity would grow. (Courtesy San Francisco Maritime Museum; John W. Proctor Collection, from *San Francisco Bay* by John Haskell Kemble.)

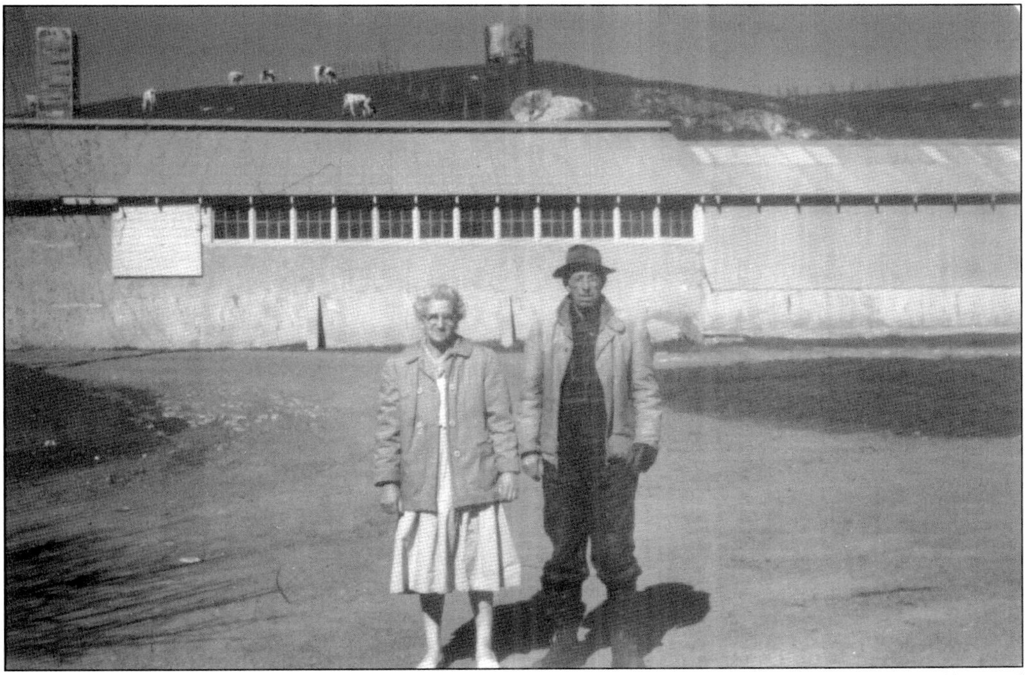

These photographs are of the Silva Dairy Ranch, which was beyond Waldo, southwest on Elk Road where it bends down into the valley. Note the cows on the hill—black and white Holsteins—and the water tank on top of Alta Road in the photograph above. Frank J. Silva married Mary Cordoza. The time of ownership was known to be between 1906 and 1960. It is presumed that this is Frank and Mary in front of the barn. (Both, courtesy GGNRA Archives, 17928-002/003.)

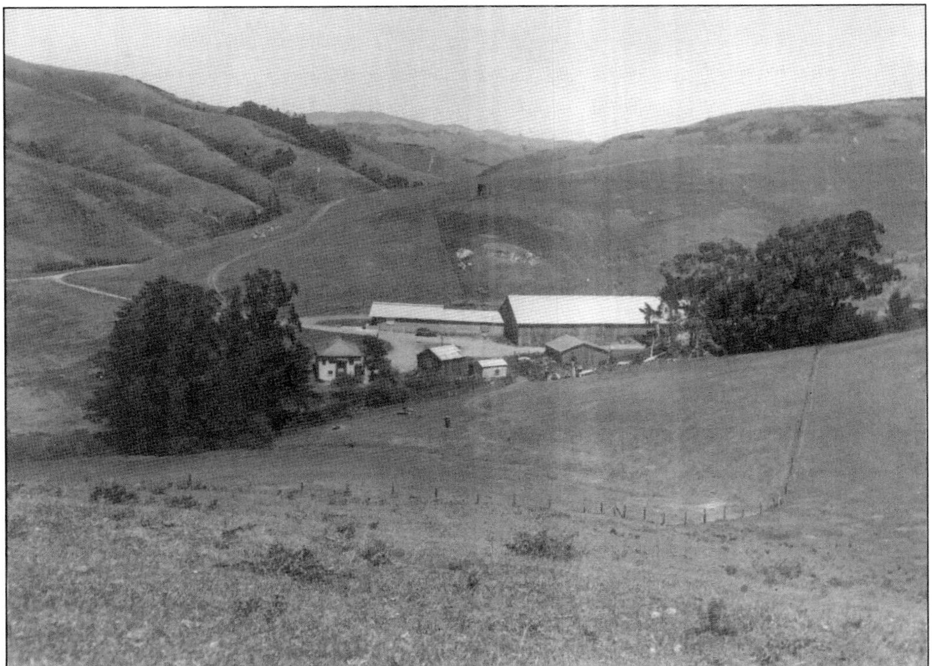

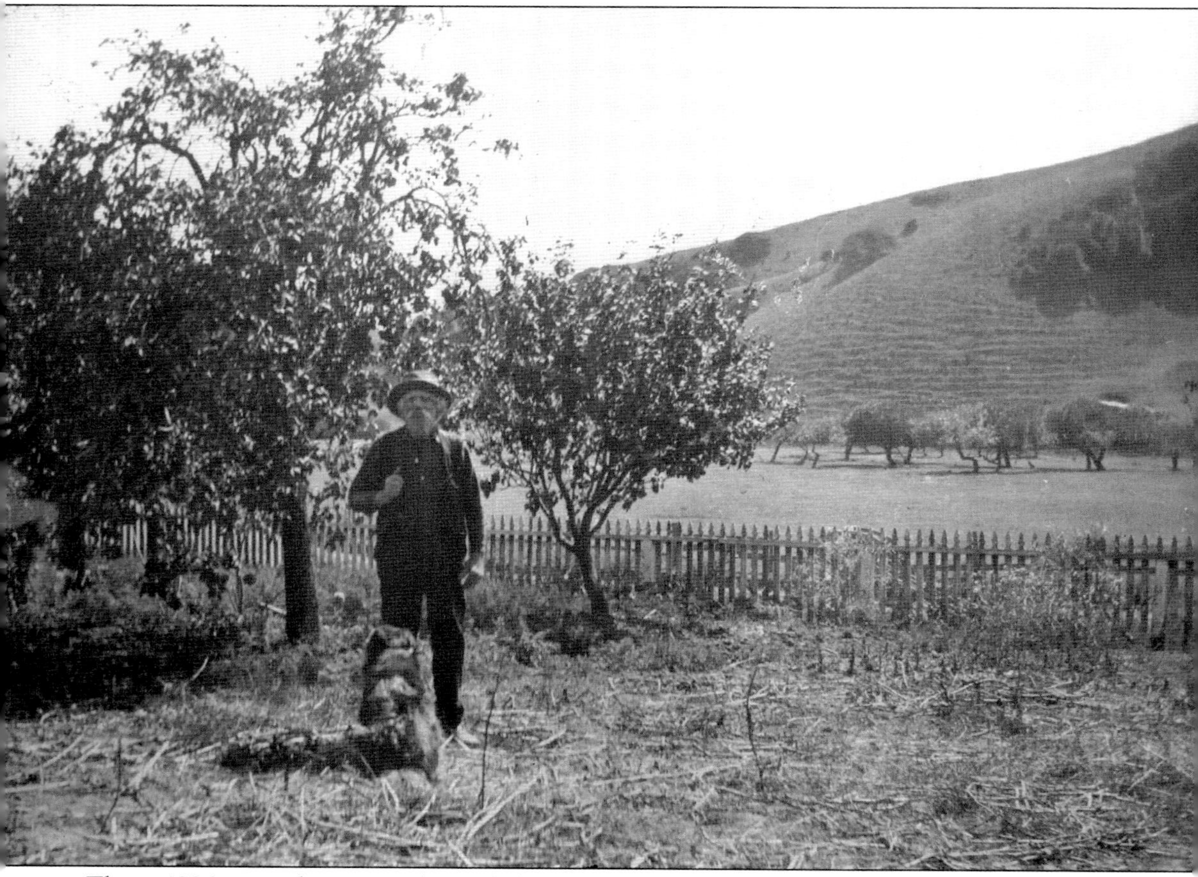

This *c.* 1906 image shows a gentleman believed to be Frank Silva in his orchard at the Silva Dairy Ranch in Tennessee Valley. (Courtesy GGNRA Archives, 19031-004.)

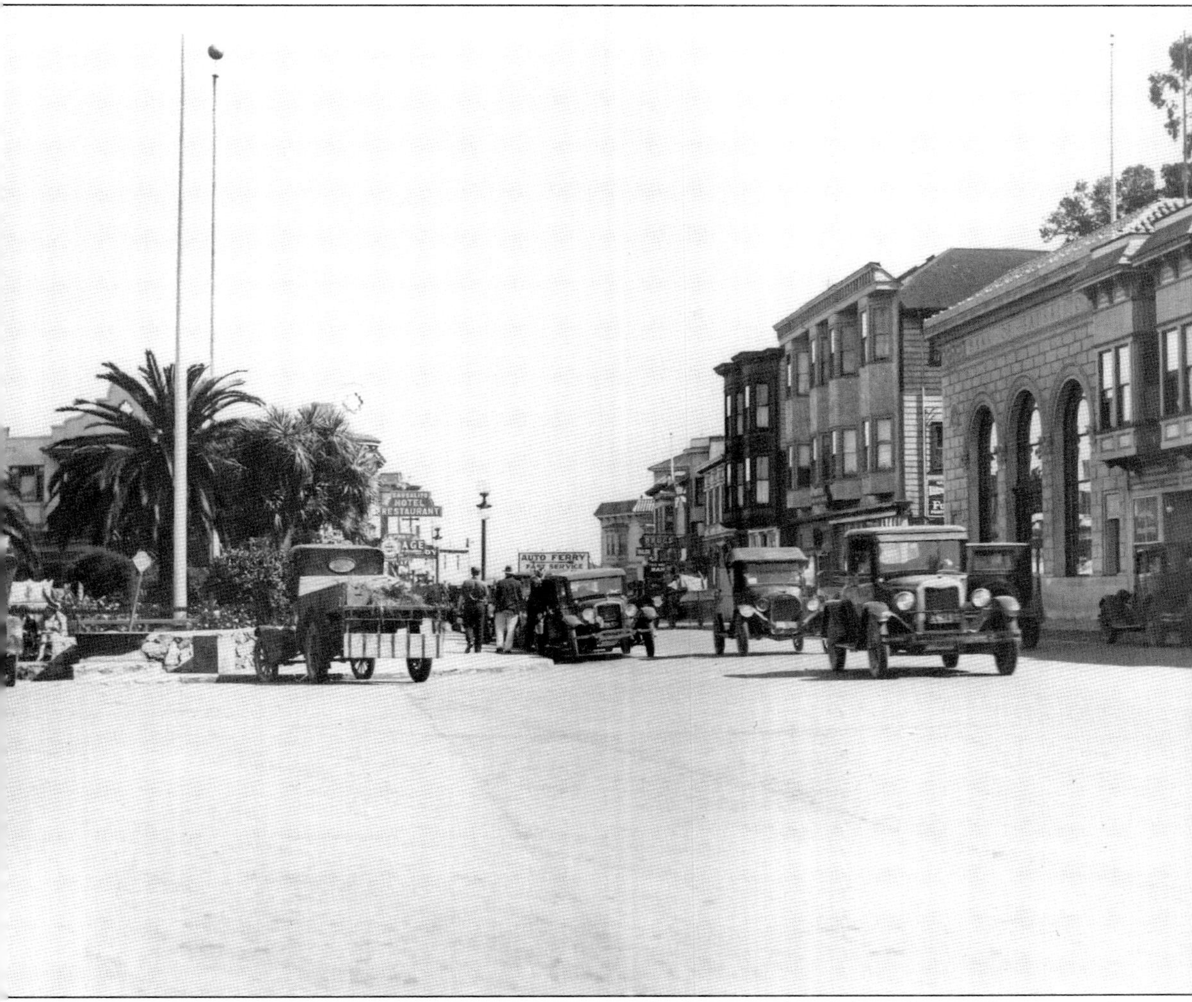

It is 1930 in Sausalito, and the automobile has arrived. The central park has a large palm tree, and there are two very tall flagpoles. Electric lighting came to the town in 1920. (Courtesy Sausalito Historical Society, 84.159.)

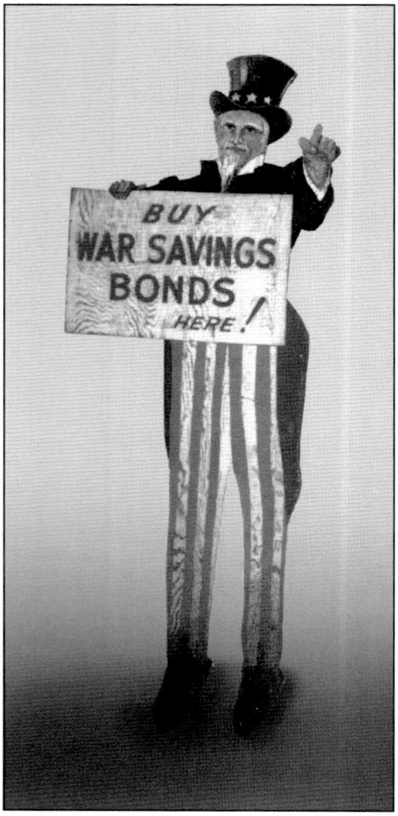

World War II comes to Sausalito, as seen in this familiar poster of Uncle Sam soliciting war bonds. This tall rendition is part of a World War II exhibit at the U.S. Army Corps of Engineers Bay Model prepared by the Sausalito Historical Society. (Photograph by Dorothy Gibson.)

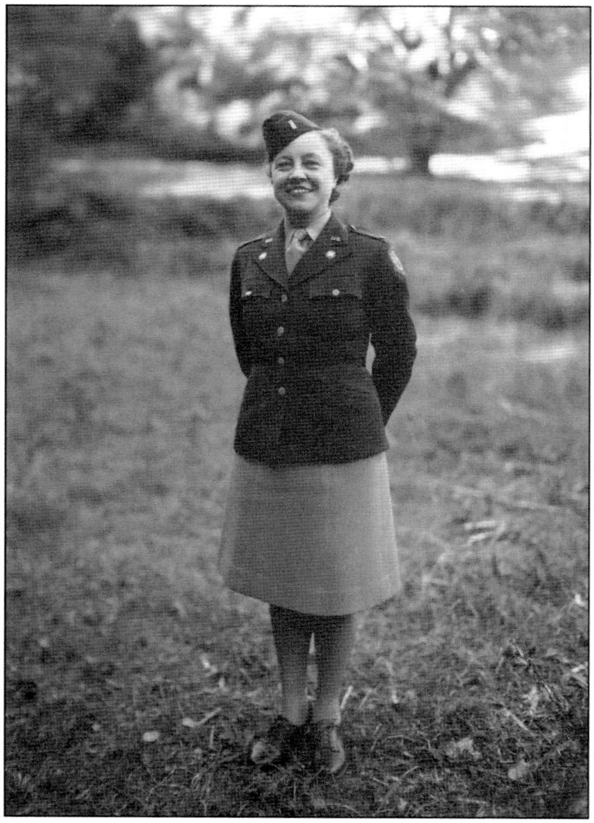

Longtime Sausalito resident Vera Clouette writes of this photograph, "This is a picture of me in my WAC uniform during World War II. I was stationed at Hampton Roads, Virginia and was sent to Fort Mason in San Francisco to be in charge of the selling of War Bonds. I was the officer in charge of the Port of Embarcation. I had no real plans to stay in San Francisco. I was heading back to Virginia, but this naval architect, George Harlan, who was supposed to report to me if he had made any War Bond sales, was reporting every morning even though he hadn't sold any bonds. Well, we married and came to Sausalito where his family had been for three generations." (Courtesy Sausalito Historical Society, 81-80.)

Workers are building a Liberty ship at Marinship during World War II. Within three months after December 7, 1941—the bombing of Pearl Harbor and the declaration of war by the United States—the chairman of the U.S. Maritime Commission sent a letter to W. A. Bechtel, an affiliate of the Six Companies, Inc., requesting a proposal for a shipyard at one of the West Coast ports. Sausalito was chosen. The contract was signed in three days. Within two more weeks, the property was condemned and all Marin residents informed. By March 28, heavy equipment had moved in. Pine Point, with its 40 houses and small commercial enterprises, was leveled to fill in the bay-side marshes. (Courtesy Sausalito Historical Society, 77-230a.)

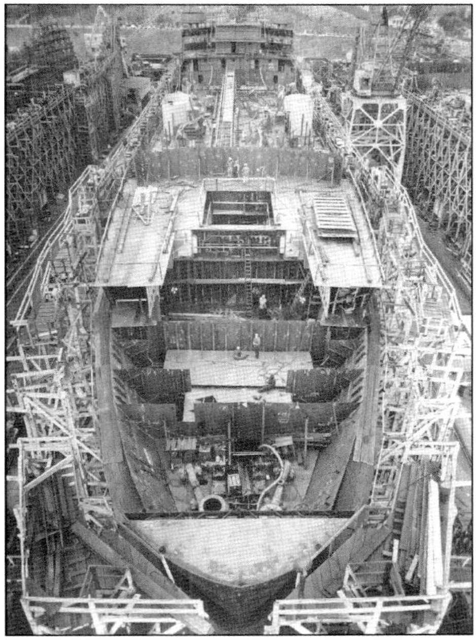

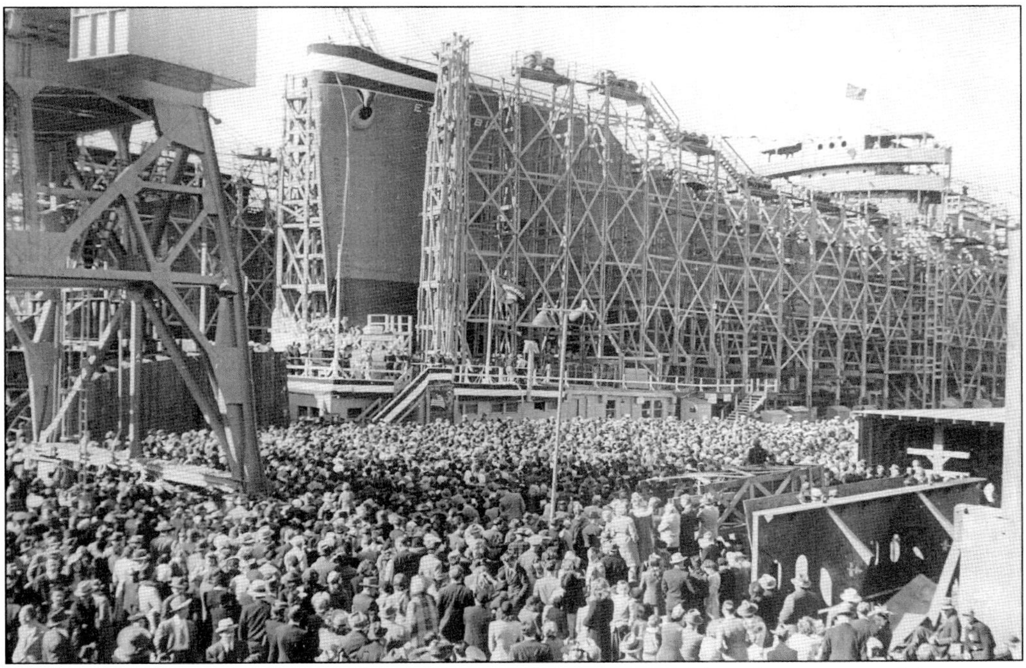

Pictured here is the celebration at the christening of a Liberty ship. Note the presence of dignitaries. The Marinship, as the area came to be affectionately called, was a city within a city. The first year, 20,000 workers, both men and women, were recruited from every state in the Union. Many came from the Southeast. They were provided with everything needed: housing, meals, uniforms and equipment, medical care, and a good wage. Marinship welcomed all nationalities willing and able to learn the skills and to work around the clock. (Courtesy Sausalito Historical Society, 2006.4.)

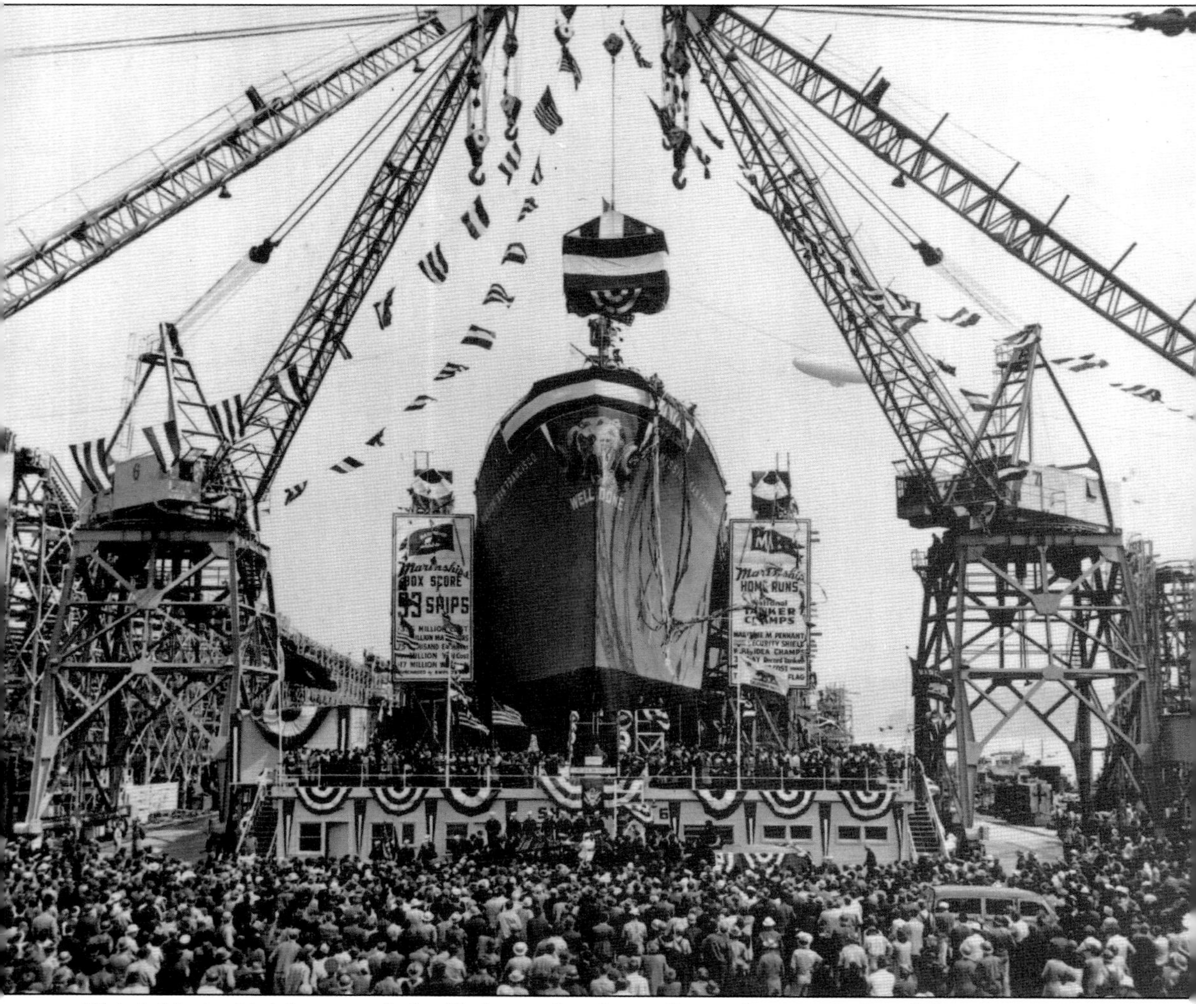

This is Marinship's last vessel, the 93rd, a tanker. It was September 18, 1945, and the war was over. After the autumn of 1952, the company switched to making only oil tankers to meet the need for fuel. The workforce grew to 75,000, and a new tanker was being launched every 10 days. In three and a half years, 15 Liberty Ships, 16 fleet oilers, 62 tankers, and 20 army invasion barges had been built, three British coasters were outfitted, and 20 vessels repaired. (Courtesy Sausalito Historical Society, 2005.35)

Seven

Marin City and Tennessee Valley

Fred Perry (1904–1996), an old-timer, when interviewed for an oral history in the 1980s, said, "On Sundays, we'd go to grandma's and grandpa's. There was Old Town, New Town and Out There." "Out There" was Waldo. Waldo Point (named for Whig Party Oregon gubernatorial candidate William Waldo) was where the northern terminus of Wolfback Ridge, the ridge behind Sausalito, descended into marshland at Richardson Bay. Here Sausalito's Water Street met the County Road, passing Fernwood Cemetery and the Elk Valley Creek and road as it went on to Mill Valley. A small community called Waldo developed facing a pasture. It included the original 1880 Livermore-Burgess estate on an old Native American midden, smaller homes and pastures, a dairy, and a school. In the days of the railroad, there was a Waldo station stop opposite Waldo Point. The building of the Golden Gate Bridge in 1937 included a highway—the Redwood Highway—with a tunnel through Wolfback Ridge. It came to be called Waldo Tunnel. Automobiles coming out of the tunnel descended the Waldo Grade. World War II changed the entire area. The U.S. government found Sausalito to be a prime area for a shipbuilding yard, from Napa Street to Waldo, and it was called "Marinship." The Federal Housing Authority, representing the Maritime Commission, requested use of the land at Waldo for temporary housing. Twenty-five acres of the Burgess estate and the surrounding area ended up as housing for workers who had been recruited from all over the country. Complete with services, the area was called "Marin City." After the war, Marinship lay fallow, but many people decided to stay. Over time, Marinship was rezoned for waterfront industrial and commercial use by Sausalito. At Gate Five Road, a houseboat community blossomed as houseboats became a popular lifestyle. The original housing, meant to be temporary, was replaced with permanent structures, and two separate additions have been made, one descending down from the water tower on the north side and the other in the lowland adjacent to community services and town center. As for Elk Valley, later renamed Tennessee Valley after the famous shipwreck there, it continued much the same—cattle grazing is gone, but the Miwok Riding Stables are still there. Some houses have been built on the bend—the entrance to the valley. Fernwood Cemetery has become fuller, reflecting the nationalities of the area: Portuguese, Italian, German, and French. And recently, the federal government has acquired some of the land, adding to its territory for the headlands of the Golden Gate National Recreation Area.

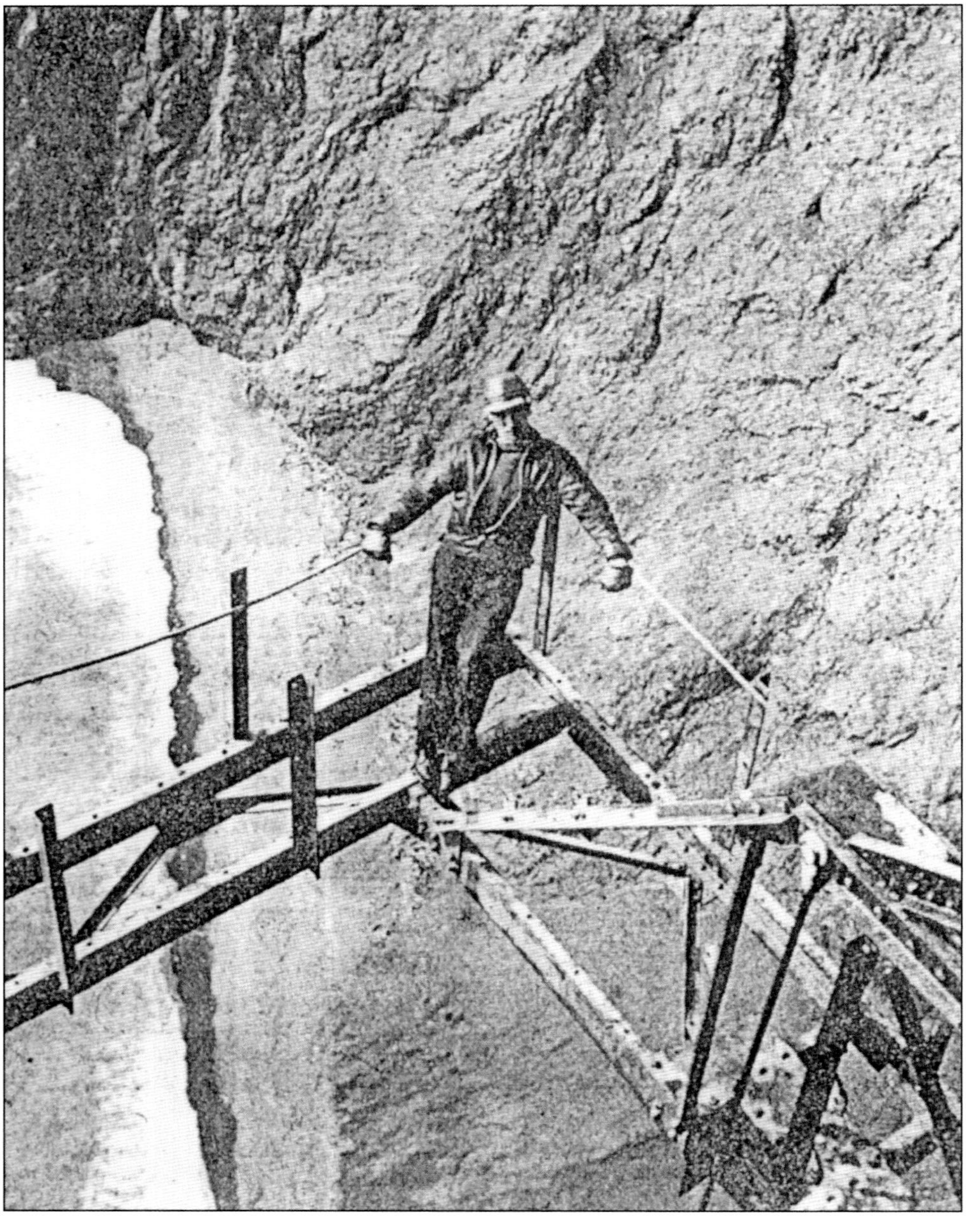

Ed Ashoff says of this photograph, "That's me in 1936, 20 years old, standing on a scaffold on the north tower of the Golden Gate Bridge. This scaffold was about 20 below the top of the tower, so I'm about 730 feet above the beach at Lime Point. No, I didn't have much of a problem with heights although for some reason I wasn't as nervous about working on the south tower. We had a little platform on top of the tower. That's where we'd have lunch and take our breaks. You were on the tower from 'bell to bell'—when your shift began to where it ended. It blew hard up there. We were spinning the cables for the deck suspension between the towers. The wind would often screw up the equipment. I was an assistant to the riggers, doing whatever I was told. We were "punks"—that was our job description. $7.32 a day and glad to have it." (Courtesy Sausalito Historical Society; Ed Ashoff, 1996 oral history.)

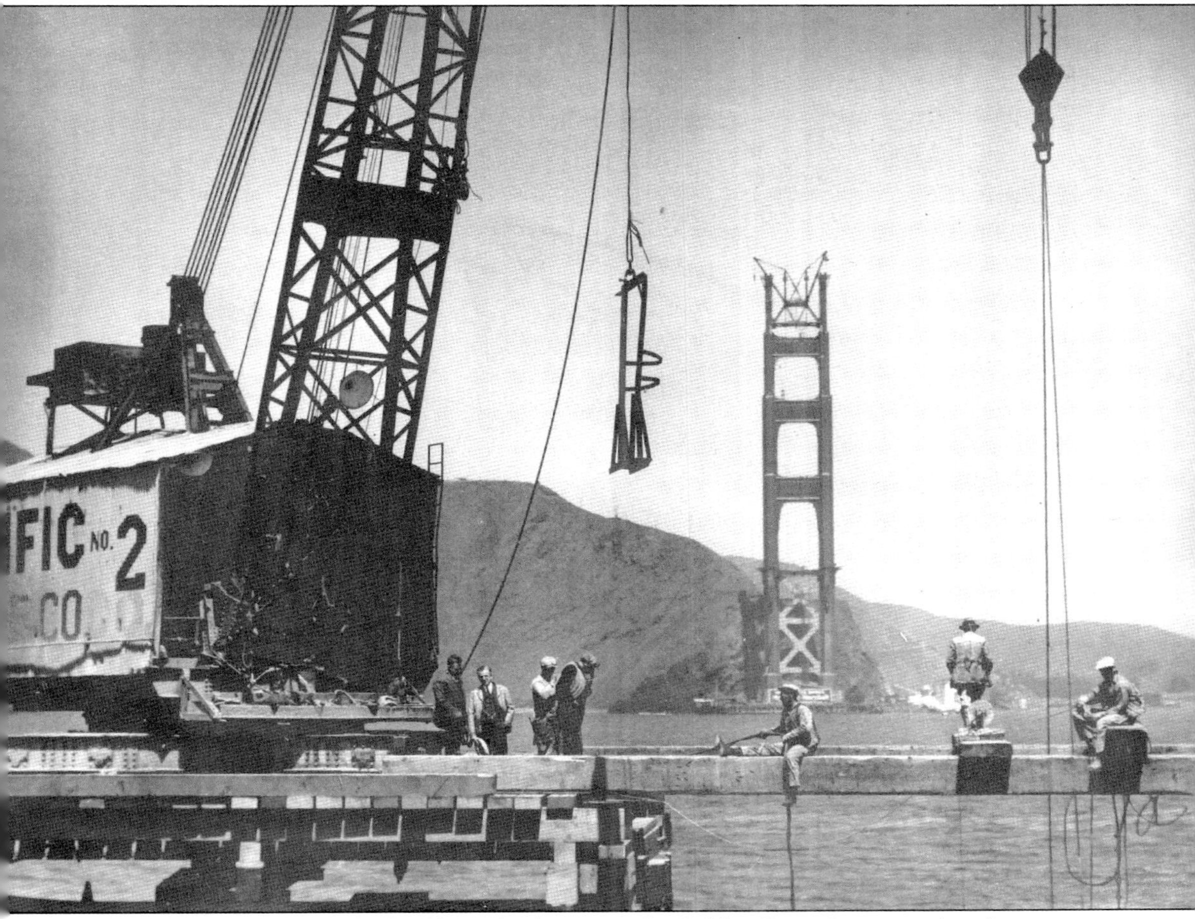

Despite the altruistic goal of building a bridge across the Golden Gate, there was a lot of controversy at the time. Owners and workers on the ferries and trains worried that their business would become extinct. It seemed fairly certain that would be the case. (Photograph by Dulcie Duncan Ray; courtesy Sausalito Historical Society, 82-185f.)

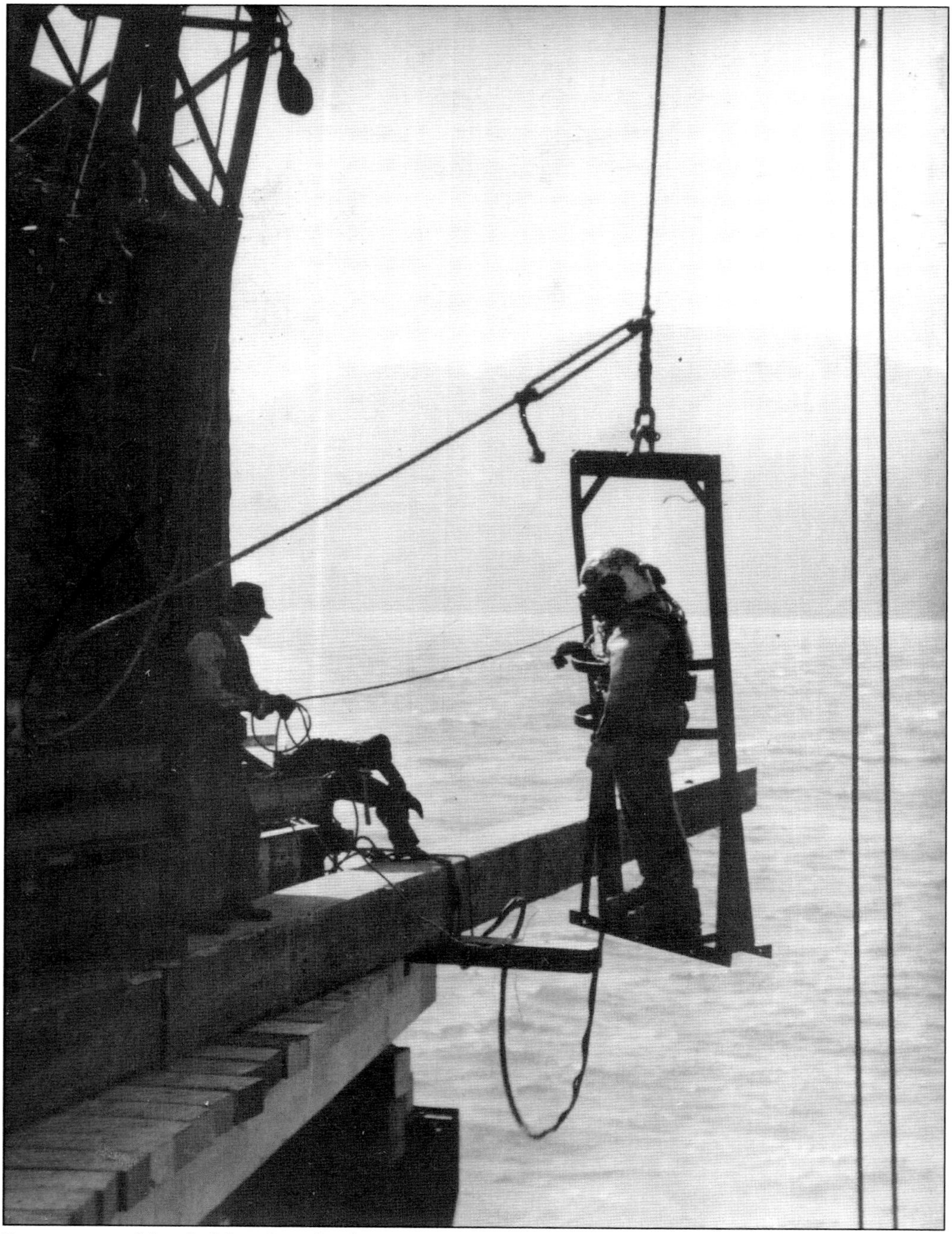

Proponents of the Golden Gate Bridge saw opportunity for growth and development, with people coming to Marin County to buy real estate and to patronize hotels and restaurants. While both fears and hopes continued, Joseph P. Strauss, the future builder, persuaded San Francisco that it would be feasible. A $35-million bond issue was put to the people. It passed November 4, 1930. (Photograph by Dulcie Duncan Ray; courtesy Sausalito Historical Society, 82-185e.)

The bridge would need to be strong enough to support a span for heavy traffic and high enough to let seagoing vessels through. It would have to be flexible and strong enough to withstand the winds and currents and impervious enough to hold up against rain, fog, and heat. Work would be continuous, and workers would need to be skilled, strong, dedicated, and daring. The bridge would accommodate walkers and drivers, and in the headlands, the bridge would connect to the new four-lane Redwood Highway with a tunnel penetrating the grade of Wolfback Ridge. (Photograph by Dulcie Duncan Ray; courtesy Sausalito Historical Society, 82-185d.)

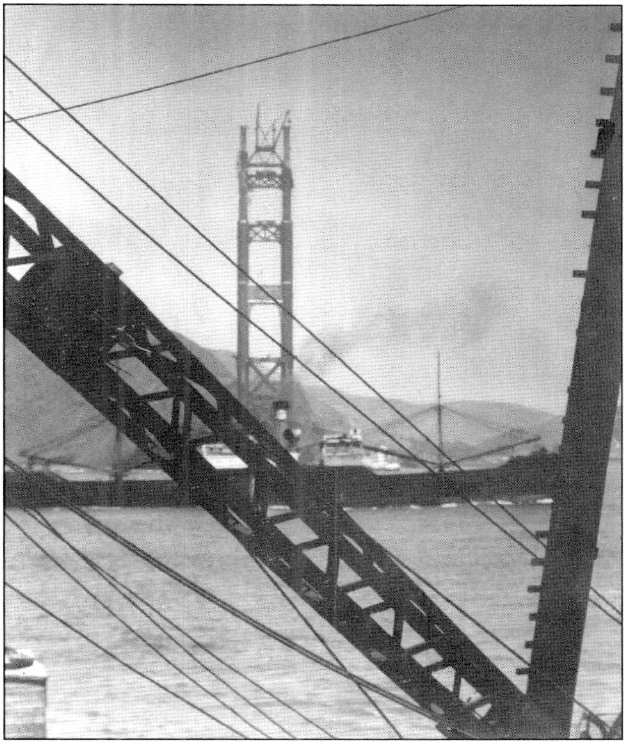

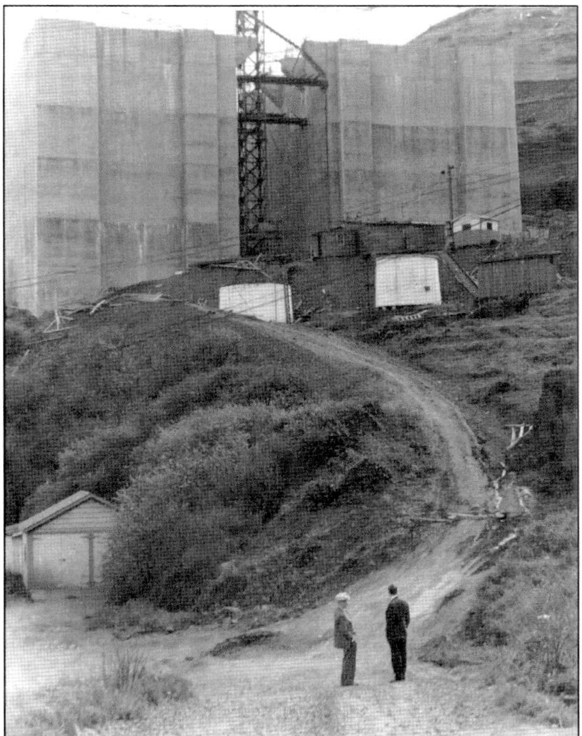

Lewis Straus (in white hat) interacts with a bridge worker at the north footings in 1936. (Photograph by Dulcie Duncan Ray; courtesy Sausalito Historical Society, 82-185a.)

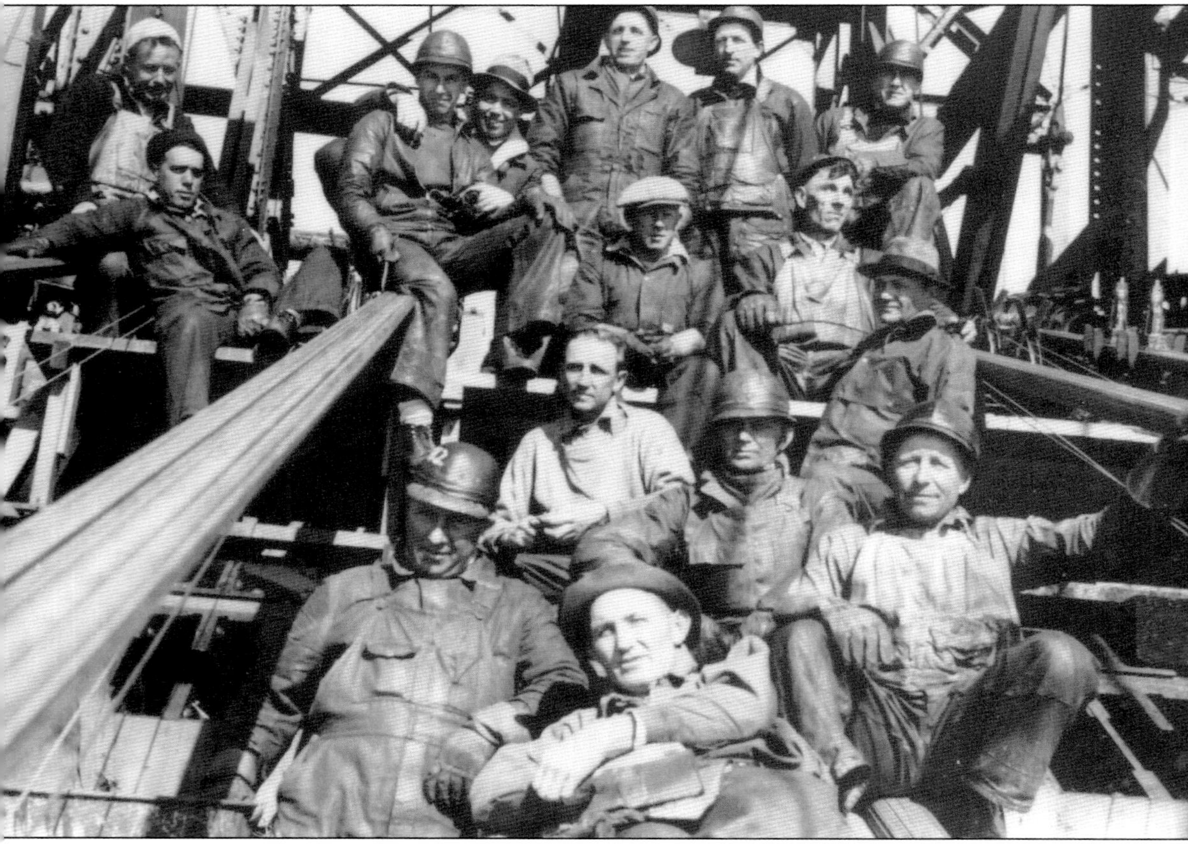

Written on the back of this photograph is: "Time out for a photo—workmen on the Golden Gate Bridge spanning crew, 1936. In rear—second from left Ed Ashoff. Far right one of the supervisors Daggis Disela next row far left Monk in front of Ed, Harrison Pederson (Swede's Brother) to Monk's left. Pomeroy in center—the back span contractor. To his left Ray McCloud." (Courtesy Sausalito Historical Society, 05-19.)

Divers for the bridge could work below as well as the high flyers above. People in Sausalito were not so concerned with the building, although it was fascinating, nor with the outcome. Most favored it as beneficial to the growth of the town. Rather, the main issue was the highway. There was a movement to have it go east along the shore, completely through the town, but the original plan held. There would be a tunnel and a highway down the Waldo Grade. (Photograph by Dulcie Duncan Ray; courtesy Sausalito Historical Society, 82-185b.)

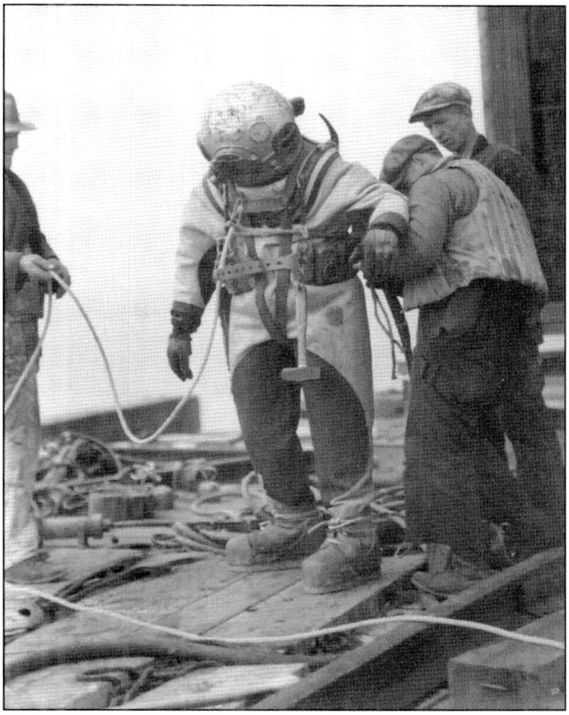

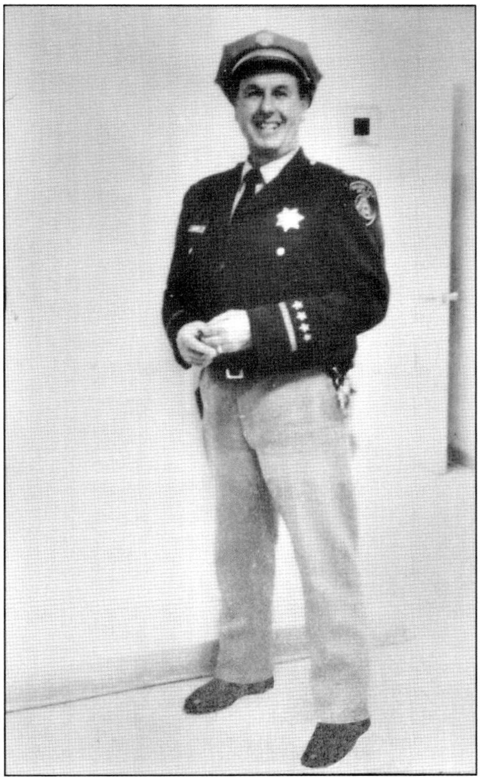

During the Depression, as work continued on the bridge, tunnel, and highway, things were slow in Sausalito. The ferryboat *Marin* (from Sausalito to Tiburon) made her last voyage, replaced by the Greyhound bus. The Northwestern Pacific Railroad was losing money, and there was talk of abandoning the interurban runs. The bridge opened May 28, 1937. Over 200,000 people walked across it that day. No doubt Ed Ashoff was one of them. Here he is sporting his new uniform; he is now an officer with the Golden Gate Bridge Authority. (Courtesy Sausalito Historical Society Oral History Project.)

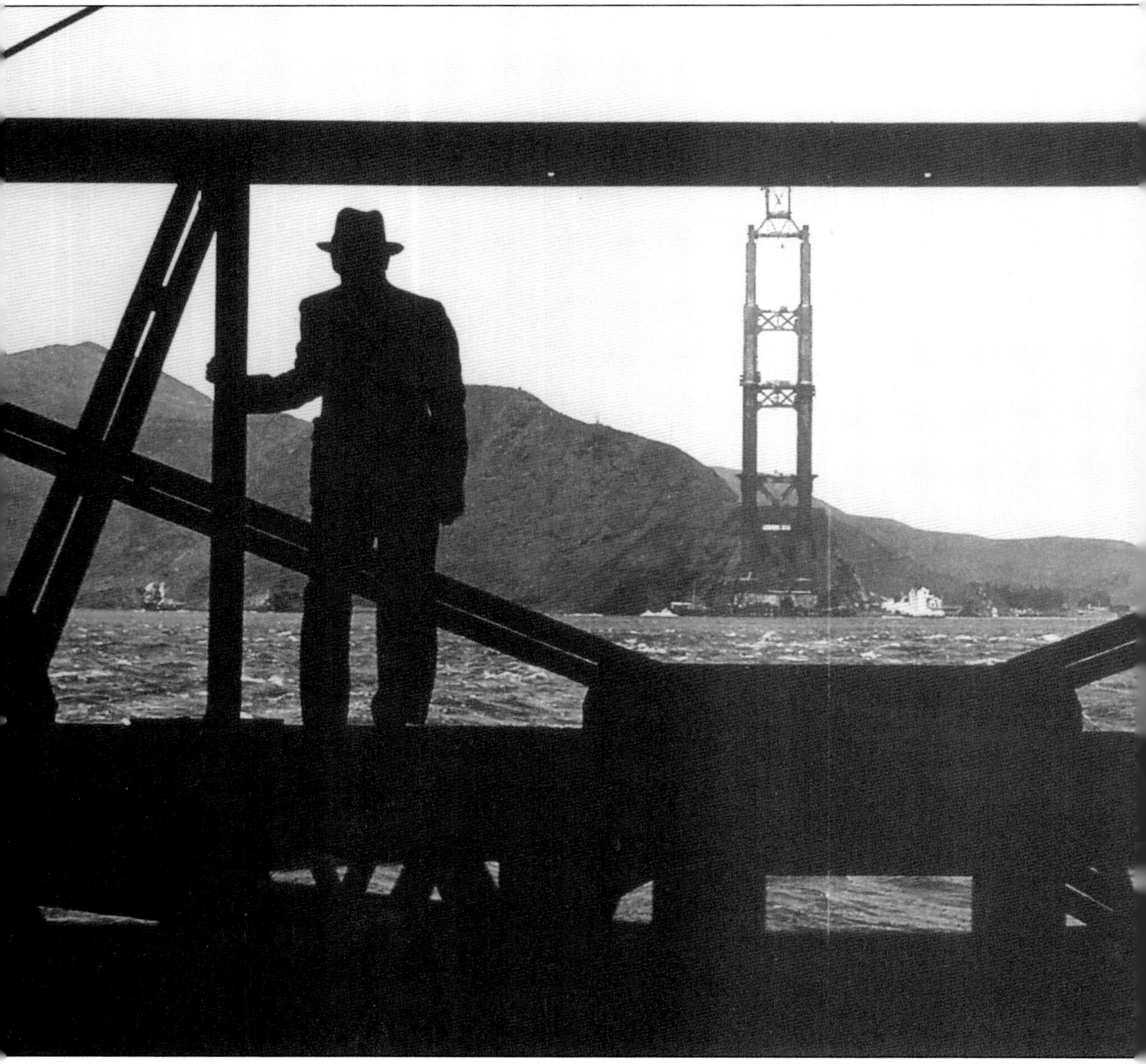

An unidentified man, probably a supervisor, is captured on the San Francisco Fort Point side of the Golden Gate in this 1937 photograph. (Courtesy Sausalito Historical Society, 84-89.)

On the west side of the highway at Waldo's base, a whole new community had been born—a planned little city for the Marinship workers. The huge trucks shovel and level the land, filling in the marsh opposite Strawberry Point, shoving aside and out those few families (including a dairy farm) who lived there. By 1942, enough houses were built to house 6,000 of the "guest workers" who had migrated from all over the United States to build the Liberty ships and tankers. Marin City, still going strong today, is 5 miles north of San Francisco. This photograph is from 1941. (Courtesy Marin History Museum San Rafael/Novato.)

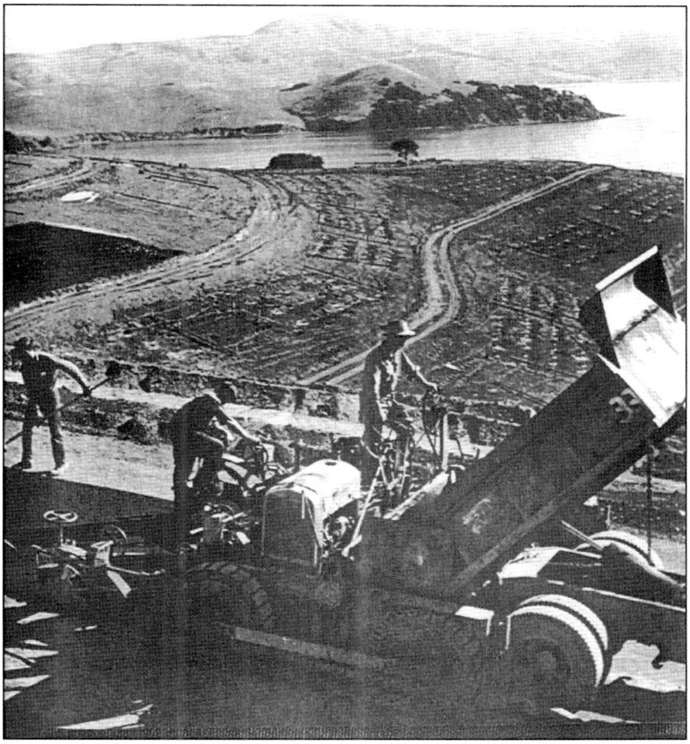

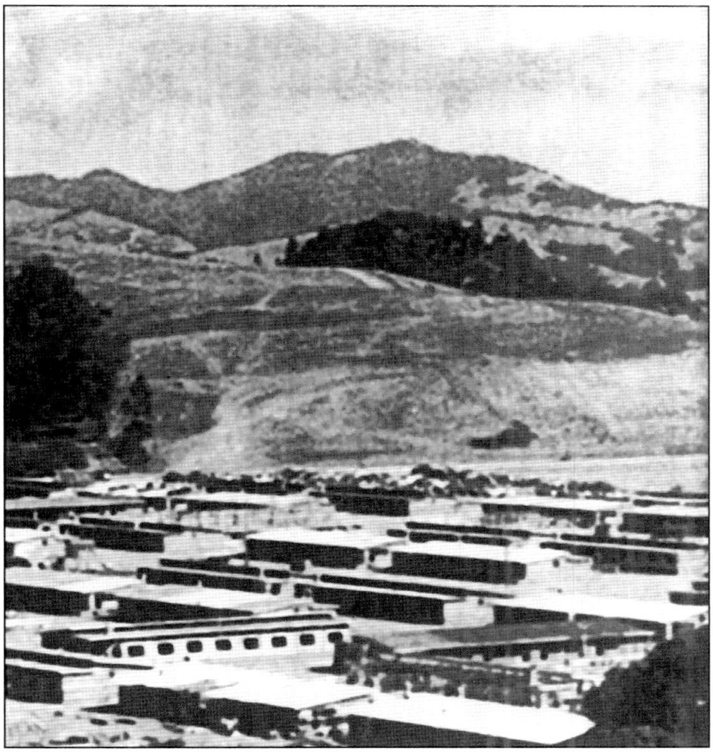

Marin City was "born" in 1942. On the left of the photograph, the housing is halfway finished, and to the right, it is complete. The whole lower flatland is filled with housing—rectangular barrack-like units for families and singles. Units were built on the downhill slopes to the south. To the left in these photographs is the Burgess estate, much of it taken by the government. (Courtesy Marin History Museum San Rafael/Novato.)

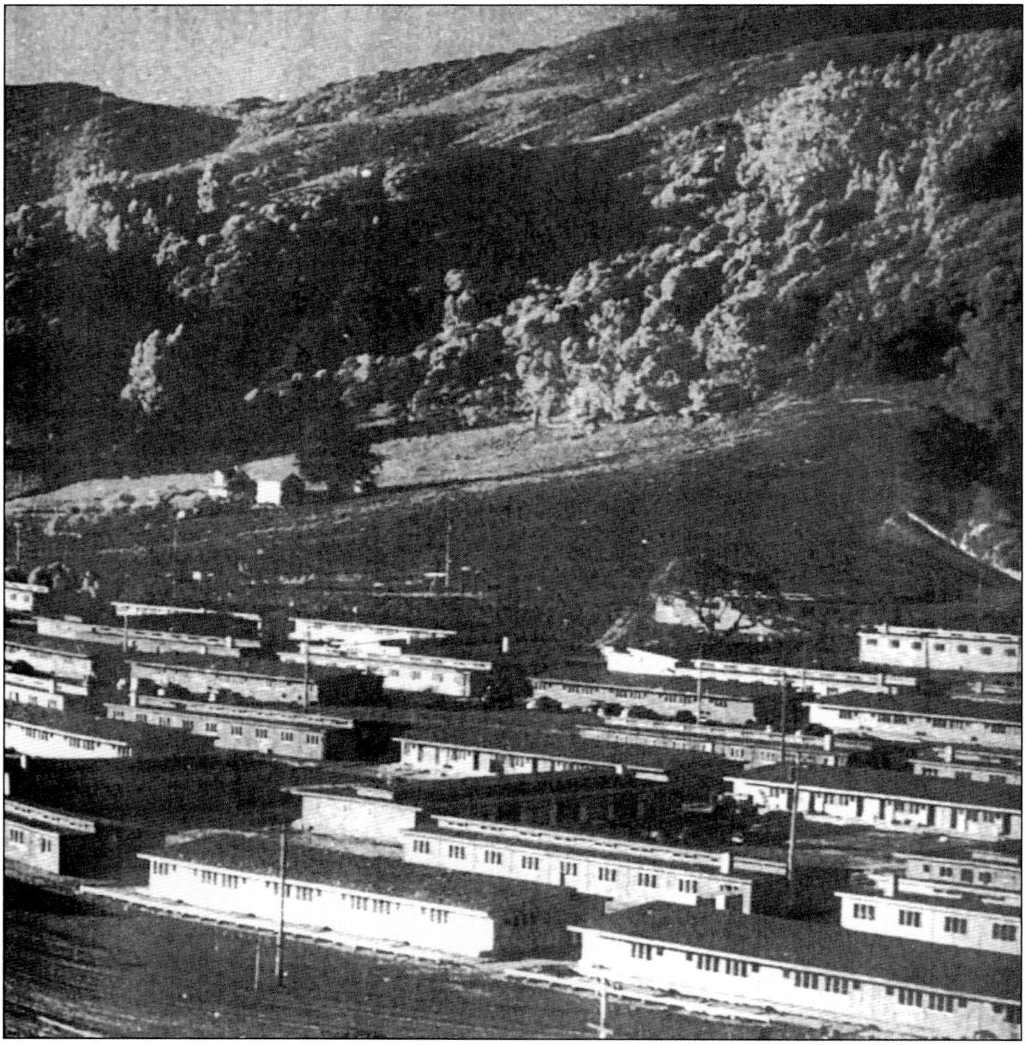

Much of Marin City's population from the Southeast was African American (40 percent). The federal government provided all services, including a full-time recreation director, 24-hour physician service, USO, Traveler's Aid, casework and family help, and fire and police protection. In 1943, a Citizens' Council was formed and a newspaper published. The housing was intended to last five years after the war. However, many wanted to stay. The County Board of Supervisors heard the situation and a master plan for redevelopment followed. Marin's Housing Authority purchased the property in 1955, and the Redevelopment Agency purchased 121 acres of the 365-acre site in 1959. The population then was 2,519 (2,040 black). There have been two major housing projects since, one to the east up the grade and the other on the flat behind city services. Population is increasingly mixed. (Courtesy Marin History Museum San Rafael/Novato.)

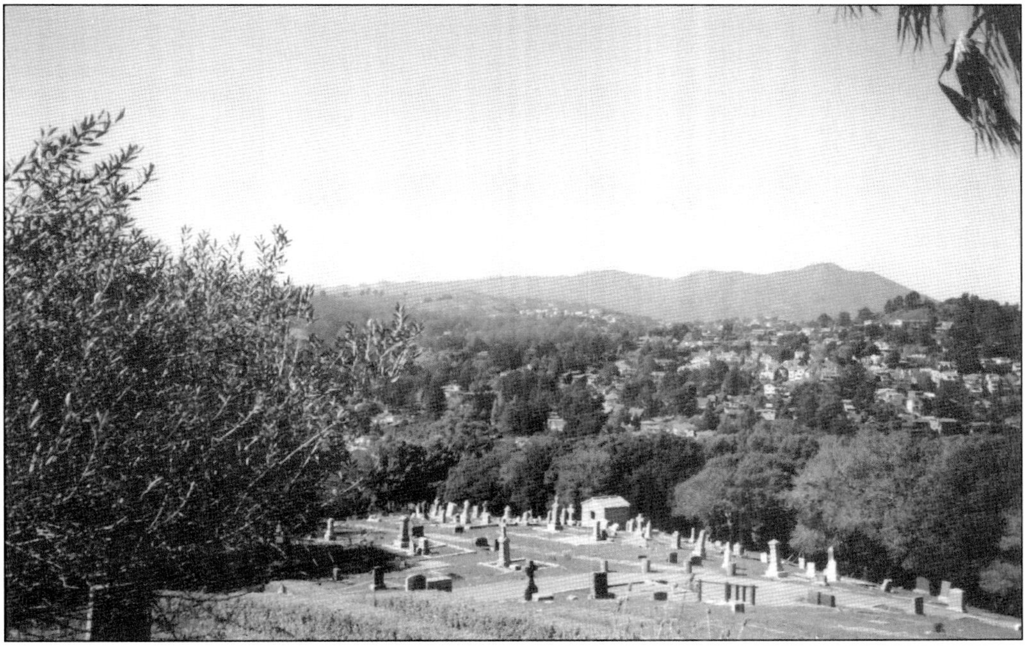

Fernwood Cemetery, with Mount Tamalpais, the Sleeping Lady, reposing in the background, is around the bend from Marin City and Waldo, on the west side toward Tennessee Valley. It is reached by foot or auto that way or by foot or horseback from Alta Road coming down. Fernwood Cemetery dates before 1890 and has outlasted the others in the Marin Headlands. (Photographs by Dorothy Gibson.)

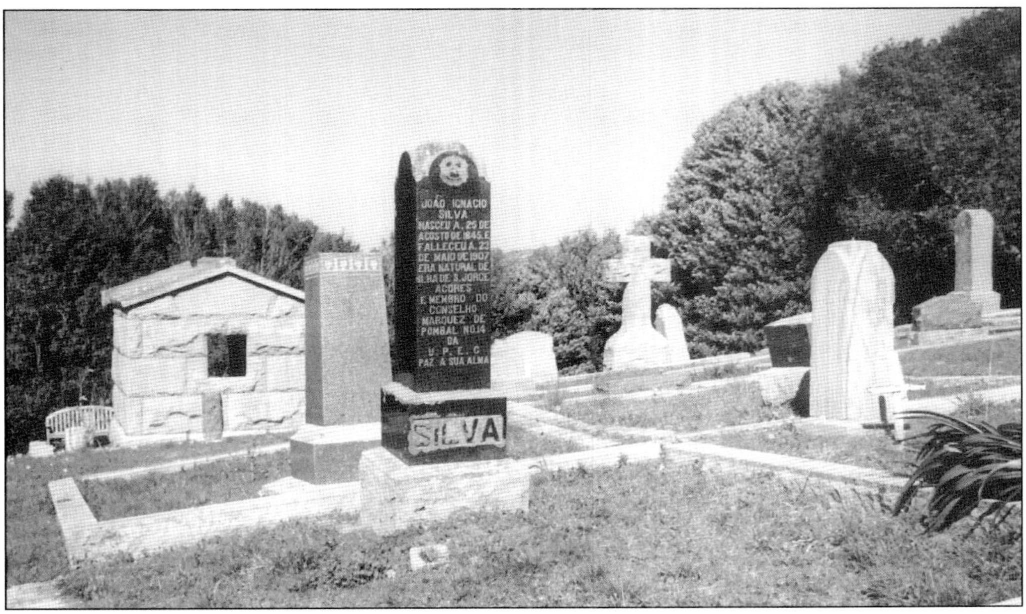

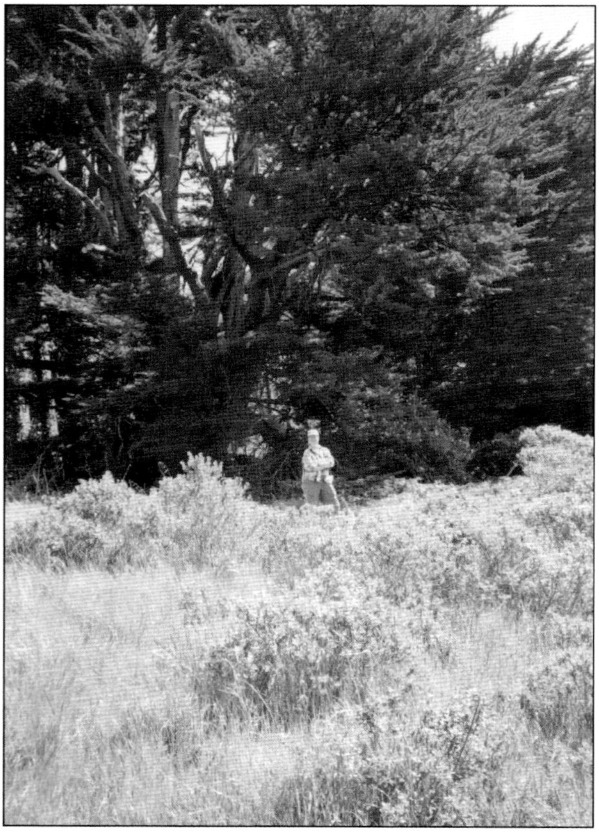

The grove west of the Redwood Highway is on the north side of Rodeo Avenue as it winds up to Alta Road. It is about all that is left of Cypress Cemetery (also known as Sunny Hills). There is a flat area suggesting burials were here and a rather deep well with a fragile fence around it. There are no markers and little to suggest its earlier status. It is in a lovely setting with a sweeping view of the North Bay across Rodeo and Nevada Valleys. The graves were transferred out when the highway cut them off from Sausalito proper. It is not certain where all were transferred, nor how many. The cemetery was active roughly from 1890 to 1937. (Photographs by Dorothy Gibson.)

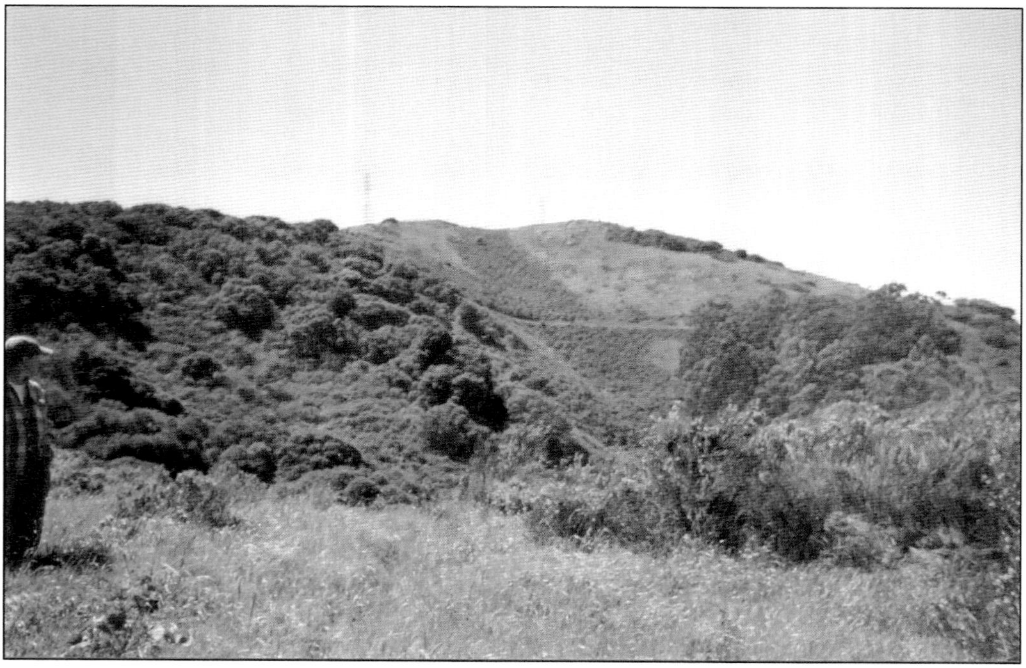

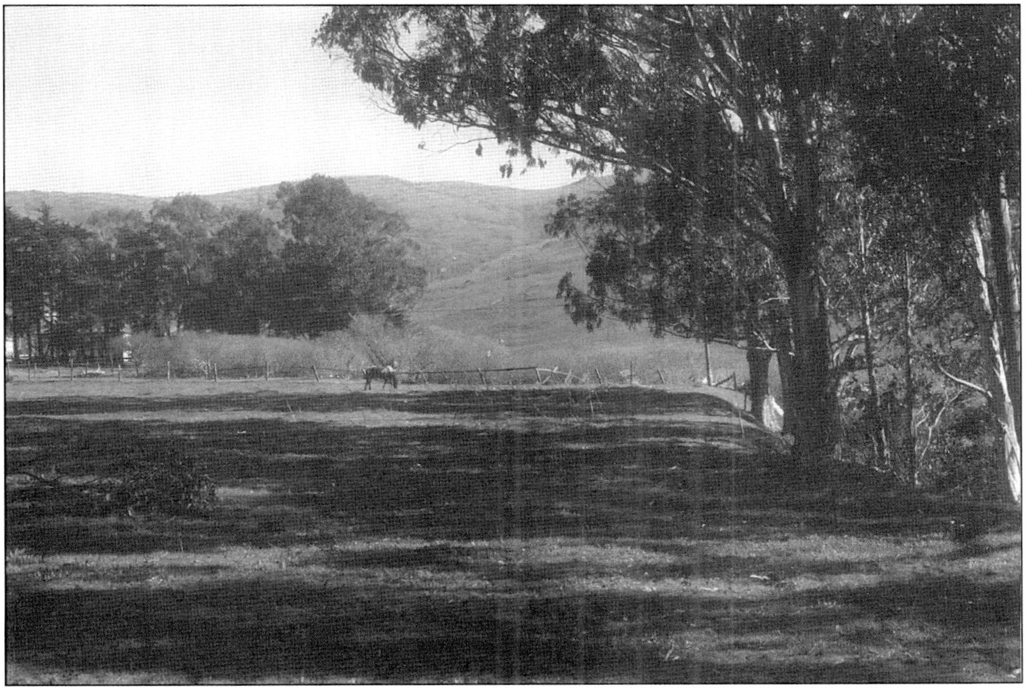

Set high on Wolfback Ridge, Alta Road is a straight dirt road dead-ending at Spencer Avenue to the south. Midway on Alta Road is a trail into the deep Oakwood Valley leading to a small reservoir, and along a stream farther down are the remnants of a farmhouse. Cows would have grazed along here and in Tennessee Valley to the ocean until the military territory became a national park in 1972. (Photographs by Dorothy Gibson.)

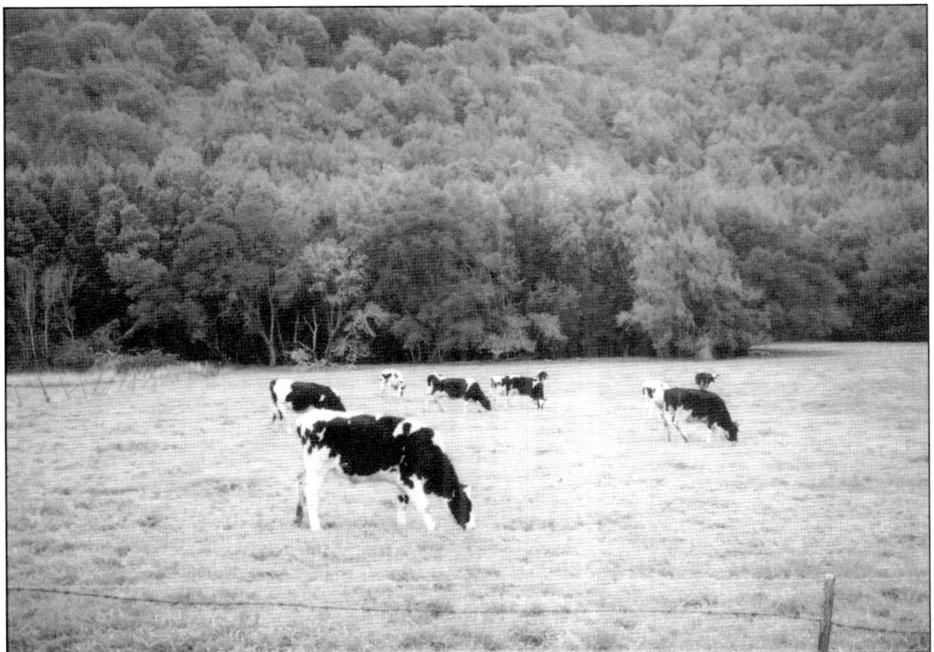

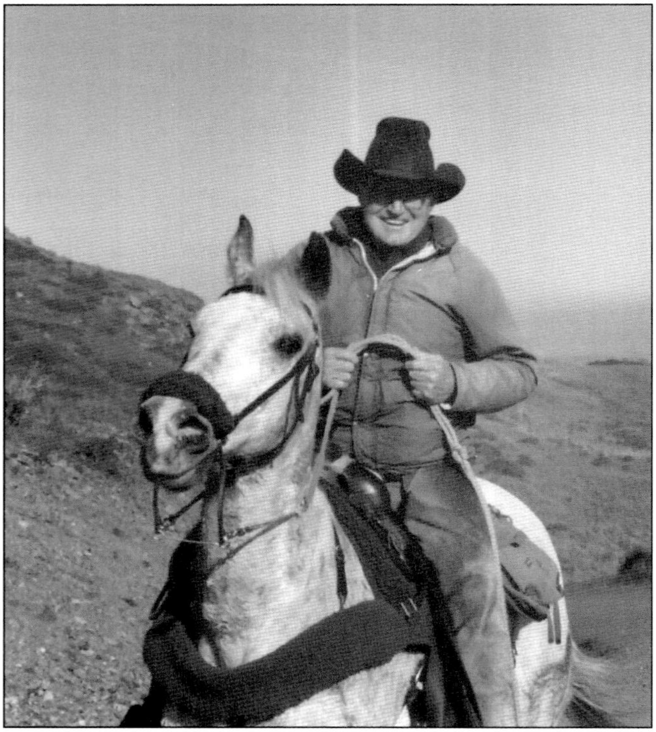

Former Sausalito firefighter Gene Poole has been riding the headlands for many years. Here he is pictured on his horse Appy on the Chunia Dairy Ranch in Tennessee Valley around 1973. Gene was born and raised in Sausalito and stationed at the post near Muir Cove in World War II to spot enemy activity. After several months of inactivity, he did spot a Japanese submarine. He gave the signal, and rather quickly, the sub was "down to the bottom with the other shipwrecks." On his horse Appy, Gene led many Fourth of July parades in Sausalito. Appy died several years back, but Gene still walks down the hill every day to visit the fire department and the fellows there. (Courtesy Gene Poole.)

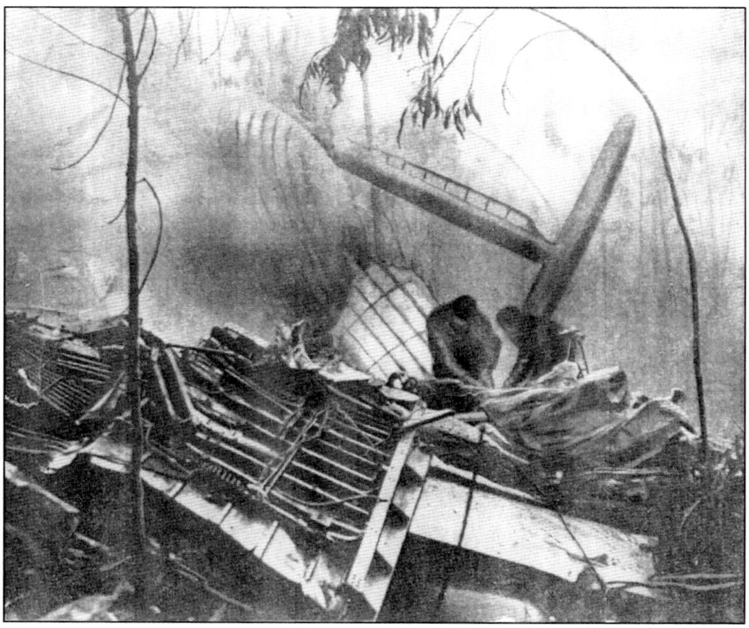

Along the picturesque hillside over the Waldo Tunnel, tragedy struck in 1942 when heavy fog contributed to a devastating airplane crash. An unidentified source noted with the photograph: "In this smoldering wreckage of what a few moments before had been a four-motored bomber, nine persons met their death yesterday." (Courtesy Sausalito Historical Society, 81-80.)

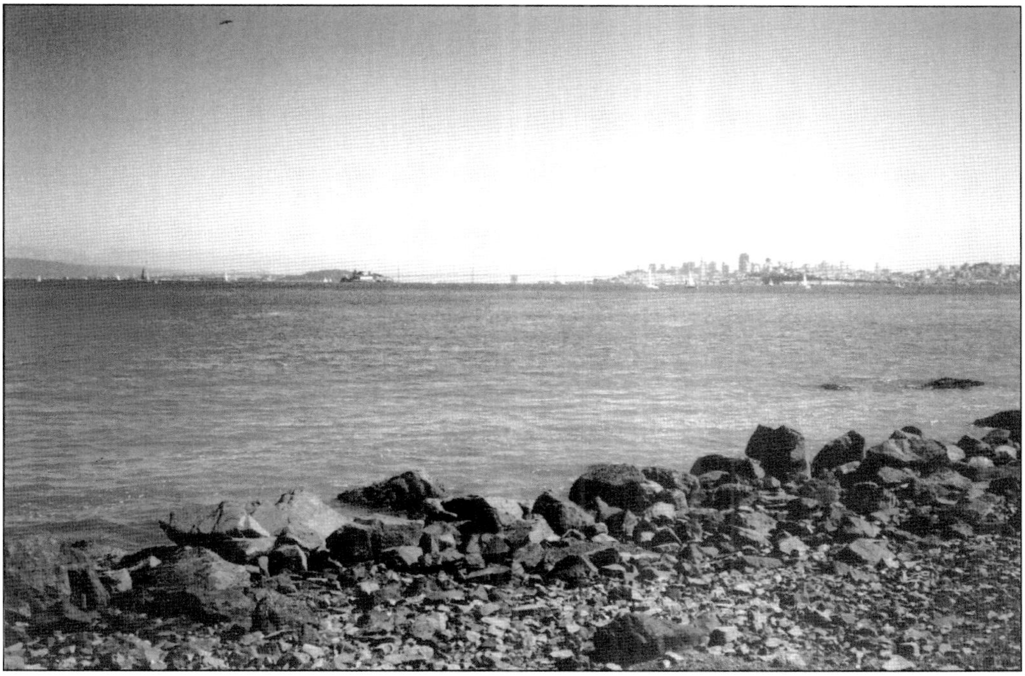

Tide Gauge Beach waits at the end of an overgrown, unmarked switchback trail in East Fort Baker. The trail leads from the southernmost extension of Alta Avenue atop Wolfback Ridge to the old fire road to Marion Avenue and South Street. (Photograph by Dorothy Gibson.)

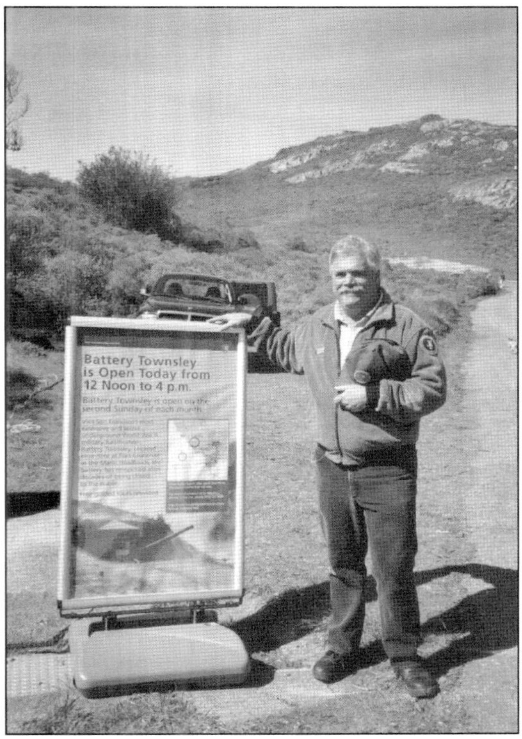

In 1972, Forts Baker, Barry, and Cronkite were transferred to the Department of the Interior to be a part of the Golden Gate National Recreation Area. John A. Martini, the recently retired park historian, serves as a volunteer at the Marin Headlands. Here he is on a guided tour of Battery Townsley at Fort Cronkite in 2008. (Photograph by Dorothy Gibson.)

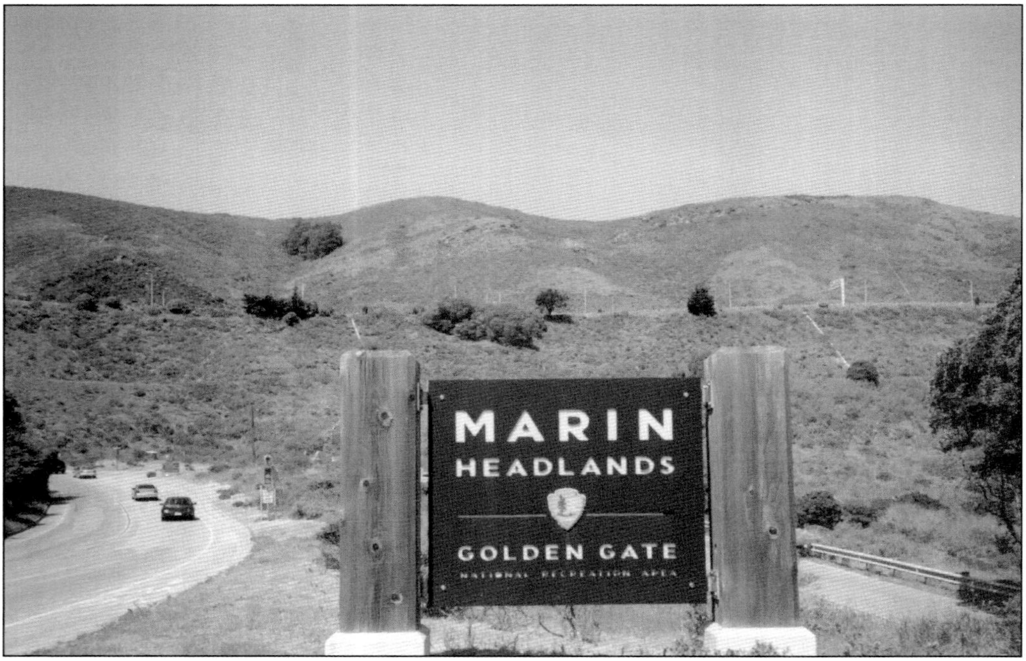

This is the east entrance to the tunnel leading to West Fort Baker, Fort Barry, and Fort Cronkite. The narrow, dimly lit tunnel is open in opposite directions for five minutes at a time. (Photograph by Dorothy Gibson.)

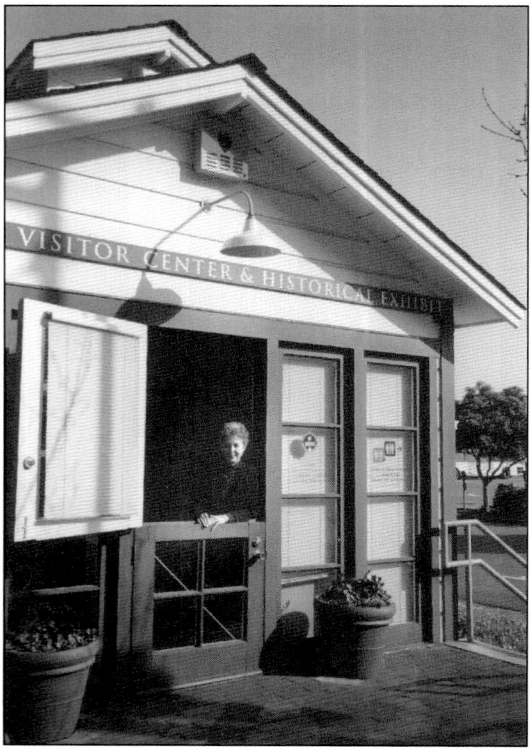

This is historian and writer Doris Berdahl in the doorway of the Sausalito Historical Society's visitor center, affectionately known as "The Ice House." Doris greets and shares historic information with all visitors. As for the nickname, the building did have that function when it was used by the Northwestern Pacific Railroad at the train station at Litho and Caledonia Streets. (Photograph by Dorothy Gibson.)

BIBLIOGRAPHY

Aker, Raymond, and Edward Von Der Porten. *Discovering Francis Drake's California Harbor*. Palo Alto: Drake Navigators Guild, 2000.
American Bird Conservancy. *All the Birds of North America*. New York: HarperCollins, 1997.
Audubon Society. *Field Guild to North American Rocks and Minerals*. New York: Alfred A. Knopf, 1979.
Beals, Herbert K. *Juan Perez on the Northwest Coast*. Portland: Oregon Historical Society, 1989.
Chin, Brian. *Artillery at the Golden Gate*. Missoula, MT: Pictorial Histories Publishing, Inc., 1994.
Goerke, Betty. *Chief Marin: Leader, Rebel, Legend*. Berkeley: Heyday Books, 2007.
Howard, Arthur D. *Geologic History of Middle California*. Berkeley: University of California Press, 1979.
Howell, John Thomas, and Frank Almeda, Wilma Follette, and Catherine Best. *Marin Flora*. San Francisco: California Academy of Sciences, 2007.
Langellier, John Phillip, and Daniel B. Rosen. *The Presidio de San Francisco: A History under Spain and Mexico, 1776–1846*. Spokane, WA: Arthur H. Clark Company, 1996.
Mason, Jack. *Early Marin*. Petaluma, CA: House of Printing, 1971.
Miller, Robert Ryal. *Captain Richardson*. Berkeley: La Loma Press, 1995.
Teather, Louise. *Place Names of Marin*. San Francisco: Scottwall Associates, 1986.
Tracy, Jack. *Sausalito: Moments in Time*. Sausalito, CA: Windgate Press, 1983.
Veronico, Betty. *Lighthouses of the Bay Area*. Charleston, SC: Arcadia Publishing, 2008.
Wright, Robert B. *California Missions*. Los Angeles: Sterling Press, 1970.

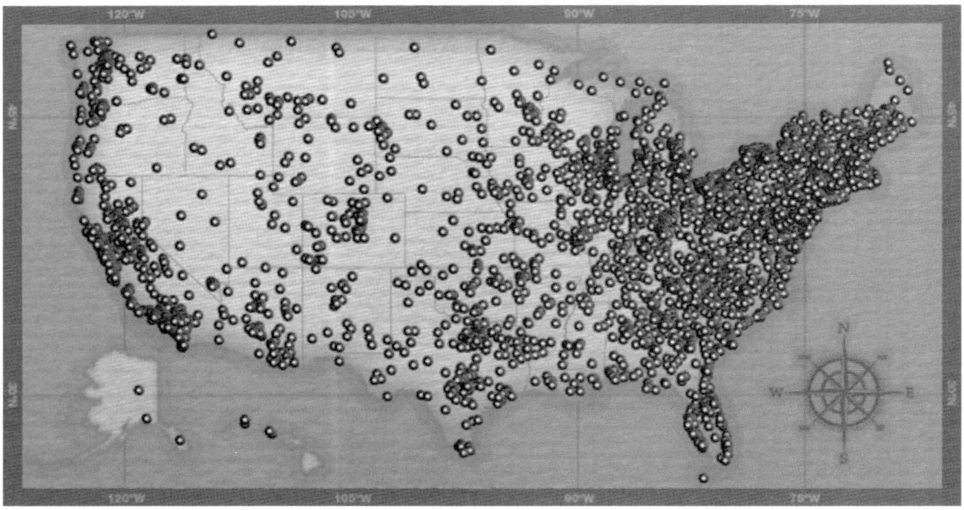